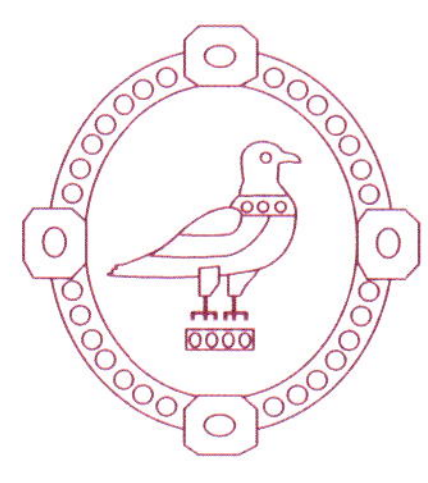

AudioVision
in the Middle Ages

SAINTE-FOY AT CONQUES

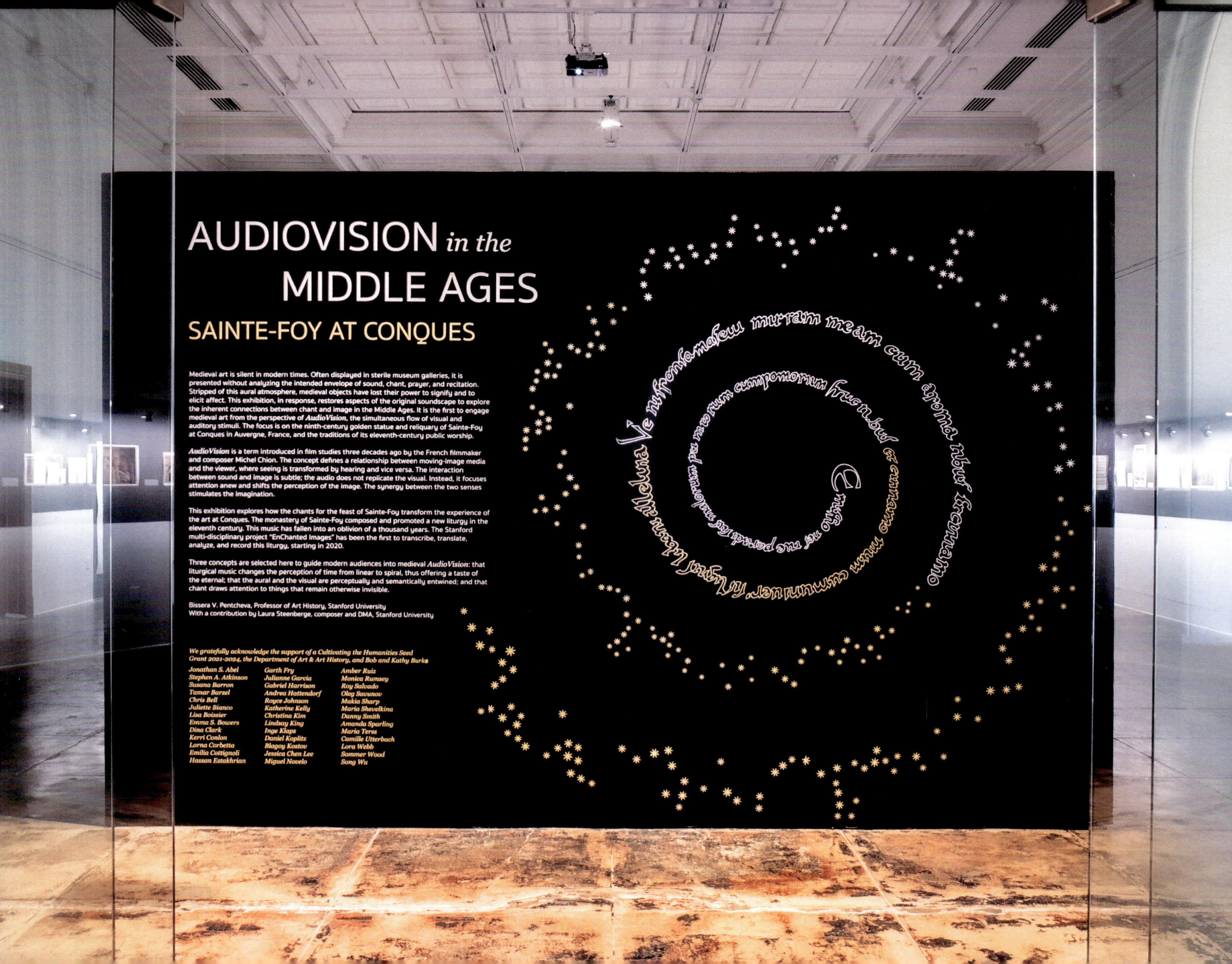

AUDIOVISION in the MIDDLE AGES
SAINTE-FOY AT CONQUES

Medieval art is silent in modern times. Often displayed in sterile museum galleries, it is presented without analyzing the intended envelope of sound, chant, prayer, and recitation. Stripped of this aural atmosphere, medieval objects have lost their power to signify and to elicit affect. This exhibition, in response, restores aspects of the original soundscape to explore the inherent connections between chant and image in the Middle Ages. It is the first to engage medieval art from the perspective of AudioVision, the simultaneous flow of visual and auditory stimuli. The focus is on the ninth-century golden statue and reliquary of Sainte-Foy at Conques in Auvergne, France, and the traditions of its eleventh-century public worship.

AudioVision is a term introduced in film studies three decades ago by the French filmmaker and composer Michel Chion. The concept defines a relationship between moving-image media and the viewer, where seeing is transformed by hearing and vice versa. The interaction between sound and image is subtle; the audio does not replicate the visual. Instead, it focuses attention anew and shifts the perception of the image. The synergy between the two senses stimulates the imagination.

This exhibition explores how the chants for the feast of Sainte-Foy transform the experience of the art at Conques. The monastery of Sainte-Foy composed and promoted a new liturgy in the eleventh century. This music has fallen into an oblivion of a thousand years. The Stanford multi-disciplinary project "EnChanted Images" has been the first to transcribe, translate, analyze, and record this liturgy, starting in 2020.

Three concepts are selected here to guide modern audiences into medieval AudioVision: that liturgical music changes the perception of time from linear to spiral, thus offering a taste of the eternal; that the aural and the visual are perceptually and semantically entwined; and that chant draws attention to things that remain otherwise invisible.

Bissera V. Pentcheva, Professor of Art History, Stanford University
With a contribution by Laura Steenberge, composer and DMA, Stanford University

We gratefully acknowledge the support of a Cultivating the Humanities Seed Grant 2021-2024, the Department of Art & Art History, and Bob and Kathy Burke

Jonathan S. Abel
Stephen A. Atkinson
Susana Barron
Tamar Barzel
Chris Bell
Juliette Bianco
Lisa Boissier
Emma S. Bowers
Dina Clark
Kerri Conlon
Lorna Corbetta
Emilia Cottignoli
Hassan Estakhrian

Garth Fry
Julianne Garcia
Gabriel Harrison
Andrea Hattendorf
Royce Johnson
Katherine Kelly
Christina Kim
Lindsay King
Inge Klaps
Daniel Koplitz
Blagoy Kostov
Jessica Chen Lee
Miguel Novelo

Amber Ruiz
Monica Rumsey
Roy Salvado
Oleg Savunov
Makia Sharp
Maria Shevelkina
Danny Smith
Amanda Sparling
Maria Terss
Camille Utterbach
Lora Webb
Sommer Wood
Song Wu

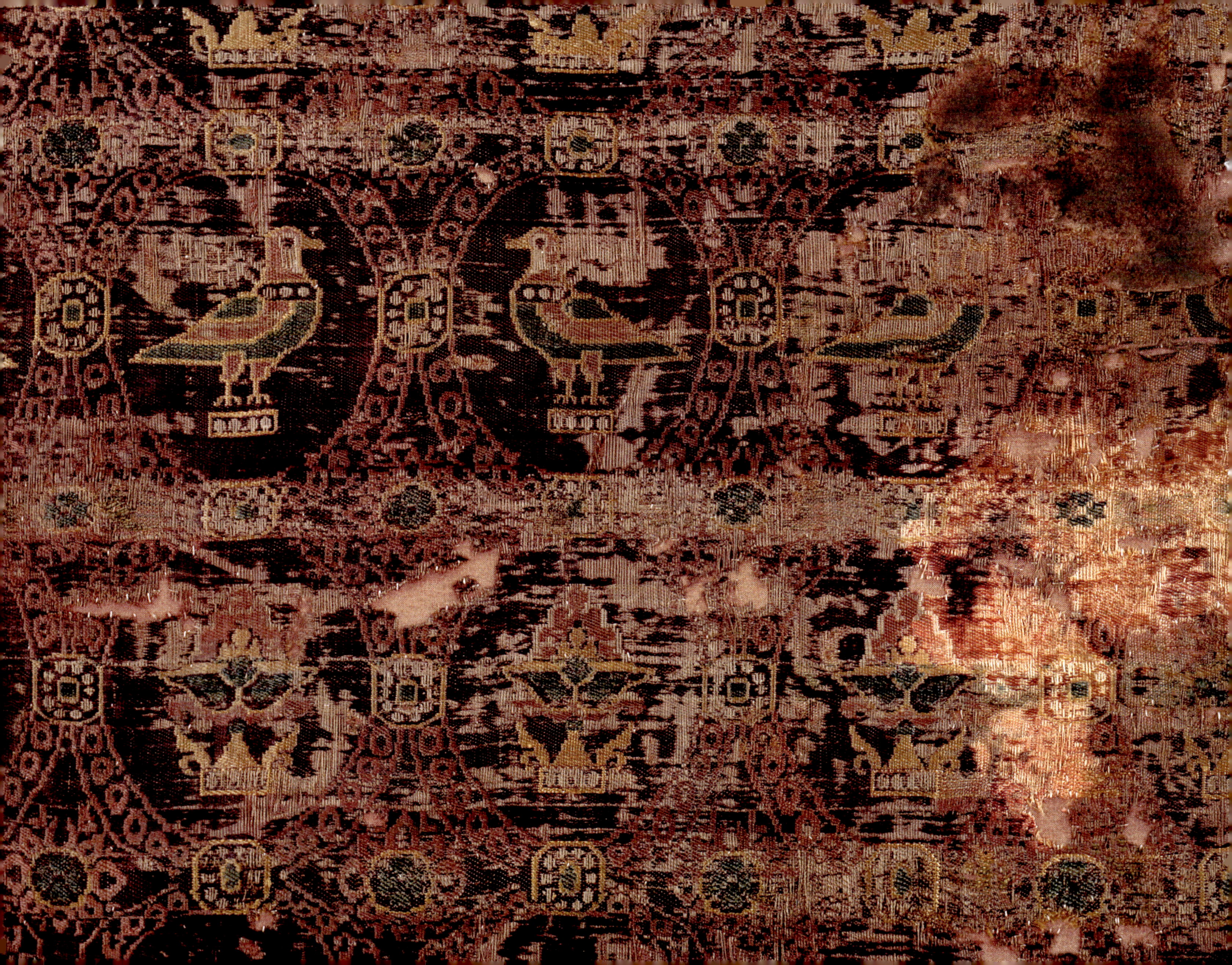

AudioVision in the Middle Ages: Sainte-Foy at Conques
Exhibition at the Stanford Art Gallery, curated by Bissera V. Pentcheva

January 24–March 17, 2023

This exhibition has been generously supported by Stanford University's Cultivating
the Humanities Grant; Department of Art & Art History; ArtsCatalyst Grant,
Bob and Kathy Burke, and Samuel H. Kress Foundation Publication Fund

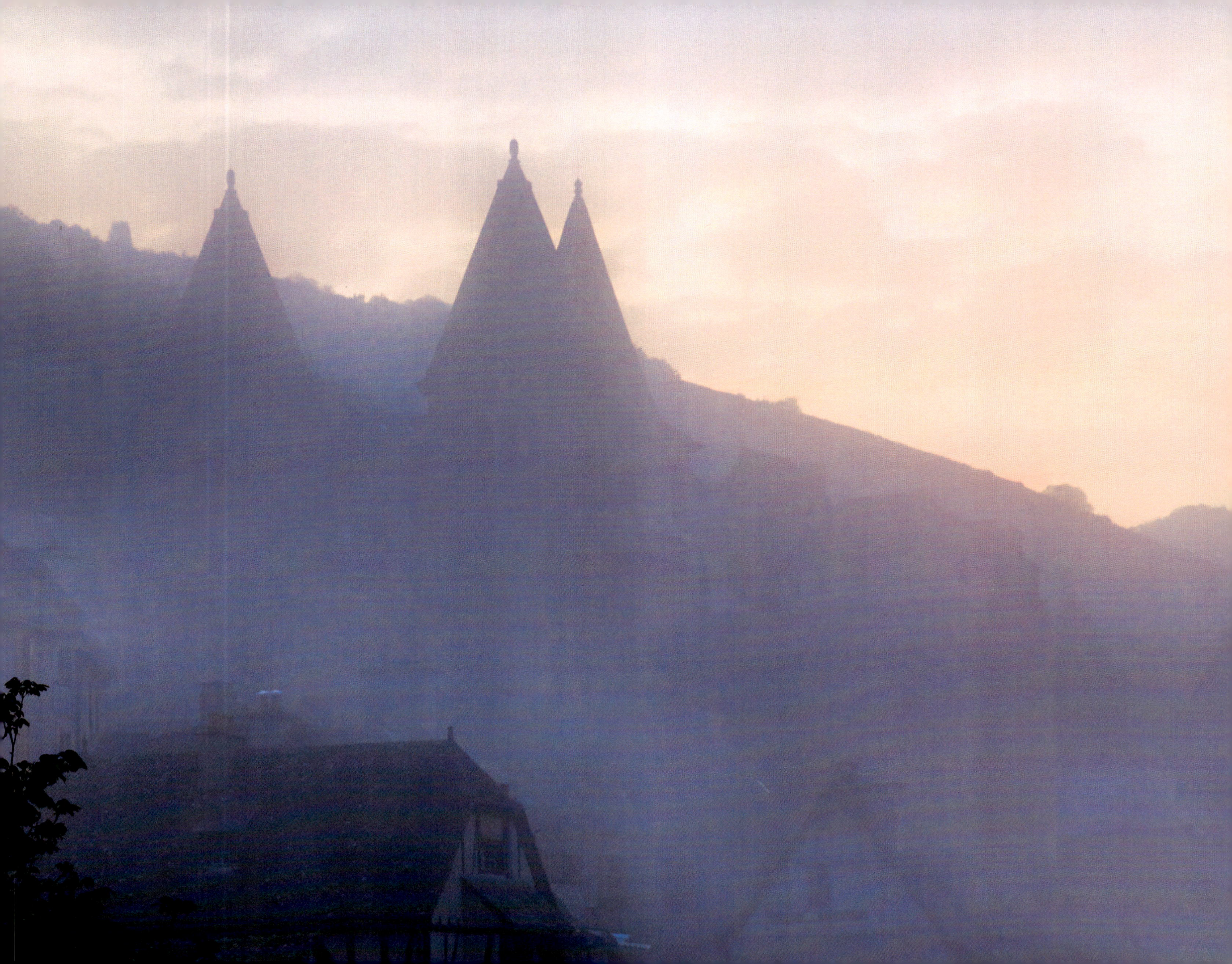

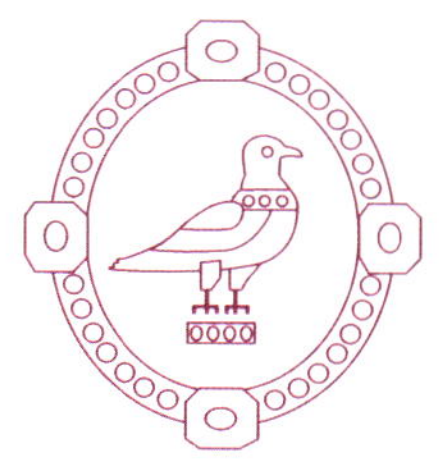

AudioVision
in the Middle Ages

Sainte-Foy at Conques

BISSERA V. PENTCHEVA

STANFORD ART GALLERY

ACKNOWLEDGMENTS

Special thanks to:

Juliette Bianco

Lisa Boissier

Dina Clark

Thomas Dale

James Grier

Gabriel Harrison

Inge Klaps

Pavle Levi

Francisco Prado-Vilar

Gabriella Safran

Debra Satz

Amanda Sparling

Danny Smith

Laura Steenberge

Maria Terss

Camille Utterbach

Manuscript editing by Monica Rumsey

Book design by Dina Clark

Printed by Community Printers
Santa Cruz, CA

Distributed by Stanford University Press

Published with Bowes Faculty Research Funds, a grant from the School of Humanities and Sciences at Stanford University, and Samuel H. Kress Foundation Publication Fund

Library of Congress Control Number 2022923729

ISBN: 979-8-218-12137-2

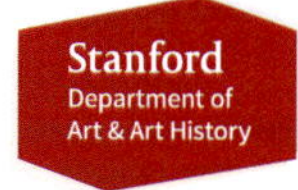

Cover images:

Front:
Statue of Sainte-Foy, 9th-11th cent.
Photograph: Miguel Novelo; digital visualization of the responsory *Emissiones Tue*: Jessica Chen Lee

Back:
AudioVision in the Middle Ages Exhibition at the Stanford Art Gallery
Photograph: Susana Barron

Opening photos (in page order):

Erich Lessing/AKG Images

Susana Barron

Philippe Raveton

CONTENTS

Introduction

Medieval art is silent in modern times. Often displayed in sterile museum galleries, it is presented without any analysis of the intended envelope of sound, chant, prayer, and recitation. Stripped of this aural atmosphere, these objects have lost their power to signify and to elicit affect. This exhibition, in response, restores aspects of the original soundscape to explore the inherent connections between chant and image in medieval times. It is the first to engage medieval art from the perspective of *AudioVision*, the simultaneous flow of visual and auditory stimuli (Pentcheva 2022a). The focus is on the ninth-century golden statue and reliquary of Sainte-Foy at Conques in Occitania, Southern France, and the traditions of its eleventh-century public worship.

What makes the gilded effigy of Sainte-Foy special is the fact that it is the earliest surviving three-dimensional statue in the Latin West. It eschews naturalistic representation (*mimesis*) (Taralone 1978; Taralone 1997; Dahl 1979; Hahn 2012, pp. 117–33; Fricke 2015, pp. 149–212; Dale 2019, pp. 95–103; Foletti 2018; Pentcheva 2021a). Instead of showing the delicate shape of a twelve-year old virgin, it presents an enthroned male-looking figure of great authority. The authenticity of the statue issues not from the form, but from its function as a reliquary; it contains the skull of the saint and keeps it hidden from view (Pentcheva 2021a; Pentcheva 2022a).

AudioVision is a term introduced in film studies by the French theorist and composer Michel Chion (Chion 1994). The concept defines a relationship between moving-image media and the viewer, where seeing is transformed by hearing and vice versa. The interaction between sound and image is subtle; it dupes the mind into thinking that the audio replicates the visual, while in fact, it focuses attention anew and shifts the perception of the image. The synergy between the two senses stimulates the imagination. In the original context of the Middle Ages, hearing the chants while seeing images covered in gold and gems compelled the audio-spectator to conjure the invisible celestial realm and its inaudible and ceaseless cosmic music (*musica mundana*).

The gilded effigy-reliquary of Sainte-Foy forms the ritual focus at Conques. The monastery composed and promoted a new liturgy for her feast in the eleventh century. This music has fallen into an oblivion of a thousand years. The Stanford multi-disciplinary project "Enchanted Images" has been the first to transcribe, translate, and record this liturgy, starting in

2020. This masterful music and poetry narrate Sainte-Foy's martyrdom and glorification, eliciting visions of her ascent to heaven amidst stars and flowers. The circular structures of some of these chants bend linear time (Pentcheva 2020a; Pentcheva 2023a). Others draw attention to what is otherwise invisible: the skull of the saint, hidden in the recesses of the gilded statue-reliquary (Pentcheva 2022a).

This exhibition and accompanying documentary film explore how the combination of glittering material splendor and music were integral to a viewer's experience of the divine at Conques. This sensorial immersion attuned the participants to the ephemeral presence of Sainte-Foy and invited the faithful to consider the very structure of time and the world itself. Three concepts are selected here to guide the modern audience into medieval *AudioVision*: that liturgical music changes the perception of time from linear to spiral, thus giving a taste of the eternal; that the aural and the visual are perceptually and semantically entwined; and that chant draws attention to things that remain otherwise invisible.

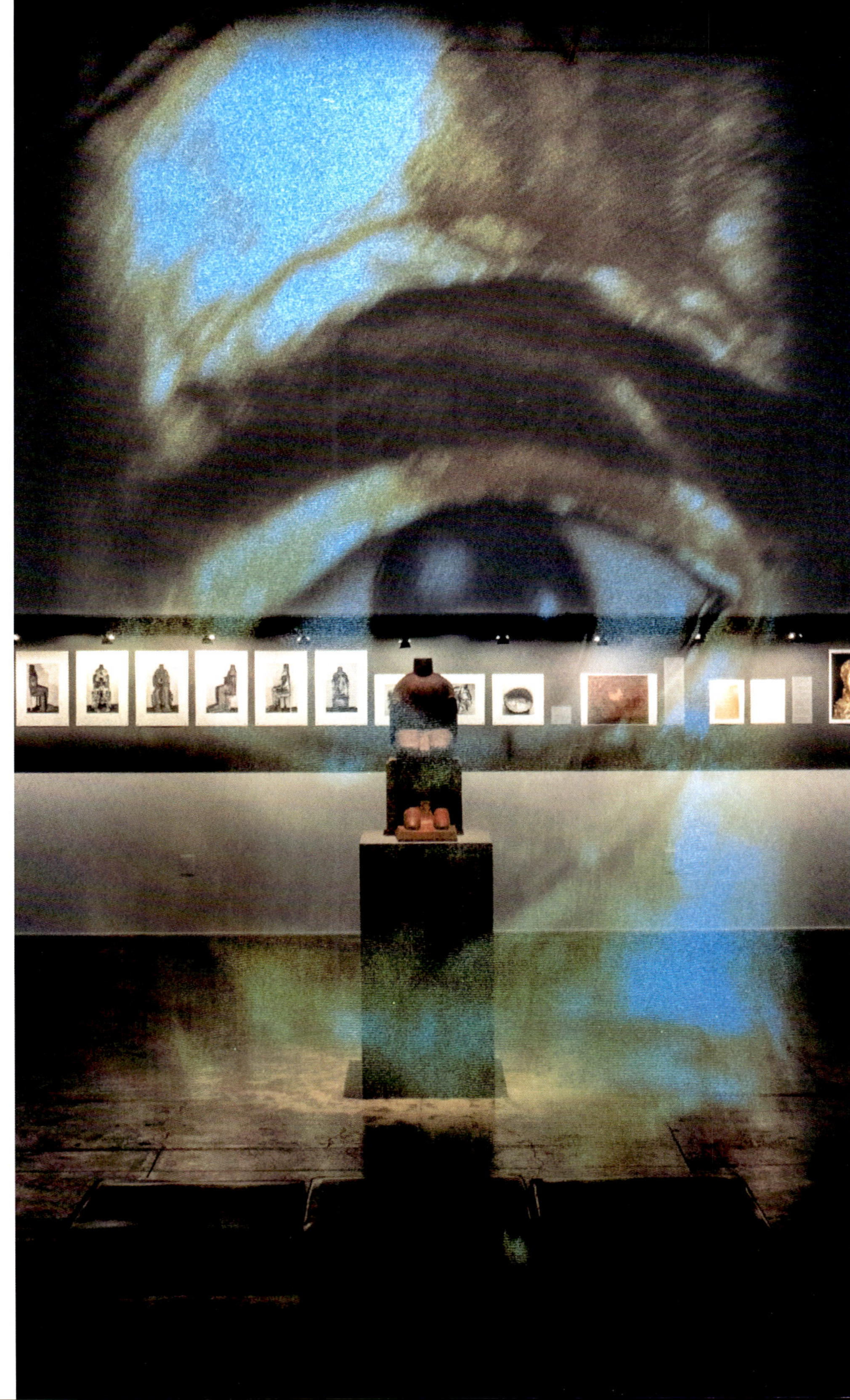

The exhibition *AudioVision in the Middle Ages* at the Stanford Art Gallery, interior

Photograph: Susana Barron

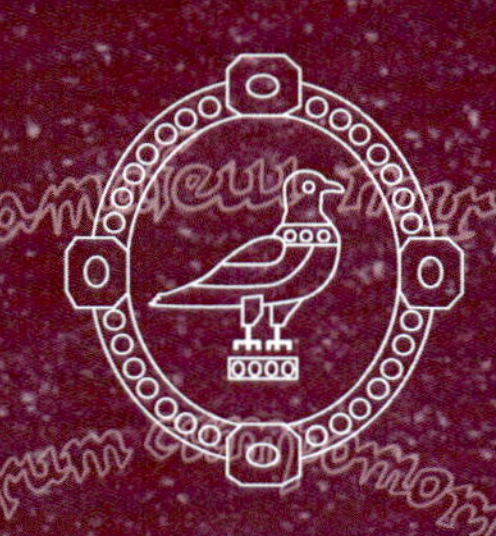

Choroi (Circles)

Spirals and the Warping of Time

Circular structures define life in a medieval monastery, but they are difficult for a modern visitor to perceive. From the repetition of the liturgy through the hours of the day to the details of the music and iconography, time in the Middle Ages was presented as an intricate pattern of circles and spirals that attuned the mind to the eternal (Pseudo-Dionysius, *De caelesti hierarchia*, bk. 7, ch. 4). The concept of circularity is invested in the ancient Greek term χορός (*choros*). This word identifies both action and place: dance, song, and the circular shape of the stage where they unfold. In the ancient Graeco-Roman world, this *choros* of singing and dancing around the altar appeased the divine (Lonsdale 1994–95; Isar 2006; Isar 2011). During the fourth century, when Christianity underwent a change in status from a persecuted sect to a legitimate religion in the Roman Empire, it privileged chant over dance, so the term *choros* became closely associated with

singing (Pentcheva 2017). Translated in Latin as *chorus*, this word is at the root of our modern "choir" (Pentcheva 2020a).

In medieval times, the cosmos is envisioned as a series of rotating spirals (*choroi*). The Lord rules the center, while angels and saints, arranged in concentric circles, ceaselessly sing praise to the divine. Theirs is the cosmic music of the spheres (*musica mundana*); this is the sound produced by the rotation of the stars. Humanity could only imitate this heavenly music in their imperfect performance of liturgical chant (*musica humana*) (Pentcheva 2017; Pentcheva 2020a). Ideal Christian life was imagined as a *choros* beginning and ending with God: birth and baptism, life, death, and a hoped-for return to God at the end of time. Monastic life, too, was envisioned as a *choros*. Led by the abbot, the brethren both strove toward and prayed to return to the divine (*The Rule of Saint Benedict*).

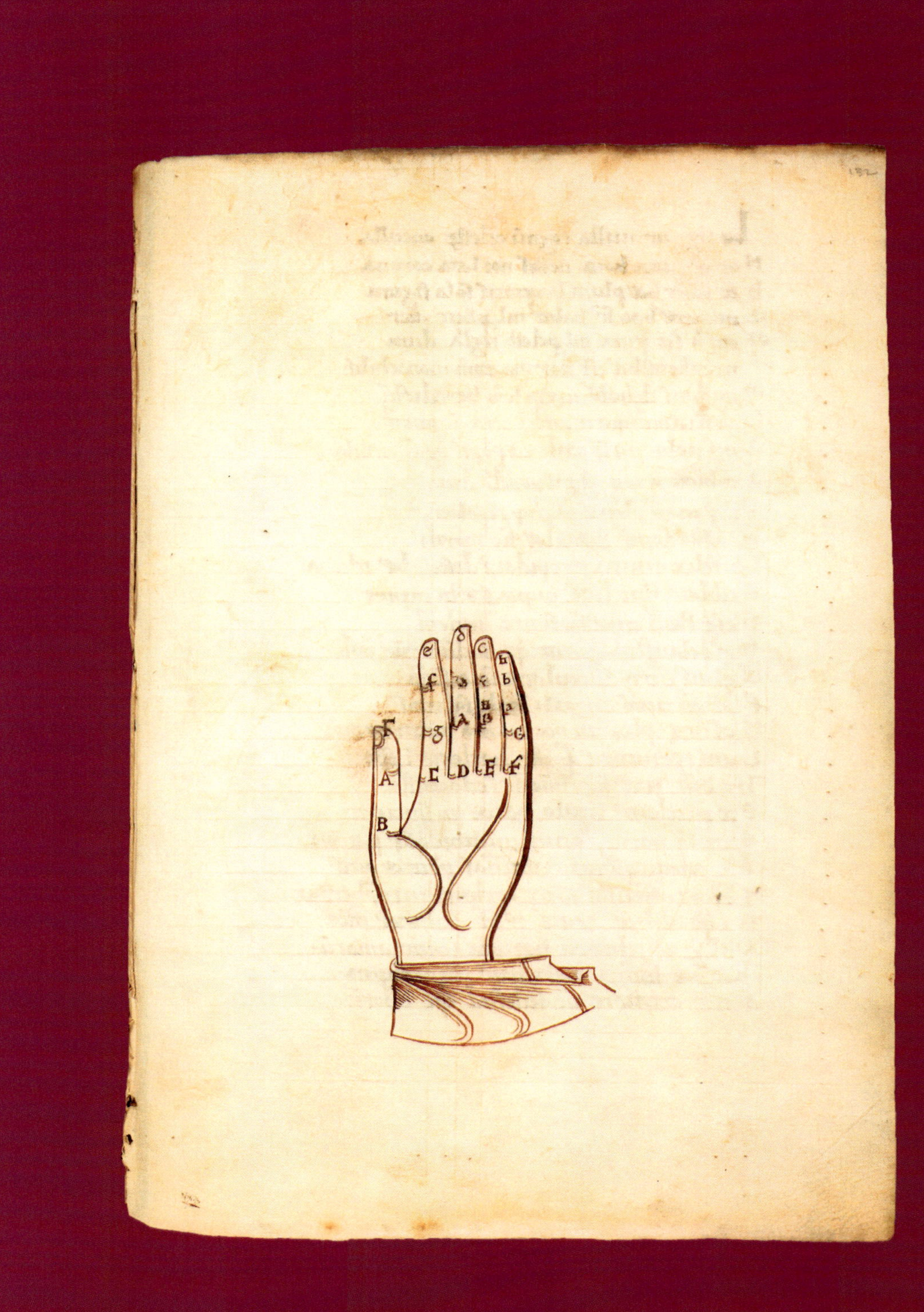

Liber enchiriadis de musica
(A Handbook on Music)
(12th – 13th century)

Collection of texts on music, including those by
Cassiodorus (490 – died about 585) and Guido
d'Arezzo (born about 991 – died after 1033)
Paris, BnF, MS Lat. 7211, fol. 132r

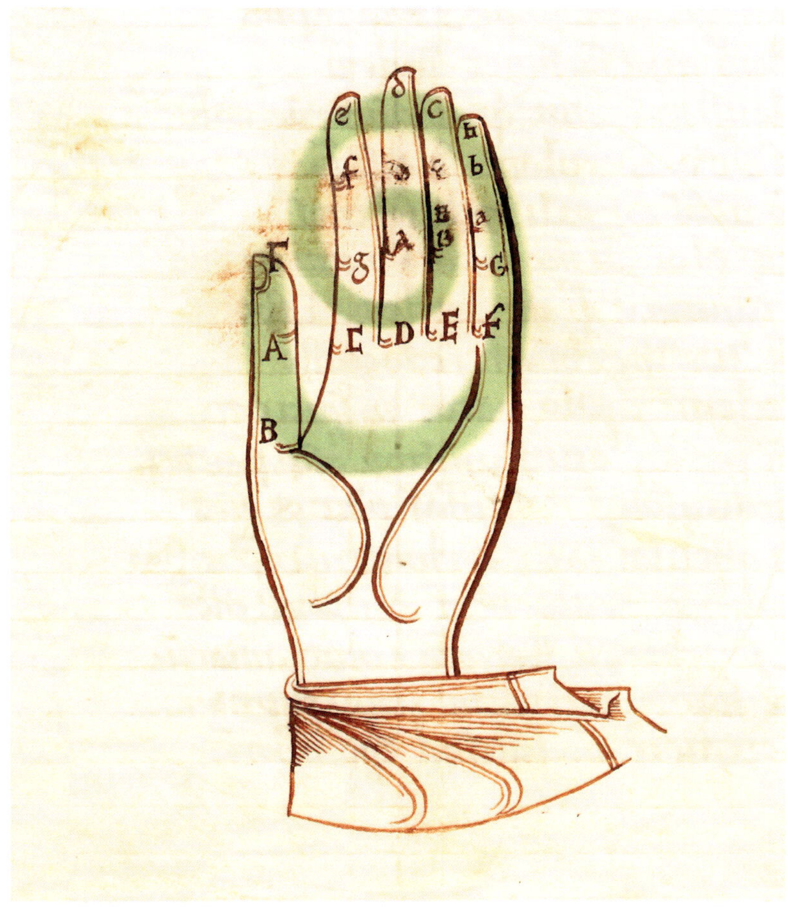

Coloring: Jessica Chen Lee

C hant as a conduit of prayer and salvation commands a *choros*-structure. The musical scale, known as a gamut, is the complete building unit of the system. In medieval times, the ascent through the scales was envisioned in the left human hand, each tone passing through each knuckle. This mnemonic device is known as the Guidonian hand, named after Guido d'Arezzo, an eleventh-century music theoretician (Fassler 2014, pp. 95–102). By contrast, today we conceptualize the musical scale as a piano keyboard—linear and disembodied, and thus we miss its spiraling structure and its capacity to uplift to the divine.

When a monastery composed a new liturgy, it could share it with other institutions by means of a *libellus* (booklet). This example, from Paris, BnF, MS Nouv. Acq. Lat. 443, contains the eleventh-century Office of the Feast of Sainte-Foy at Conques. This *libellus* was eventually bound with other small-format *libelli* whose texts were performed on the same occasion: the *Passio* (Passion), *Liber Miraculorum*, (Book of Miracles), and a vernacular *Canso* (Song) of Santa Fides. At some point in the twelfth century, this compilation was brought to the monastery of Saint-Benoît-sur-Loire. Today, this manuscript has been divided and the parts are kept at four different collections: Paris, Orléans, Vatican City, and Leiden (Grémont 1969; Huglo 1971; Huglo 2009; Pentcheva 2021b; Pentcheva 2022ab; Pentcheva 2023a).

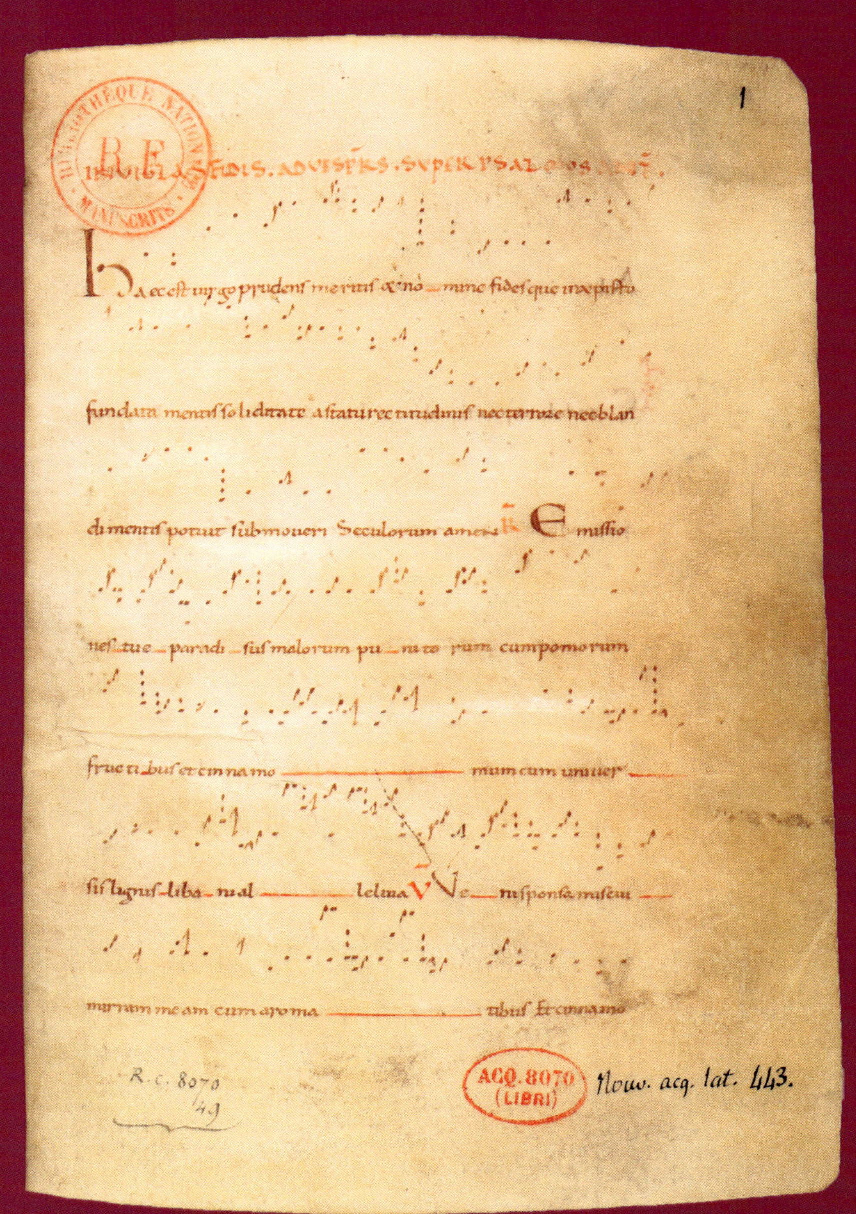

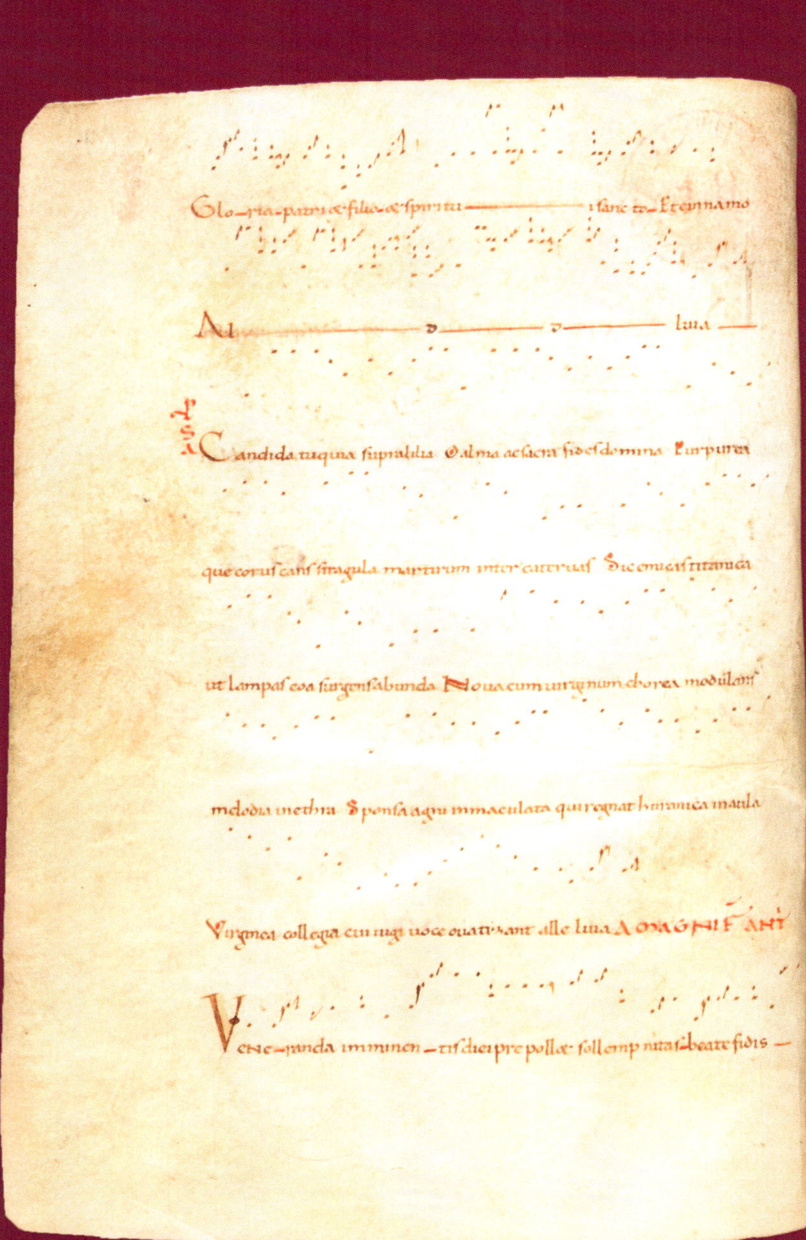

The first two pages, known as folios 1recto and verso (fols. 1rv), contain the responsory *Emissiones Tue* (Your Aromas) for the vespers liturgy of Sainte-Foy at Conques (Cantus n.d. chant ID 600779 and 600779a). A responsory is an elaborate chant that is sung after reading aloud such texts as the passion of the saint during the feast (Hiley 1993). Responsories are connectors; they enable the faithful to retain the vivid images they have just encountered in listening to the narrative text and then hear these ideas again in song. Responsories help the participants discover nuances as they retell the narrative in poetry and music.

Pages from a *Libellus* or small-format book of the *Office of Sainte-Foy* (1037–1065)

Paris, BnF, MS Nouv. Acq. Lat. 443, fols. 1rv.

Responsory *Emissiones tue* and
Prosa Candida tu quia

Respond: Emissiones tue paradisus malorum punitorum cum pomorum fructibus

Refrain [Repetendum]: *et cinnamomum cum universis lignis libani. Alleluia* **(Melody A)**

Verse: Veni sponsa miscui mirram meam cum aromatibus (Melody B)

Refrain: *et cinnamomum cum universis lignis libani. Alleluia* (Melody A)

Doxology: Gloria patri et filio et spiritui sancto (Melody B)

Refrain: *et cinnamomum cum universis lignis libani* (Melody A)

Untexted Melody based on the cadence (end melody) of the Refrain: *Alleluia* (Melody A¹)

**Prosa Candida tu quia repeating the
melody of the Untexted Alleluia (Melody A¹)**

1a Candida tua quia supra lilia,

1b o alma ac sacra Fides domina.

2a Purpurea que coruscans stragula martyrum inter catervas,

2b sic emicas titanica ut lampas eoa surgens ab unda.

3a Nova cum virginum chorea modulans melodia in ethra,

3b sponsa agni immaculata, qui regnat huranica in aula.

4 Virginea collegia cui jugi voce ovatizant alleluia.

Respond: Your aromas are a paradise with fruits of pomegranate and apples
Refrain [Repetendum]: *and cinnamon with cedars of Lebanon, Alleluia*
Verse: Come, my bride, mix my myrrh with the perfumes
Refrain: *and cinnamon with cedars of Lebanon, Alleluia*
Doxology: Glory to the Father, and the Son, and the Holy Spirit
Refrain: *and cinnamon with cedars of Lebanon, Alleluia*
Untexted Melody based on the cadence (end melody) of the Refrain: *Alleluia* (Melody A^1)

*Prosa **Candida tu quia** repeating the*
melody of the Untexted Alleluia (Melody A^1)

1a [You are] brighter than the lily,

1b O nourisher and holy mistress, Fides.

2a Glittering in your purple dress among the gathering of the martyrs,

2b you shine like a star, rising from the Titans' eastern wave.

3a New, in the choir of virgins, [you] sing melodiously in the heavens,

3b as the bride of the immaculate lamb, who rules in the celestial courts.

4 In whom the choirs of virgins exult with their concordant praise "Alleluia."

Latin from the *Office of Sainte-Foy*, ed. Bouillet 1900, p. 644,

English translation: Bissera V. Pentcheva

Heavenly Re-singings:
Poetry, Music, and Imagination

Choroi (Circles)

To the medieval mind, the cosmos was a vision of perfection, where the celestial spheres produced music called *musica mundana* that remained inaudible to humans. This music issued from the ceaseless and harmonious revolutions of the stars around a fixed axis. Humanity aspired to these eternal rotations (*choroi*) and emulated them in their own ring structures of the daily liturgy and its melodies. The vespers responsory is an elaborate chant performed after the faithful have just tasted the beginning of the story of the saint's life. The responsory *Emissiones tue* (Your aromas) employs a ring structure, which is made perceptible through five repetitions of the melody A of the refrain (*repetendum*) (Pentcheva 2023a).

melodia in ethra, sponsa agni immaculara, qui regnat huranica in aula. Virginea collegia cui jugi voce ovatizant alleluia. Nova cum virginum chorea modulans stragula martyrium inter catervas, sic emicas titanica ut lampas eoa surgens abunda. Purpurea que coruscans lignis libani. Alleluia. Candida tua qui supra lilia, o alma et sacra Fides domina. Alleluia. Gloria patri et filio et spiritui sancto et cinnamomum cum universis lignis libani. Veni sponsa muscue mirram meam cum aromatibus et cinnamomum cum universis lignis libani. Alleluia. et cinnamomum cum

Color diagram: Jessica Chen Lee

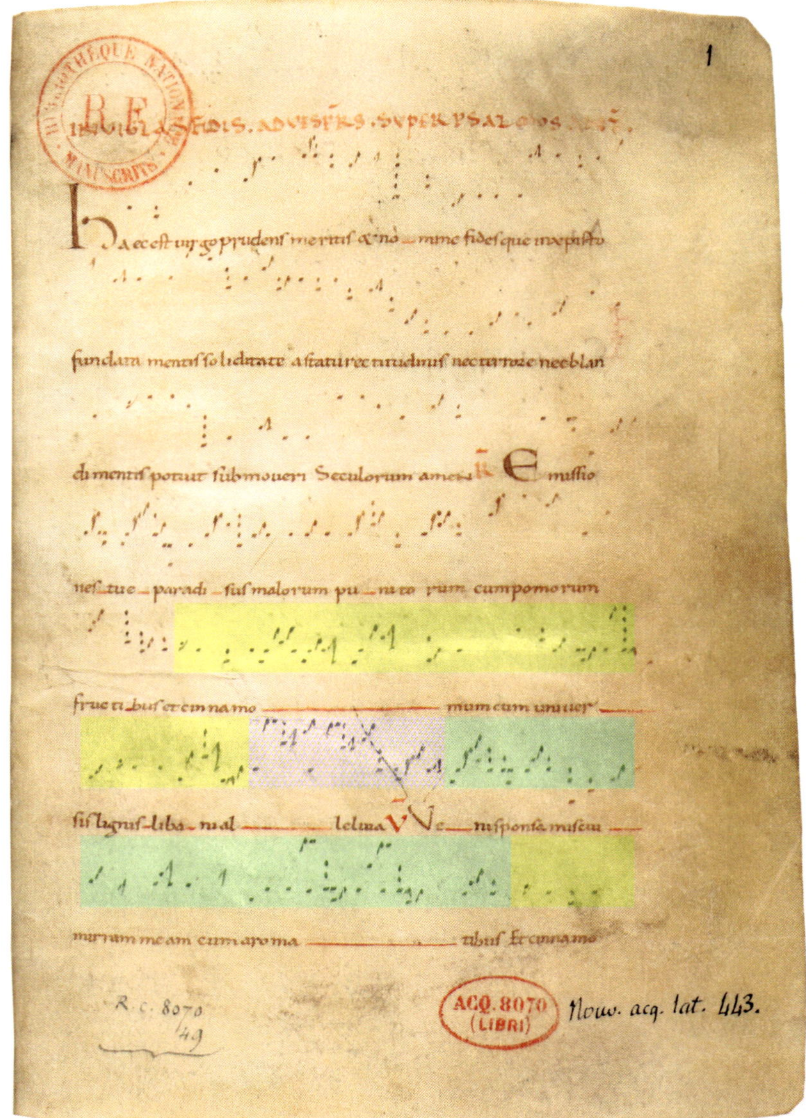

Melodic structure of the responsory
Emissiones Tue (Your Aromas)

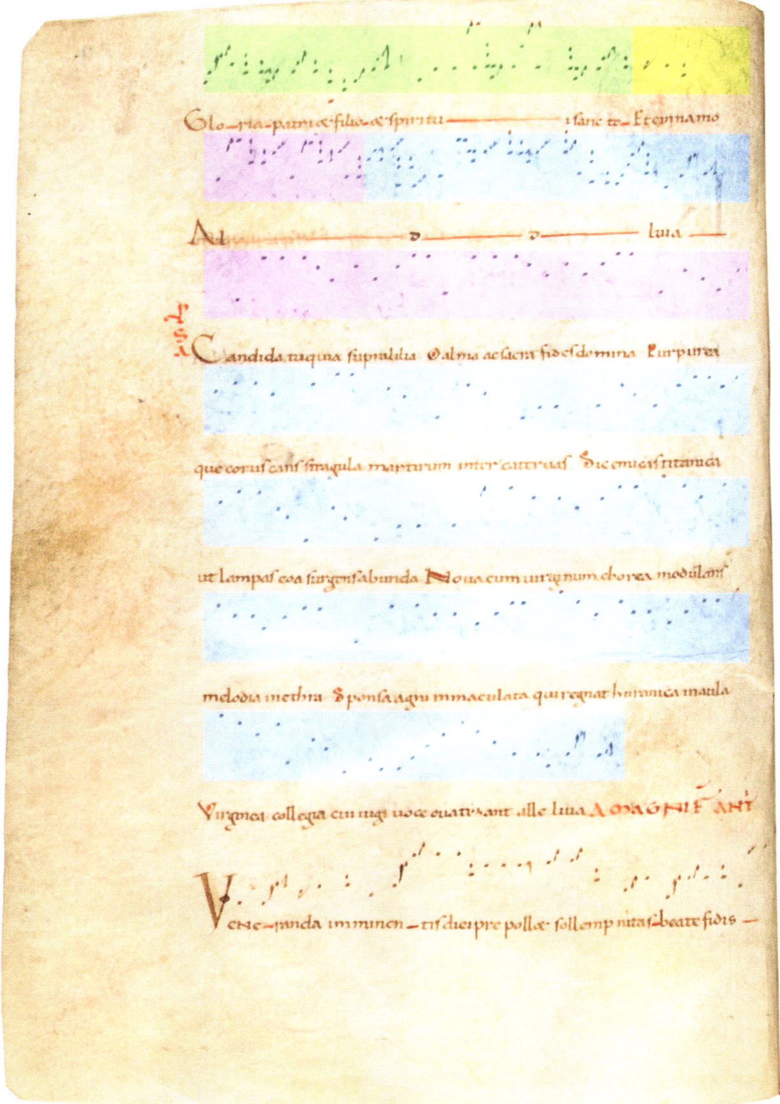

The structure of this responsory is:

Starting melody

A-melody (Refrain) et cinnamomum

B-melody Veni sponsa

A-melody et cinnamomum

B-melody Gloria Patri

A-melody et cinnamomum

A¹-melody Alleluia

A¹-melody Candida tu quia… Alleluia

Coloring: Jessica Chen Lee

The chant *Candida tu quia* (You are brighter) narrates the vision of Sainte-Foy entering the celestial courts (Cantus n.d., chant ID no. g03234; Pentcheva 2021b).[1] Its melody is first encountered when sung to the word "alleluia," a sound believed to be an angelic utterance outside the register of human language, and thus, enthralling in its incomprehensibility (Fassler 1993, p. 44). The melodic phrase of the last segment of the refrain, coincidentally also the word Alleluia, serves as the first building block of an elaborate melisma (melody A[1]); melisma is the singing of many notes to a syllable. This un-texted Alleluia (melody A[1]) stands for the *musica mundana*, the music of the heavens, lifting the imagination of the faithful to the celestial choirs. The sound of the syllables *Al-le-lu-i-a*, rich with many vowels that diversify the repeated "l," are sung over doubled and repeated variant melodic phrases. The stretching of the singing of Alleluia across long melodies emphasizes the heavenly nature of the sound that obscures the semantics of the word and pushes beyond the register of human speech.

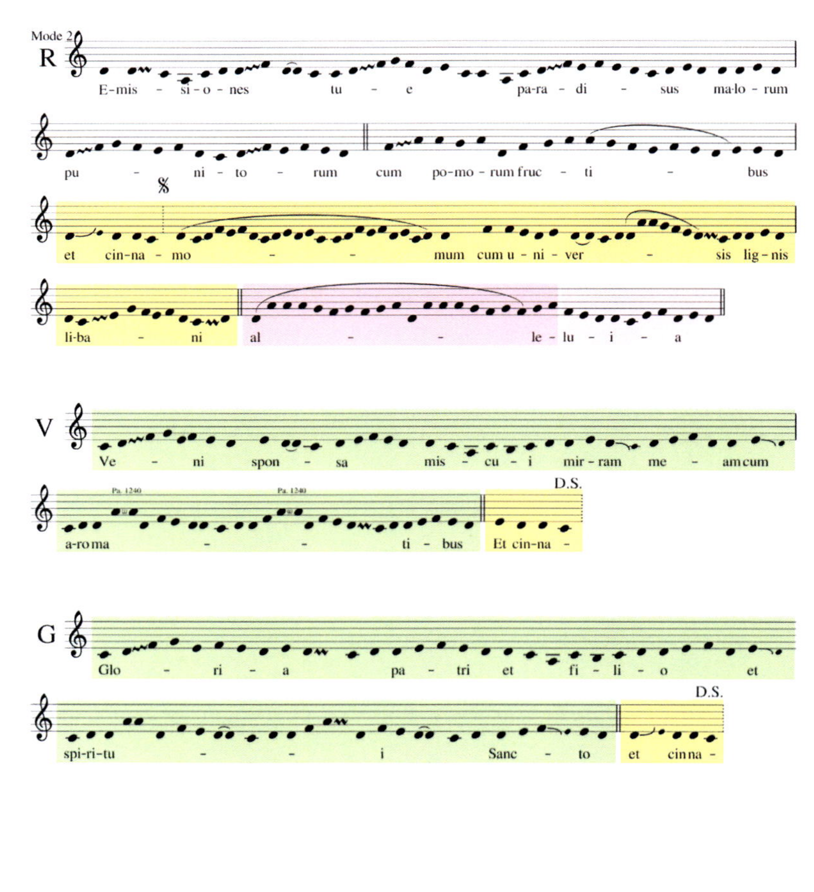

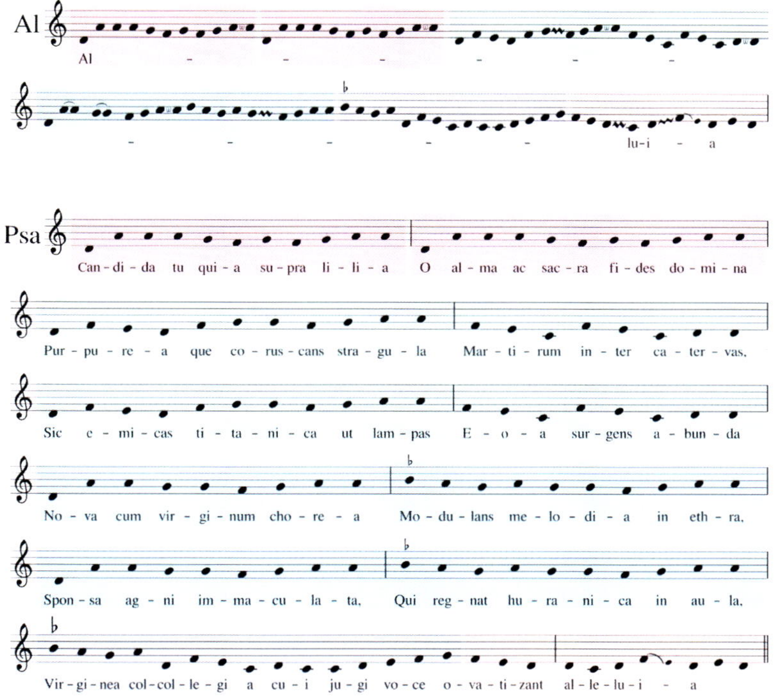

Once we have heard the melody sung to the seemingly endless Alleluia, we encounter it again in the *prosa Candida tu quia*, this time as a syllabic chant—a genre also known as *prosula* or *sequentia* (sequence) that translates the incomprehensible angelic utterance "Alleluia" into human language. Now each note is a bead in a necklace stringing together a vision of Sainte-Foy's ascent to heaven. The circular structure formed by repeating the Alleluia melody in the *prosa Candida tu quia* displays the aural equivalent of the medieval sign ⊕ capturing the entwining of celestial and terrestrial music depicted in manuscripts and the repeat of the same shape in the ring form of the diadem with which Sainte-Foy is crowned at her glorification in heaven. Furthermore, the *prosa* repeats sections of the Alleluia (melody A¹), amplifying the sense of circling that re-inscribes the ring structure of *choros* (Pentcheva 2023a).

Transcription: Laura Steenberge
Coloring: Jessica Chen Lee

---

1. In the Cantus database, this *prosa* is only identified for the feast of Santa Caecilia, without the recognition that it was originally composed for Sainte-Foy (Pentcheva 2021b).

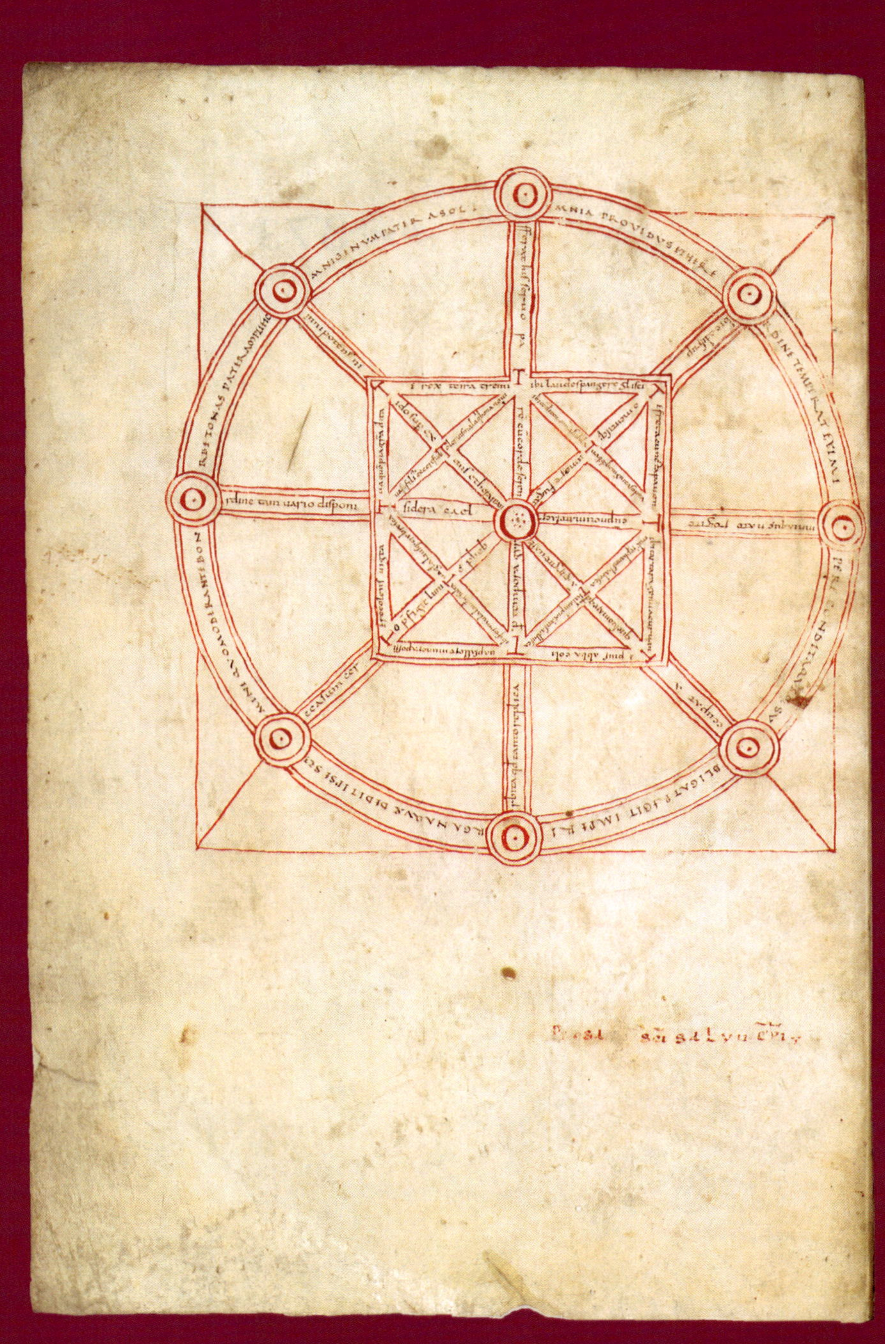

The Music of the Spheres from
MS Lat. 776 (1050–1075)

A Gradual (music MS containing the
chants for Mass) from the monastery of
Saint-Michel at Gaillac in Albi, France
Paris, BnF, MS Lat. 776, fol. 1v

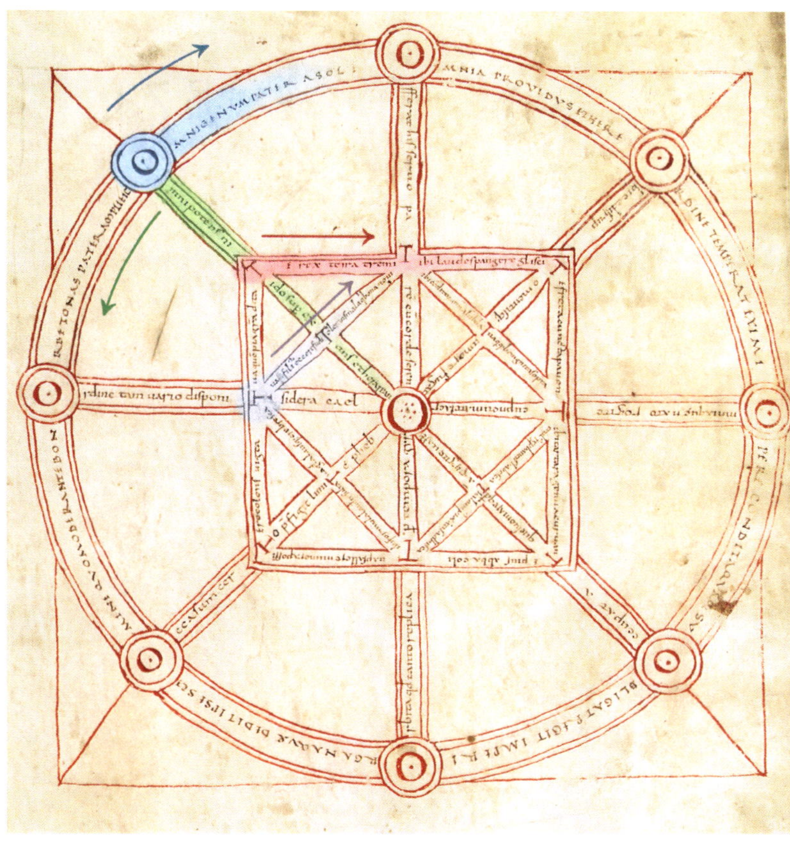

Coloring: Jessica Chen Lee

O1

O2

T3

T4

In this manuscript, four poems appear on the following geometric figures: a circle, its radii, a square, and a rhombus. This diagram serves as a preface to a liturgical manuscript. Both the content of the poems and the shapes they outline draw attention to an orbiting movement. Different circular dynamics are described: the rising and setting of the Sun, the rotation of the stars and seasons, the life of Christ, and finally, the daily liturgy. The first poem is written clockwise on the circumference of the large circle (O1); the second, set counterclockwise on the spokes of the wheel (O2); the third, on the big square (T3); and the fourth, on the enclosed rhombus (T4). The letter O with its round shape in this diagram stands for the divine. The T, which evokes the Cross and Christ's Passion, recalls mortality. The poems (O1 and O2) describe how the divine creates and directs the cosmos into a resounding polyphony. Poems T3 and T4 in the square and the rhombus, which engage with humanity, recall Christ's suffering on the Cross that conquers death and brings Salvation. Human prayer mentioned in T3 and T4 forms a cycle reflecting the larger circular movement of the celestial choirs. The abbot asks that the heavens ultimately open for the faithful, where the blessed would find joy entering the celestial *choros*. Salvation is imagined as a harmonious orbiting movement around God at the center (Pentcheva 2023b).

Omnigenum Pater a solio Poem

O.1

Omnigenum pater a soliO
Omnia providus ethereO
Ordine temperat eximiO
Opere condita quaeque suO
Obligat regit imperiO
Organa quae dedit ipse suO
Omine quo moderante bonO
Orbe tonans pater amplificO

O.2

Omnipotens niTido super exTans ethera fanO
Ordine tam vario disponiT sidera caelO
Occasum cerTo praefigit limiTe ph[o]ebO.
Orbita quod tanto replicaT per tempora gyrO
Occupat aTque suo mare quod Tam gurgite vastO
Omnia quae nato rogiTet cum pneumate sacrO
Obice disrupTo mentisque Tumore fugatO
Offerat his servo paTrem cum corde serenO

T. 3

Te rex terra tremiTibi laudes pangere glisciT
Te freta cuncta pavenTibi tartara genua curvanT
Te pius abba coliTua psallere munera possiT
Te recolens vigeaTua quam pia gratia ditaT

T. 4

Tua filius ecce refugiTolerans mala qui bona noviT
Tibi conditor omnia subdaTua quaeque benignitas optaT
Titulus reprobabtis labescaThalamus pietatis adhiscaT
Tibi formula laudis resultaTua gloria lausque crebescaT.

O.1

The Father of all living creatures from the throne,
foreseeing everything in heaven,
tunes with extraordinary precision
everything set down by his work.
He binds and rules with his command
the musical instruments that he himself creates,
guiding with a good prognostic sign,
the Father thunders in the splendid universe.

O.2

The All-Powerful residing in the luminous temple above the skies
places the stars in such a varied order in heaven.
He determines the sunset for Phoebus as a stable track,
because he replicates its cycle in the grand succession of seasons,
and because he fills the sea with his own so great eddying.
God may ask everything of the Son and the Holy Spirit
after Christ has overcome the obstacle and vanquished death's arrogance,
may the Lord offer to the servant a father with a merciful heart.

T. 3

Before you, o King-Christ, the earth shakes and bursts to affix praise,
all the seas tremble before you, and Hades bends his knees.
The pious abbot venerates you, may he sing you gifts,
worshipping daily, may he have vigor as he gets enriched by your loyal favor.

T. 4

Behold, the Son returns, enduring suffering, he renews your good tidings.
May the Creator supply all to you and whatever kindness desires!
May the condemner's name be ruined, may piety's bridal chamber open!
As your daily acclaim resounds, may your glory and praise increase!

English translation: Bissera V. Pentcheva[2]

2 . I thank Rowan Dorin, John Klopacz, and James Grier for their feedback and suggestions on my translation.

Musica Mundana Produced by the Circular Motility of the Heavenly Bodies

A computer animation enabled viewers to grasp how the diagram of Paris, BnF, MS Lat. 776, fol. 1v encodes the orbiting of the celestial bodies, which results in the music of the heavenly spheres: the *musica mundana*. In this animation, the four poems are spatially inscribed as they gradually fill up their defined visual itineraries. The diagram is transformed from a static image to a kinetic object that begins to rotate. Its central space opens as a screen on which several images are sequentially projected; these include the sixth-century mosaic showing a circle enclosing two rotated crosses from Hagia Sophia; the vision of the lamb set at the center of a cross inscribed in a circle from the Morgan Beatus (New York City, Morgan Library, MS Lat. M644, fol. 87, ca. 945), and finally a timelapse of the night sky with the circular tracks of light left by the rotating stars. All of these images projected inside the frame of the diagram articulate the medieval association of the sign ⊕ with the imagined *choros* (circular motility) engendering the *musica mundana*.

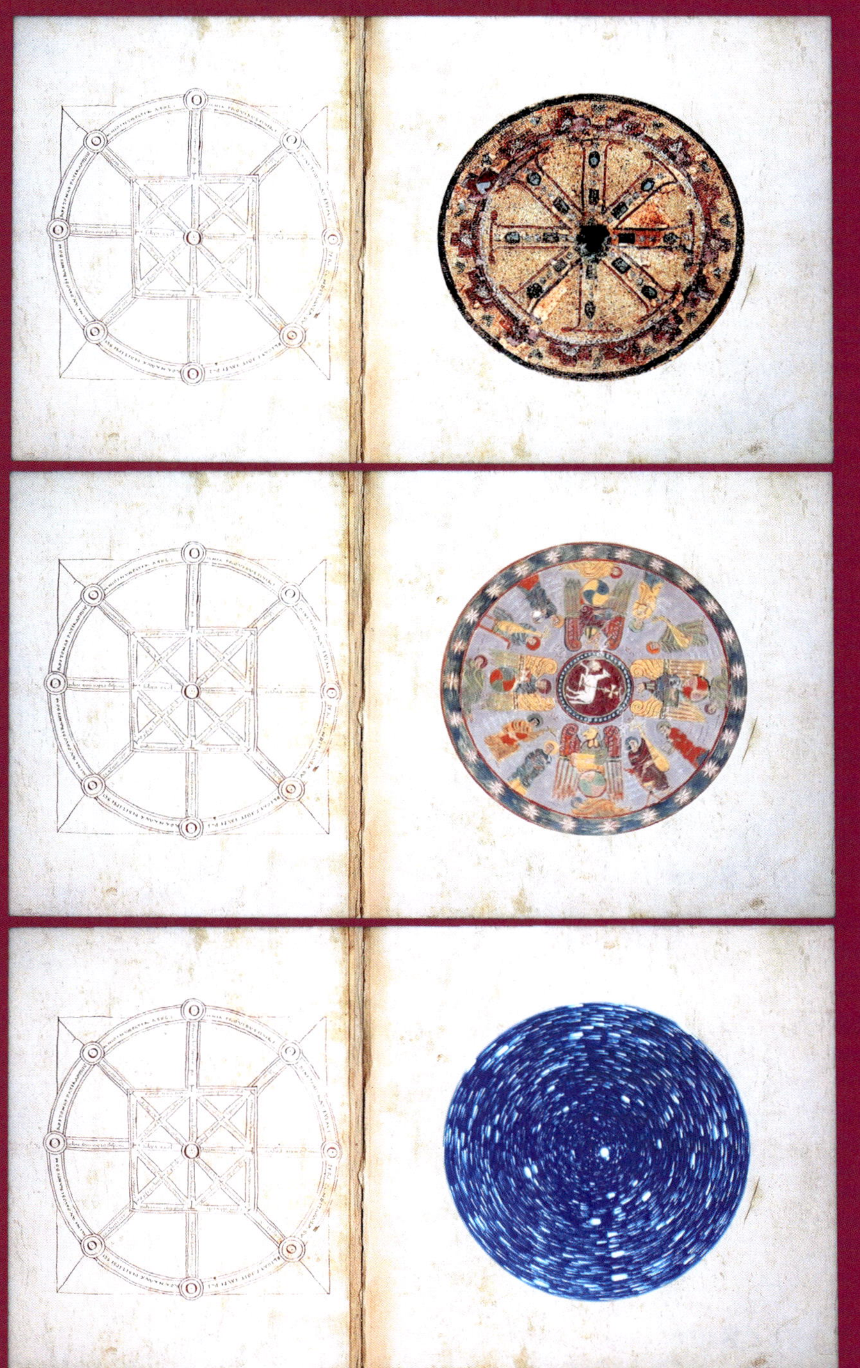

Animation: Blagoy Kostov, Illusion Box
Studio, Sofia, Bulgaria, for Stanford's
"Enchanted Images" Project

The standard medieval form of a circle enclosing two rotating crosses ⊕ marks both the shape of the crown and the form of the stars. The formal similarity between the diagram in MS Lat. 776 and the shape of the crown/star is not haphazard. In medieval culture, the orbiting star is a model of perfection; the saints turn into stars after their martyrdom and glorification (Pentcheva 2020a; Pentcheva 2023a). The miniature crown/star also stores a hidden architectural evocation. The monks on earth aspire to the perfect circular motility of the stars. The choir of the monks forms the axis around which the liturgical ritual revolves. Standing in the crossing under the dome, they occupy the architectural center, which in turn maps the diagram of the miniature in space (Pentcheva 2020a).

Plan of the Monastic Church at Conques

Lithograph after Charles Nodier, Isidore-Justin-Séverin Taylor, and Alphonse de Cailleux, *Voyages pittoresques et romantiques dans l'ancienne France*, 18 vols (Paris: P. Didot, 1833–1837), *Languedoc*, 2 vols. (Paris: P. Didot, 1835). Vol. 1, part 2, p. 264 with the diagram from Paris, BnF, MS Lat. 776, fol. 1v superimposed at the center of the transept

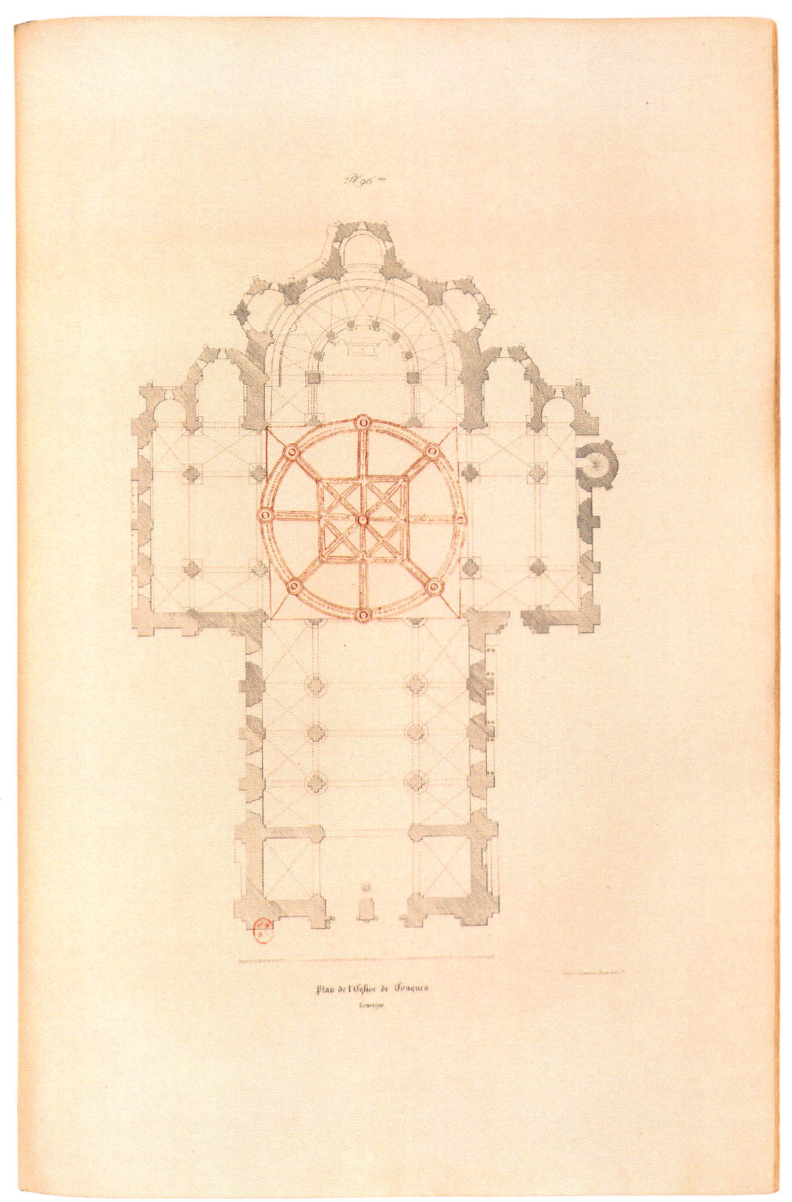

Digital design: Jessica Chen Lee

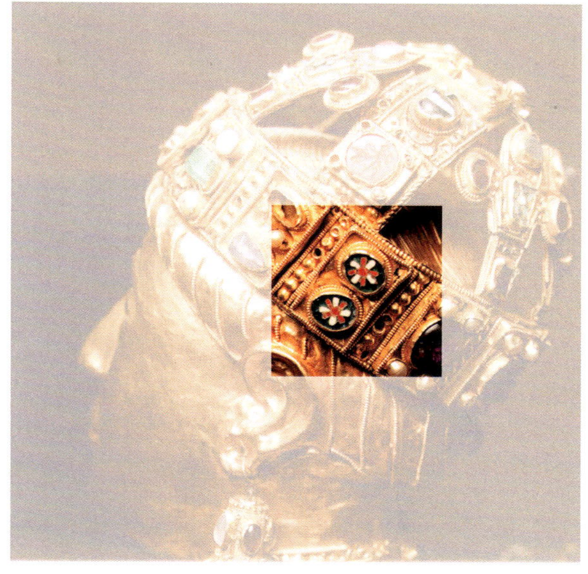

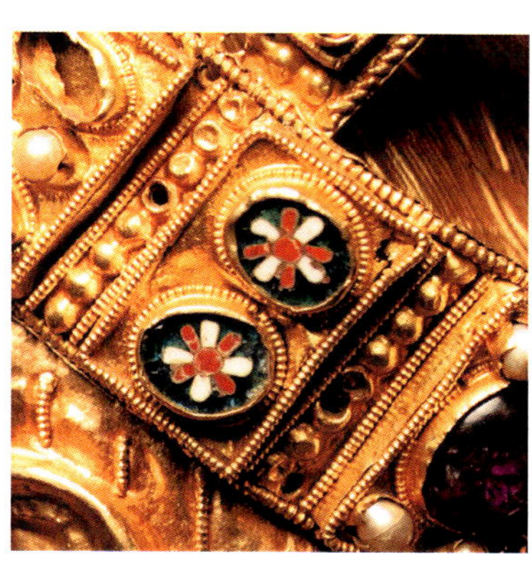

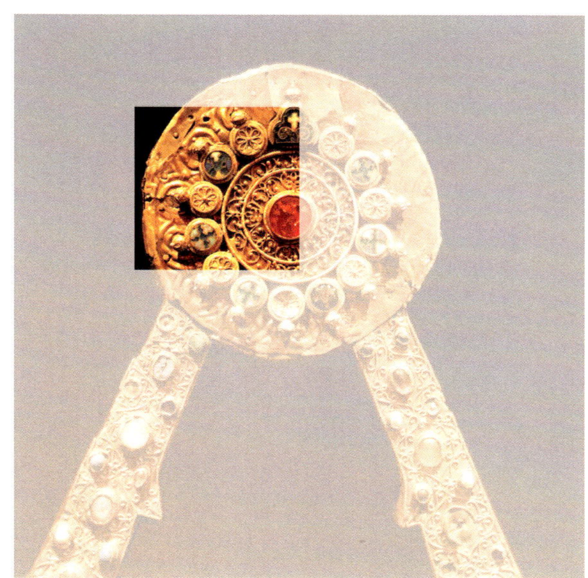

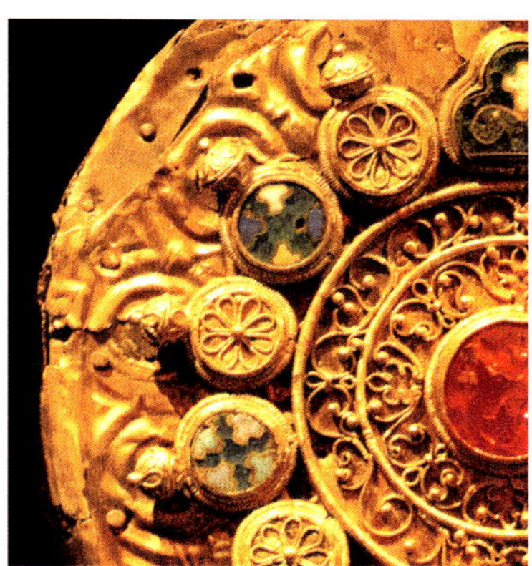

The cruciform design ⊕ of the crown as seen in the enameled roundels on the diadem of Sainte-Foy

(gold, gems, enamel, pearls, late 9th–10th centuries)

and on the
Alpha-reliquary at Conques

(gold, gems, enamels, pearls, an ancient cameo, before 1107, with materials from the 9th century and additions in the 13th century)

Photography: Miguel Novelo

The choir of monks sung under the dome in a privileged space that included the center of the transept and the sanctuary. This sacred ground was separated from the rest of the church by a low permeable barrier consisting of a stone dado and metal grille. This performance space formed the axis around which the *choros* (song and movement) of the liturgy unfolded. The Latin term for the sanctuary and its radiating chapels is *corona*, thus linking the performance space — *choros* — to the shape of the crown ⊕ (Pentcheva 2023d). The architectural *corona* that includes the altar, statue, and the singing monks, forms the field-of-vision in the medieval ecclesiastical theater. Unlike the flatness of the modern screen, the medieval stage is three-dimensional, a revolving sphere, bathed in the light of the rising and setting sun, and flickering candles, and a platform from which the human voice soared up into the tall vaults to fill the church with reverberant sound. The semicircle created by the columns framing the sanctuary's eastern end further enhanced the charisma of this *choros* performance space. A shared structural logic — the *choros* and *corona* ⊕ — unifies architecture, miniature, crown, and the ring-shape of chants.

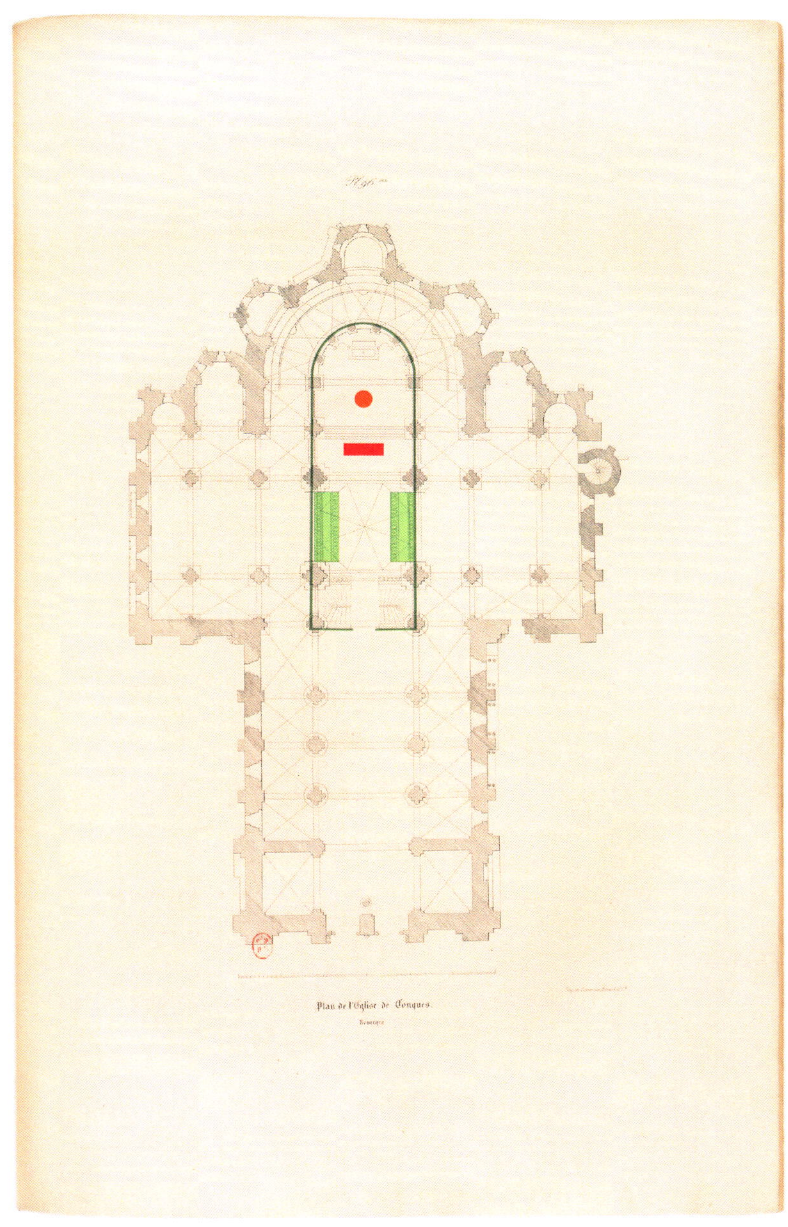

Coloring to indicate the choir, altar and statue: Jessica Chen Lee

The monastic choir forms the axis around which the liturgical ritual revolved. The enclosure of the sanctuary and the location of the monastic choir during service is shown here in green; the altar is in red, and the location of the golden statue in orange. The effigy of the saint would have stood either on the altar or on a pedestal behind the altar (Pentcheva 2020a).

Plan of the Monastic Church at Conques

Lithograph after Charles Nodier, Isidore-Justin-Séverin Taylor, and Alphonse de Cailleux, *Voyages pittoresques et romantiques dans l'ancienne France*, 18 vols (Paris: P. Didot, 1833–1837), *Languedoc*, 2 vols. (Paris: P. Didot, 1835). Vol. 1, part 2, p. 264.

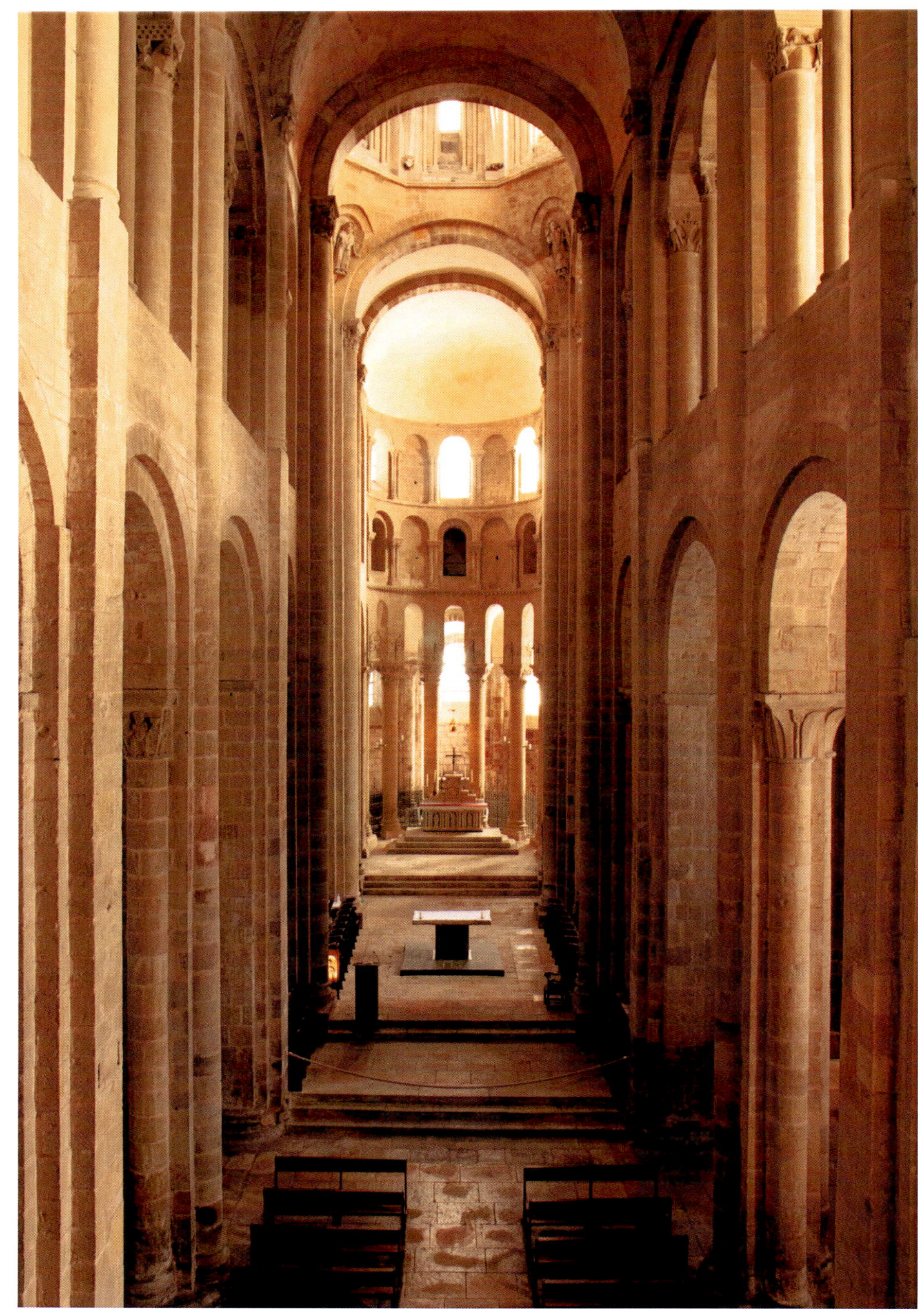

Church of Sainte-Foy at Conques,
view of the nave and sanctuary
from the western gallery

Photograph: Miguel Novelo

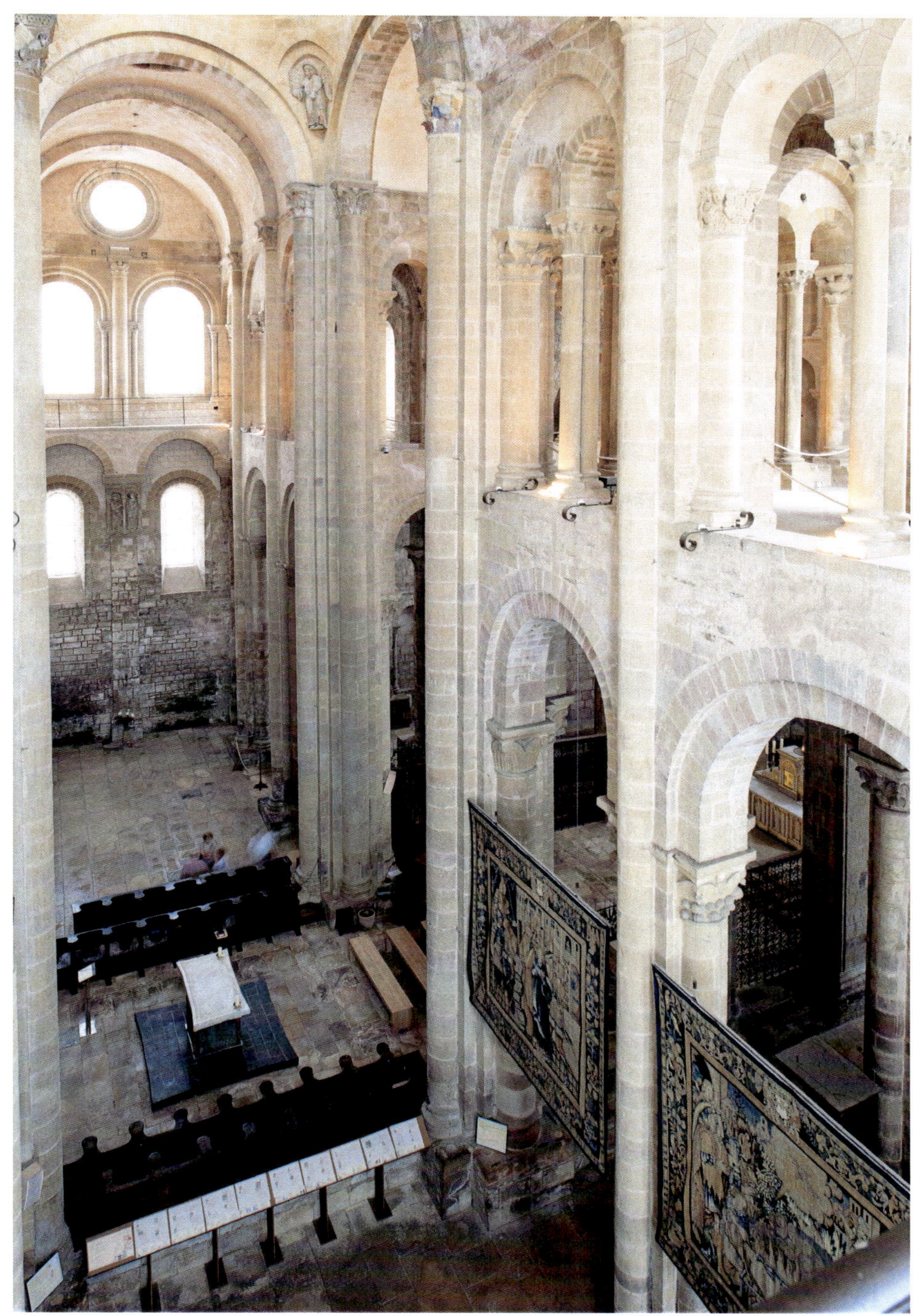

Transept of the church of Sainte-Foy at Conques, view from the southwest revealing the northern end

Photograph: Stephen Murray.
Image courtesy of the Mapping Gothic Project, Media Center for Art History. ©The Trustees of Columbia University.

Medieval Crowns:
A Cross Inscribed
in a Circle

The circular structure built in the performance of the Alleluia and *prosa Candida tu quia*, (Because you are brighter) displays the aural equivalent of the ring shape of the diadem with which Sainte-Foy is crowned at her glorification in heaven. During the Middle Ages, the shape of the crown is typically rendered as a circle with two raised and intersecting bands: a cross inscribed in a circle ⊕. This sign ⊕ communicates two ideas: first, the ideal circular motility — *choros* — through which humanity attunes to the divine and second, sacrifice through the sign of the cross that marks the saint as an emulator of Christ's Passion: an *imitator Christi* (Constable 1995; Pentcheva 2016; Pentcheva 2023ab).

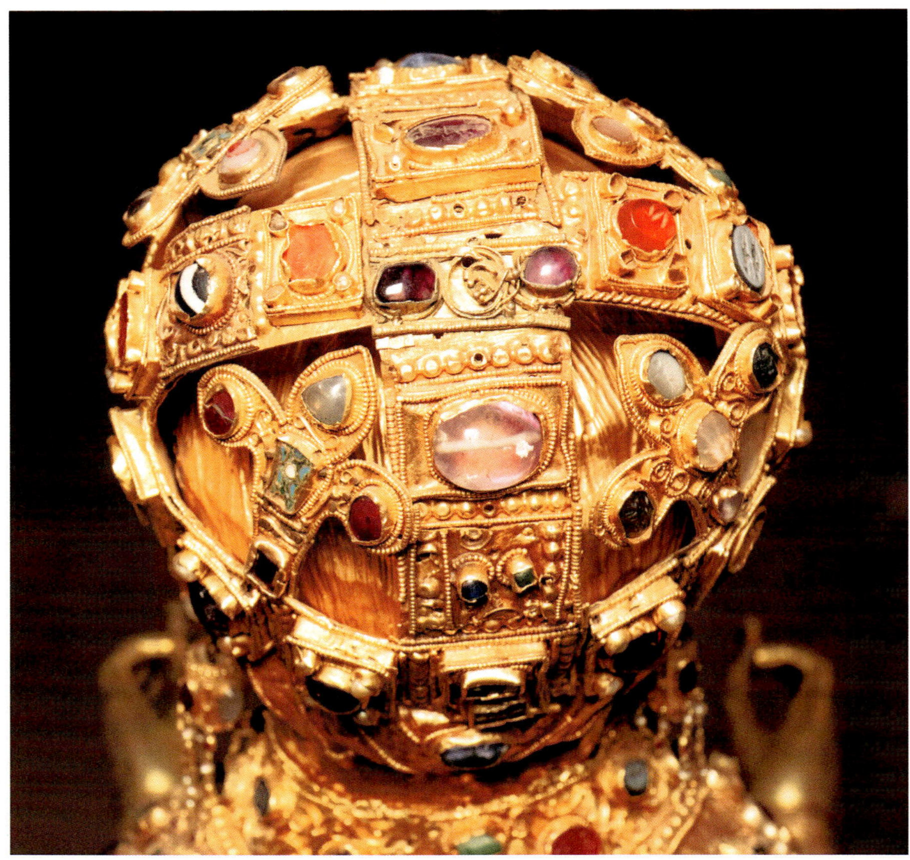

Photograph: *Miguel Novelo*

**Detail, crown of the golden image of
Sainte-Foy (late 9th or early 10th century)**

Gold, enamel, pearls, and gemstones
Abbey Church of Sainte-Foy at Conques, France

The crown is a synecdoche of the resurrected body of the saint. In the twelfth-century Life of Christian of Aumone, the protagonist sees a vision of Saint Augustine and he asks him if all saints are crowned. St. Augustine responds that indeed all are crowned with one crown, and it is Christ (Pentcheva 2016). On the facade at Conques, an angel proffers a diadem that projects in the physical space (Bonne 1984). There is no obvious figure to receive this *corona* in this upper register. But as the gaze descends, it falls on the praying figure of Sainte-Foy on the row below. The crown is for her, marking her as the *corpus spiritale*: the resurrected, star-like, inviolate body.

Through her Christo-mimesis, Sainte-Foy has become the *corona*. She now has the power with her prayer to pull divine energy down to earth. The life-giving force of the Spirit appears to the right in a sequence of progressively rising lids of tombs from which the bodies of the resurrected emerge. Sainte-Foy's glory reflects the Majesty of Christ. And while on the façade the crown hovers over her praying body, in the interior of the church, Sainte-Foy is enthroned and crowned in her golden effigy. She presides in the architectural *corona* of the performance space (Pentcheva 2023b, Pentcheva 2023d).

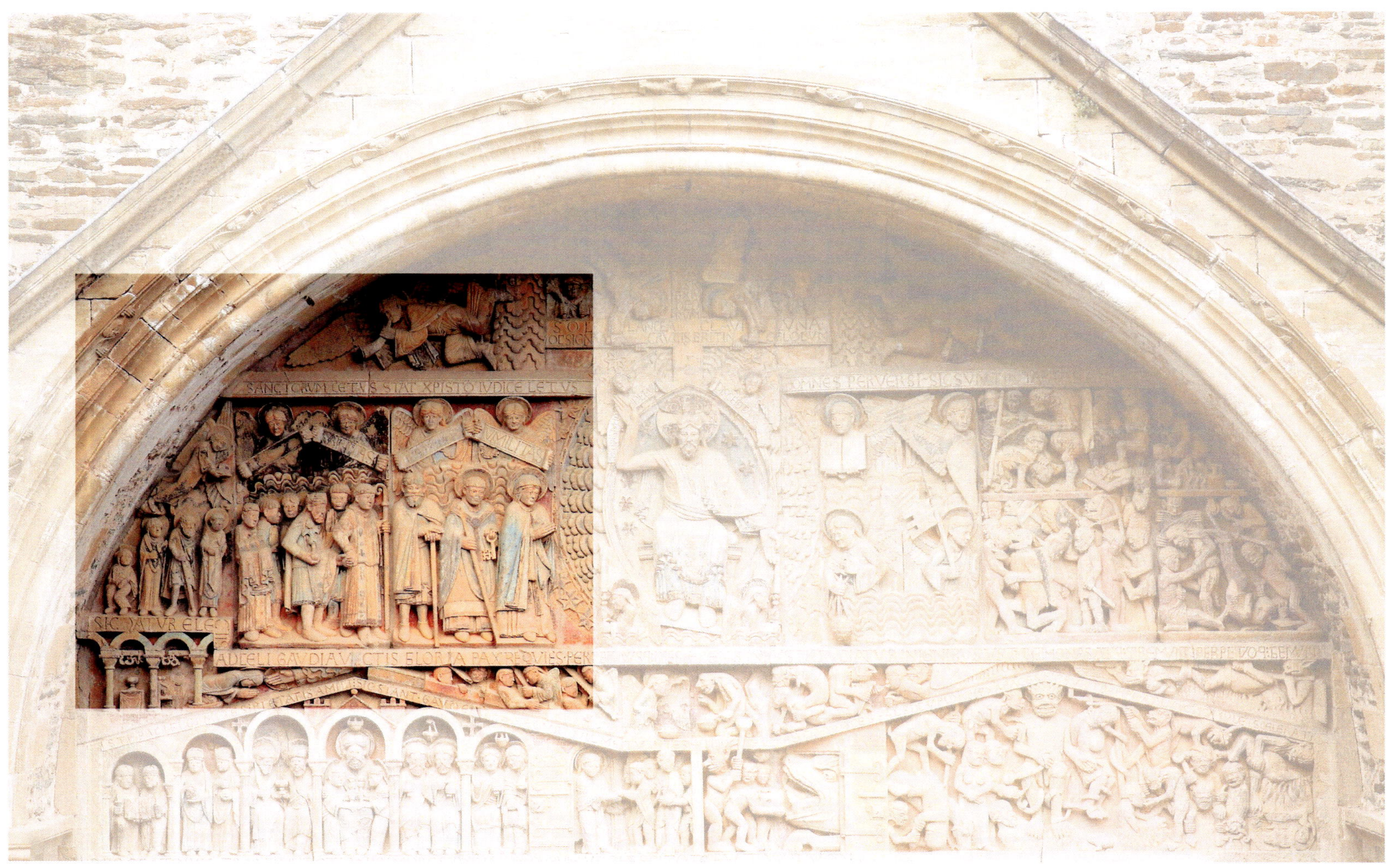

Detail, an angel presenting the martyr's crown (1105–1115)
Relief on the tympanum of the west façade Abbey Church of Sainte-Foy at Conques, France

Photograph: Boris Missirkov

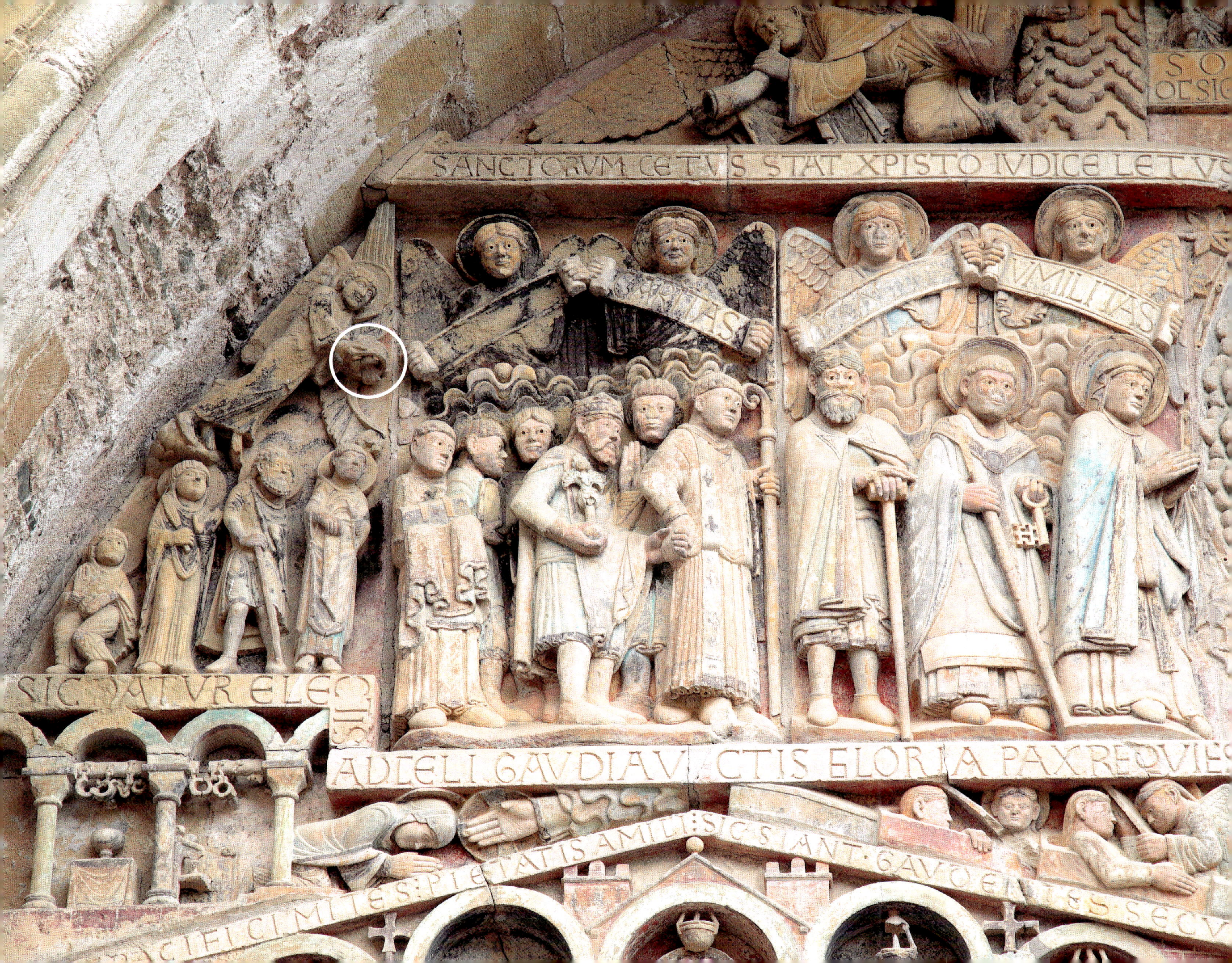
SANCTORVM CETVS STAT XPISTO IVDICE LETVS
VMILITAS
VMILITAS
SIC DATVR ELECTIS
ADELI GAVDIA VNCTIS GLORIA PAX REQVIES
PIETATIS AMILLIS SIC STANT GAVDENTES

This liturgical manuscript, designed for Sélestat, a dependency of Conques in Alsace, contains the music, the Passion, and the Book of Miracles of Sainte-Foy. The decorated initial on this folio opens the Passion of Sainte-Foy. The figural representation illustrates what the liturgy achieves: that the performance resurrects the saint. A monk on a bent knee in the lower lobe of the S pushes a book over an open tomb toward the upper segment of the S. Here, in the higher realm, the protagonists rise: Sainte-Foy, her follower Saint Caprasius of Agen (who is said to have witnessed her beheading), and their killer, the Roman governor Dacianus. Their vertical stance speaks of their emergence from the shadow of the past and their entry into the sensorial flow of the present. What was dead and horizontal is now alive and standing. This resurrection of life contrasts with the threatening advance of death. Dragons slither down the S, ready to devour lions, who in turn open their jaws to swallow the opened tomb. Biting and chewing are dimensions of death issuing from the Latin words for death (*mors*) and *morsum* (a morsel, or a piece bitten off) (Danford 2014). This decorated initial argues that it is the liturgy, exemplified by the book, that arrests the ripping bite of death. By singing the liturgy, the monk brings the past to life in the present and amplifies the voices of the saints that are otherwise no longer audible to humans. The sinuous S also elicits the infinite cycle of a song with a refrain transforming text into chant, past into present, endings into beginnings (Pentcheva 2023a).

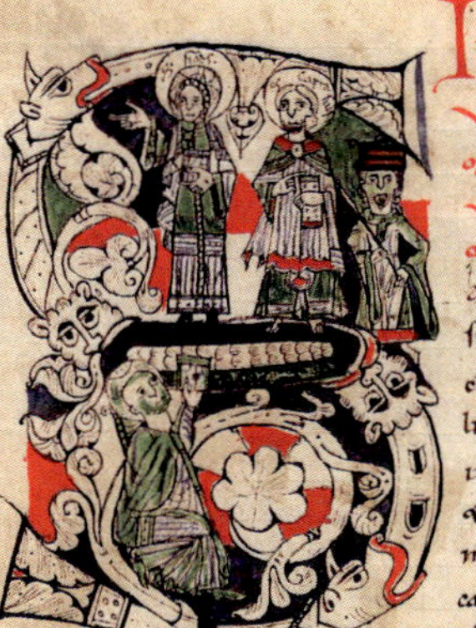

Choros of the festal liturgy
of Sainte-Foy (late 11th–early
12th century)

Sélestat, Bibliothèque Humaniste,
MS Lat. 22, fol. 5v

These two facing miniatures form a pair illustrating Salvation as a *choros* (circular motility allowing humanity to return to God) and explain how it is experienced through the senses. The image on the left shows Salvation by means of the sacraments. A spiral wends its way moving upward toward Christ. Baptism forms the beginning of this ascending *choros* and union with the divine. *Ecclesia*, a personification of the Church, meets the arrivals at the top and offers them a chalice with the blood of Christ. This illustration foregrounds the role of touch, taste, and smell in partaking in the Divine through the sacraments.

The miniature on the right introduces the sense of sight. Christ appears at the center of the O, the initial of *osculetur* (may he kiss), the first word of the Song of Songs. Angels surround His majesty. The elect climb up, seeking union with Christ. Children have gathered at the top platform. An angel touches the eyes of the rightmost child. This gesture is symbolic, showing how the faithful will be purified and will then be able to see God face to face. The spiral and the circle (*choros*) in the composition of these two miniatures visualize the dynamic through which the energy of Salvation flows: it orbits and ascends (Franze 2021; Pentcheva 2022b).

Choros as the cycle of Christian life (ca. 1000 CE)

Commentary on the Song of Songs
Bamberg, Germany, Staatsbibliothek, Bibl. MS Lat. 22, fols. 4v and 5r

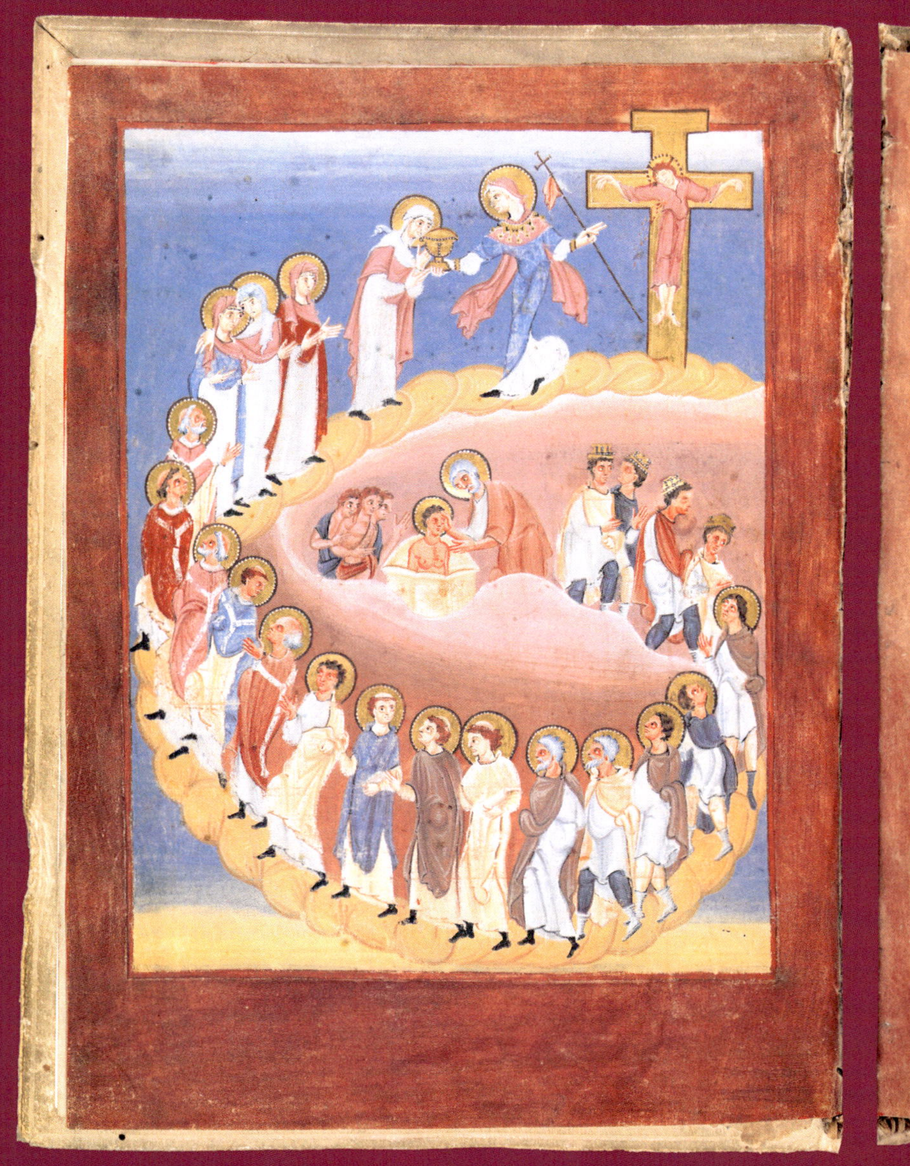
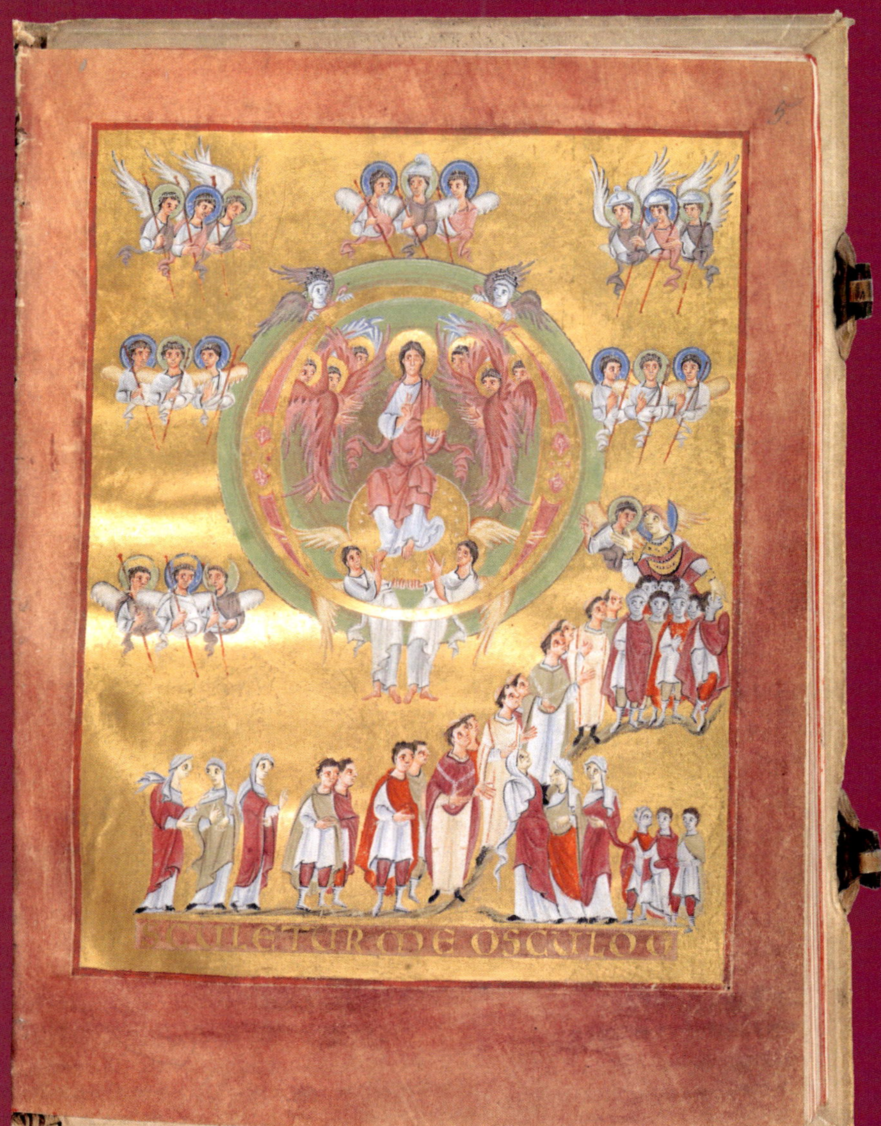
· OSCULET UR ME OSCULO ·

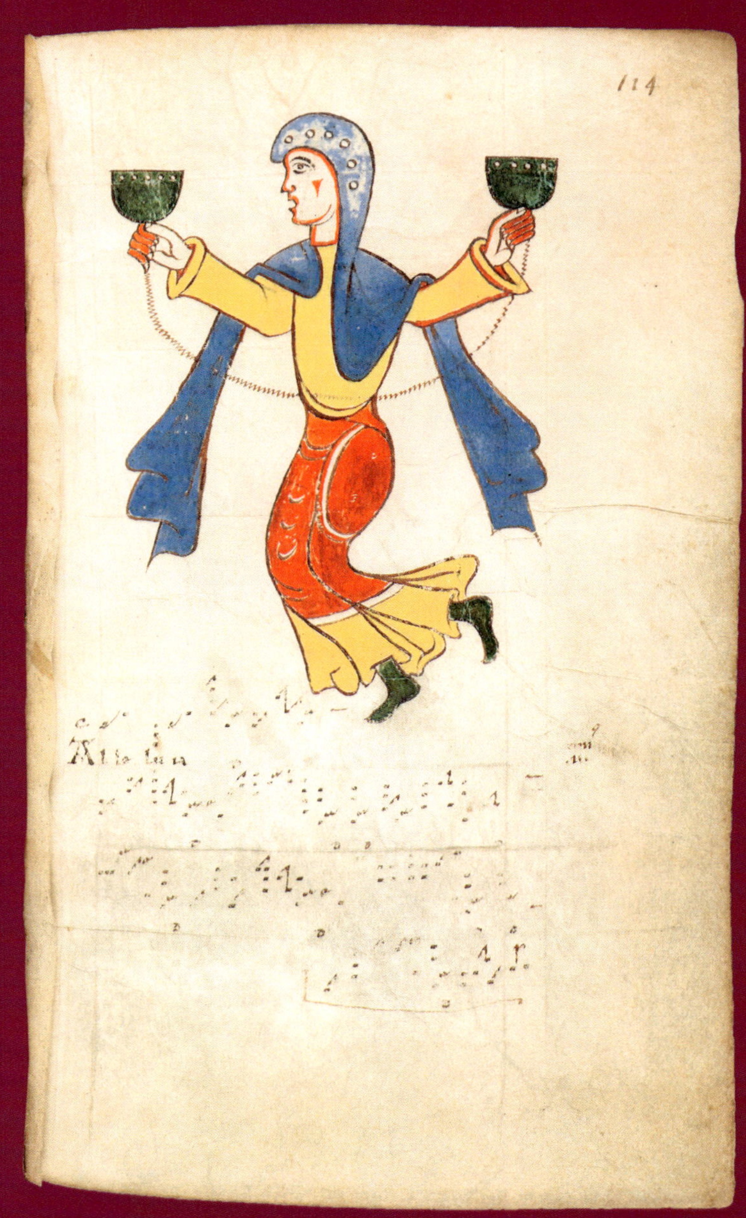

Choros in a dancer-singer (dated
987–996) and an untexted Alleluia
(music added after 1030)

Paris, BnF, MS Lat. 1118, fol. 114r
Monastery of Sant Sadurní de
Tavèrnoles, Catalonia

The diagram of a circle encompassing inscribed rotated crosses in MS Lat. 776, the ring structure in the performance of the responsory *Emissiones tue* and Alleluia and *Prosa Candida tu quia*, and finally the circle-with-a-cross shape ⊕ of the saintly crown communicate the ideal circular motility — *choros* — through, which humanity attunes to the divine (Pentcheva 2017; Pentcheva 2020a). *Choros* is both chant and dance. The miniature in Paris, BnF, MS Lat. 1118 presents an opportunity to explore *choros* as voice and movement through space.

This liturgical manuscript — a *proser-troper* identifying two genres of elaborate chants sung for the liturgy of Mass — from the monastery of Sant Sadurní de Tavèrnoles, Catalonia, is best known for the large and brightly colored illuminations found in the tonary, a reference section that groups chant melodies according to the eight modes (Collamore 2006). Musical modes define the scale, stock motifs, and general construction of a chant. The eight illustrations depicting musicians and jugglers function as a visual mnemonic for each mode.

At the end of the tonary, there is a curious ninth miniature: a dancer-singer with mouth wide open and body swayed in a swift forward motion. In her uplifted arms she holds two chained cups of a percussion instrument: an audiovisual pun on the Latin verb *tympanizo* ("to beat" and "to resound") that elicits both the sound of a voice and steps pounding in space. The notation oscillates in peaks of ascending and descending notes, meeting the dancing figure and mirroring the jagged contours in the folds of her dress. This music was added in the 1030s and represents an untexted Alleluia. A florid melisma is set to the last syllable "a" of Alleluia. Paired together, dance and chant exemplify a virtuoso performance designed to reach the level of joy equal to the imagined celestial exaltation (Pentcheva 2021b).

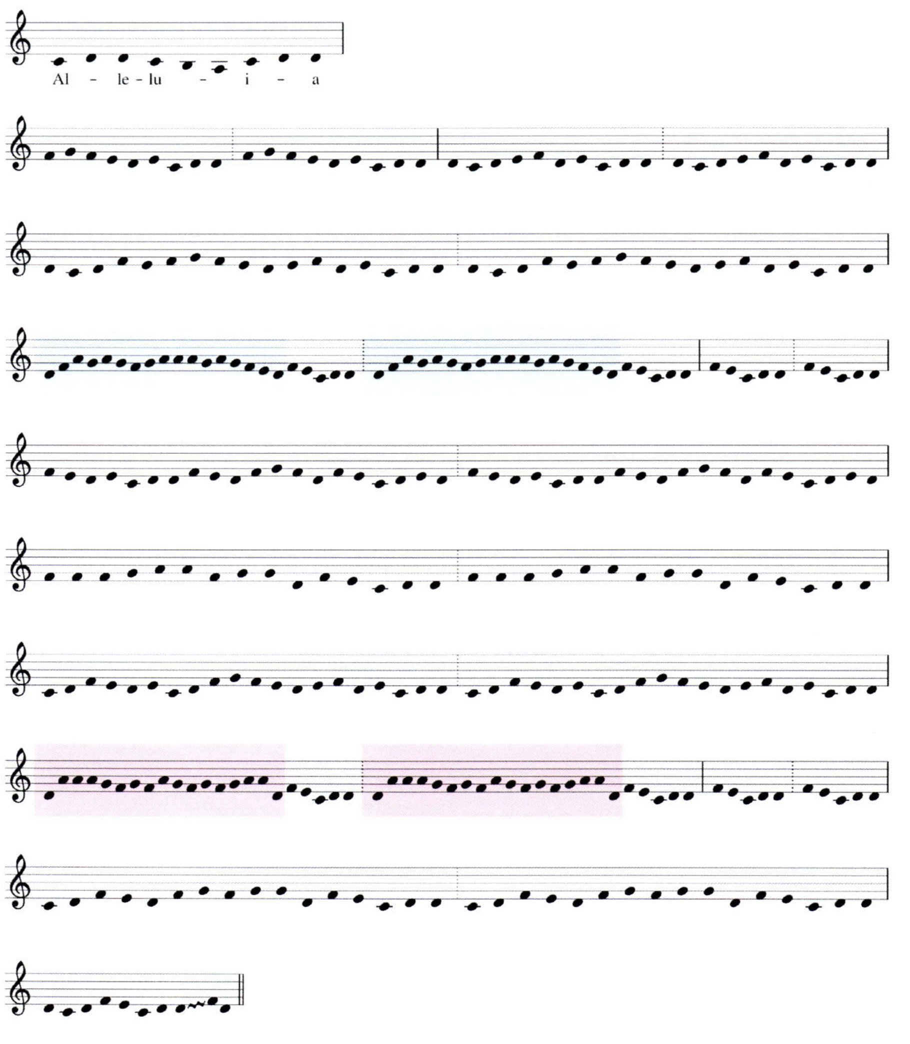

Almiphona Alleluia, MS 1118, f. 114r

The reconstruction of the chant here is assisted by comparisons to the other version of the same song on f. 131v. All repeats have been fully written out to visualize the entire length of the chant.

Transcription: Laura Steenberge
Coloring: Jessica Chen Lee

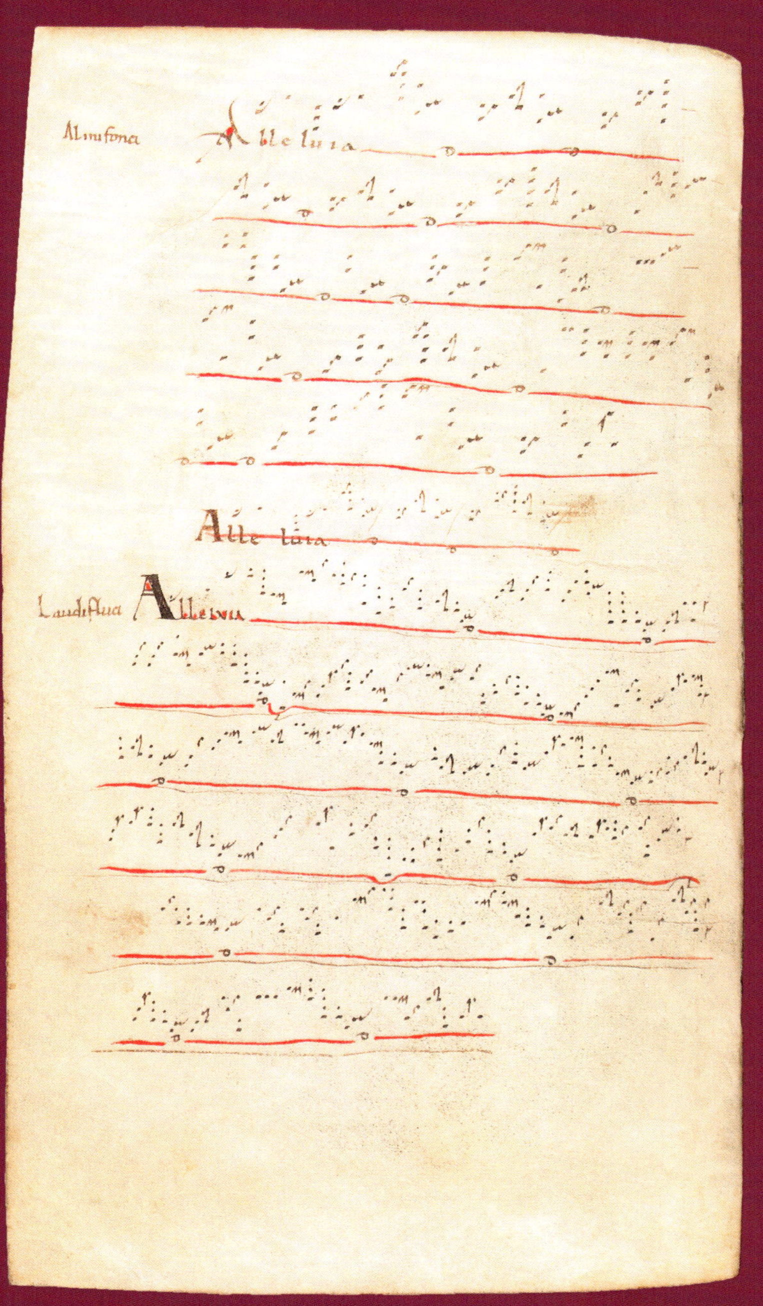

The untexted Alleluia on folio 114r suggests that as long as the breath lasts in singing the melismas, the eternal is sensorially perceptible to mortals. The beauty and artistry of the human dance and chant can elicit the perfection of the eternal celestial *choros* (the imagined round dance and chant of the stars). The Alleluia melody on folio 114r appears again on fol. 131v, which brings to the fore the idea of eternity in the instant. The poem is not written out; only its first word appears in the margin of folio 131v: *almiphona*, or "blessed-sounding." This is the incipit or first word of the sequence (*prosa*) *Almiphona iam gaudia* (Blessed-Sounding Joys Precisely Now), which describes the Holy Spirit as a voice, whose effortless song envelops the celestial gathering in a bright aura. The melodic phrases to which this vision is sung mirror sonic motifs featured in the vespers responsory of Sainte-Foy: the melismatic Alleluia and its poetic rendering as syllabic *prosa Candida tu quia* (Pentcheva 2021b).

Almiphona (Blessed-Sounding) *prosa*
(987–996)

Paris, BnF, MS Lat. 1118, fol. 131v
Monastery of Sant Sadurní de Tavèrnoles, Catalonia
(Cantus n.d., chant ID no. ah53076)

Almiphona *prosa*

1 Almiphona iam gaudia; caeli rutilant per climata; elogiantur cuncta bona.

2a Pneumatis afflata sacra flamma replentur hodie quis piorum, affabre corda pura,

2b Renovantur namque festalia typicalia dudum in Sina Moysi consignata.

3a O beata et vera gaudia homo cum celsa petit, Deus et ima in ignis forma.

3b Pace namque hodie in vera sunt copulata duo animalia: superna ima.

4a Theologa rhemata concrepet utriusque diapason vera.

4b Cherubin aetherea seraphin atque cuncta ignicoma turma

5a Tuba jubilaea tympanizet rupta vincula.

5b Prius verbigenam detinebant quae nexam drachmam.

6a Nunc vos Michael satrapa Gabriel vera police dans nuntia

6b Nos terrigenas vernulas ferte in vestras policas officinas.

7a Nunc ergo cuncta superna juncta phalanga benedicat sanctum pneuma voce sonora.

7b Cujus et munere compta testula rubra redimpendat vera symbola enharmonica

8a Esse ultima vel particula mereamur ejus in aula.

8b Amen omnia subiungant pium mente pura iam nunc redempta

9 Rite canentes alleluia.

1 Blessed-sounding joys precisely now; the heavens glow red in the midst of the constellations; may all good tidings be uttered.

2a Today the pure hearts of the pious are skillfully inspired by the Spirit,

2b For indeed the symbolic festivities once assigned to Moses at Sinai are [now] renewed.

3a O blessed and pure joys, [which] man together with the heavens seeks, divine and human [linked] in the form of fire.

3b In peace today indeed the two forms of life are united: the celestial and terrestrial.

4a May the divine words ring true, a diapason [octave] through both ends.

4b The celestial cherubin and seraphin and the entire fiery-haired crowd

5a resound with a triumphant trumpet, [for] the chains are broken,

5b which formerly detained the Word-begotten one [Christ], held hostage for [a bag of] coins.

6a Now you, Michael the general [and] Gabriel, giving true messages from heaven,

6b bring us, earthborn servants, into the heavenly workshops.

7a Now with the whole celestial army gathered together, may the Holy Spirit offer blessing with a melodious voice.

7b And through the ruddy lantern, adorned with [the Holy Spirit's] gift, may he [the Holy Spirit] offer again the true and melodious symbols.

8a May we be deemed worthy to be even the humblest part of his palace.

8b Amen; may everything join the pious, with pure and now redeemed mind

9 in duly singing Alleluia.

Latin in: Cantus n.d., chant ID no. ah53076.
Thesauri hymnologici prosarium, vol. 53, pp. 132–34

English Translation: Bissera V. Pentcheva

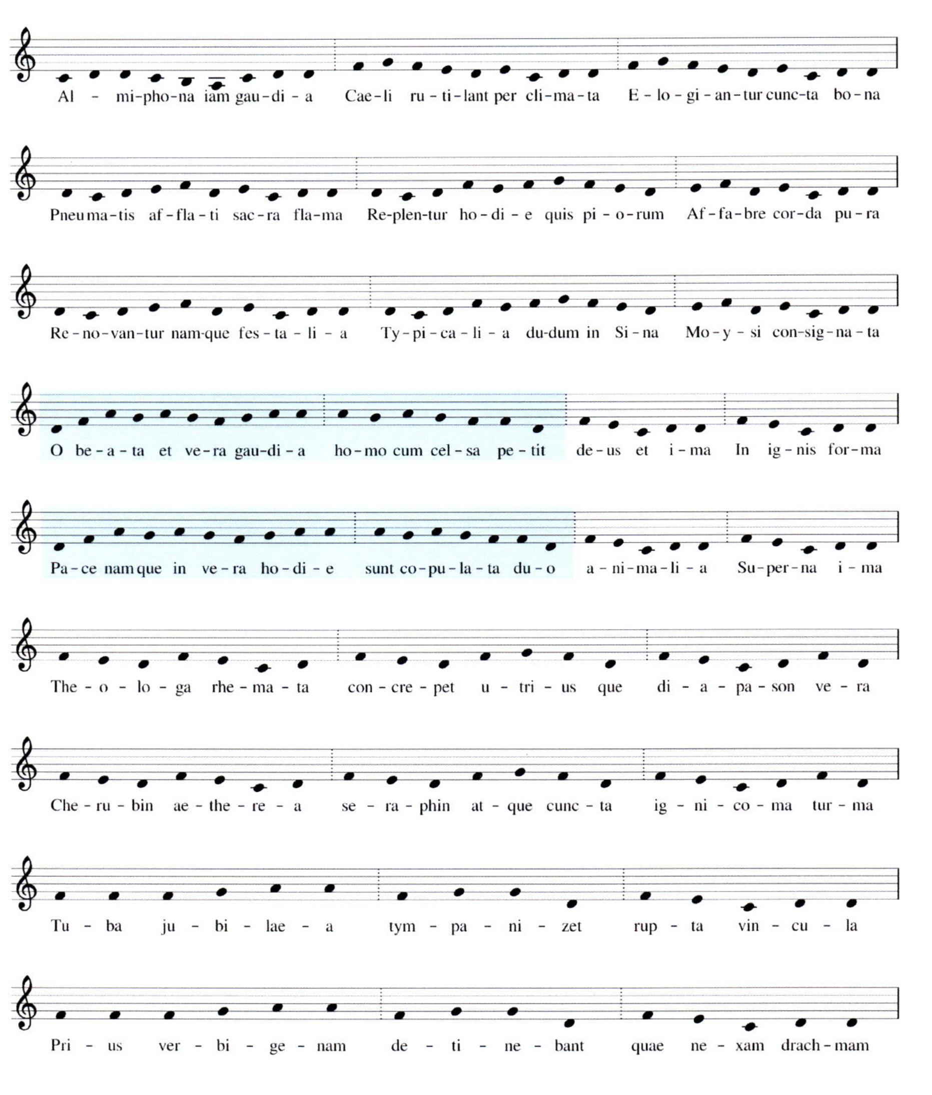

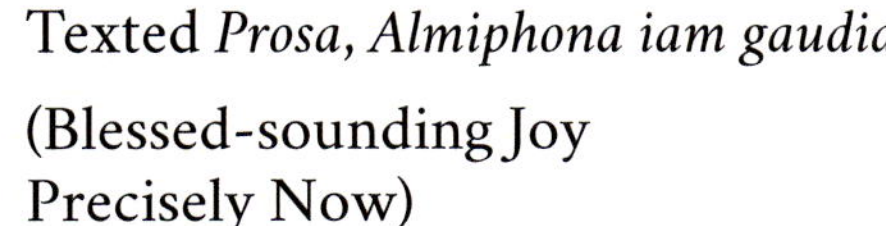

Texted *Prosa, Almiphona iam gaudia*

(Blessed-sounding Joy
Precisely Now)

Transcription: Laura Steenberge
Coloring: Jessica Chen Lee

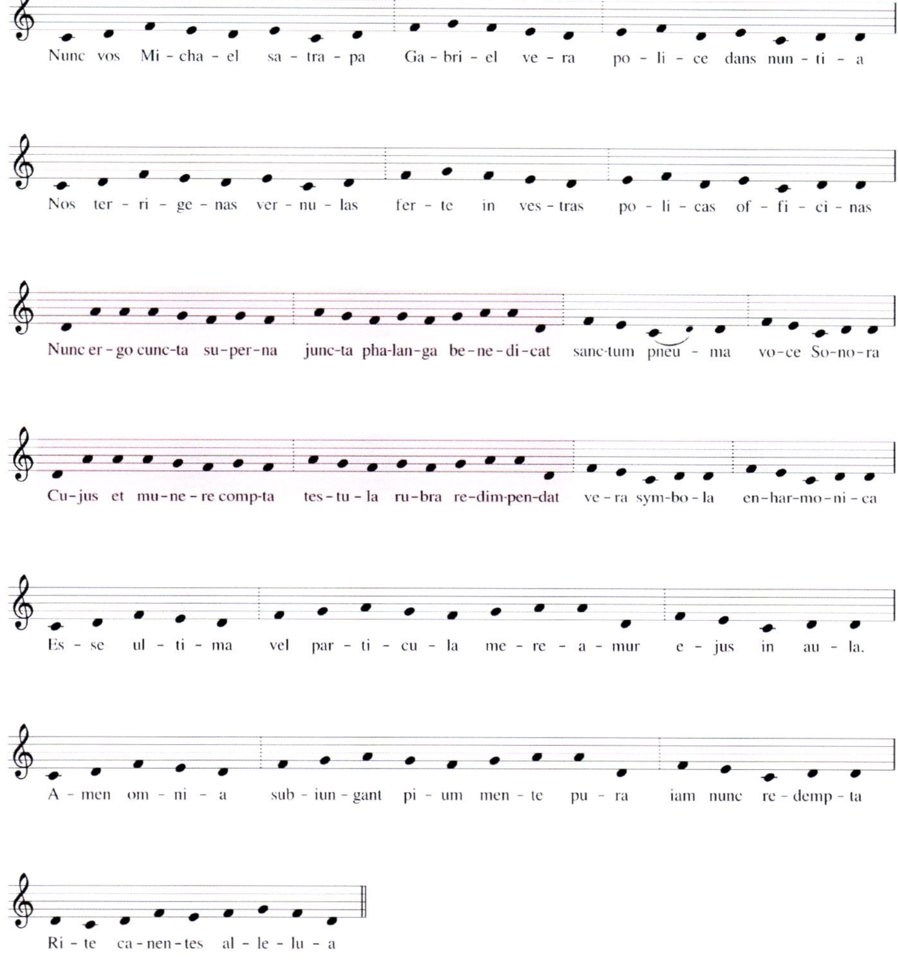

Nunc vos Mi – cha – el sa – tra – pa Ga – bri – el ve – ra po – li – ce dans nun – ti – a
Nos ter – ri – ge – nas ver – nu – las fer – te in ves – tras po – li – cas of – fi – ci – nas
Nunc er – go cunc-ta su-per-na junc-ta pha-lan-ga be – ne – di – cat sanc-tum pneu – ma vo-ce So-no-ra
Cu – jus et mu – ne – re comp-ta tes – tu – la ru-bra re-dim-pen-dat ve – ra sym-bo – la en-har-mo-ni – ca
Es – se ul – ti – ma vel par – ti – cu – la me – re – a – mur e – jus in au – la.
A – men om – ni – a sub – iun – gant pi – um men – te pu – ra iam nunc re – demp – ta
Ri – te ca – nen-tes al – le – lu – a

Virtuoso Voice and Dance

The two melodies in *Almiphona* that elicit the music of Sainte-Foy draw attention to the perception of the untexted melisma as ceaseless breath. Although there are no written Latin sources to explain the perception of virtuoso singing of extended melismas, compelling evidence survives in the Classical Arabic poetry of Ibn Rūmī (836–896), who lived in Baghdad during the height of the Abbasid period (750–1258). By the tenth century, his poetry had spread all the way to the Umayyad Caliphate in Spain. In the following segment, Ibn Rūmī describes the performance of a virtuoso dancer-singer, a *qiyān*, named 'Wahid,' an Arabic word meaning "Unique" (Pentcheva 2021b).

14 She sings so effortlessly, it seems she's not singing, and she sings beautifully.

15 You do not see her eyes bulging or her neck veins bursting from strain,

16 because of the calm of her voice, which is unbroken, and its stirring passion, which is unflagging.

17 When she sings, her breath always reaches the end of the phrase; it is long like the sighs of her lovers.

18 Her coquetry and flirtation make her voice even more delicate, and passion thins it further, till it almost dies.

19 So her voice seems to be now dying, now coming to life, delightful whether soft or raised.

20 In it are embroidery and jewelry fashioned from the melody; which the poem wears with pride.

21 Her mouth, and her voice vibrating are sweet; everything of hers bears witness to this.

22 Like cool limpid water, her kisses quench thirst, and a song from her lips evokes lost happiness.

Translation by Akiko Sumi, from *Description in Classical Arabic Poetry: Wasf, Ekphrasis and Interarts Theory* (Boston and Leiden: Brill, 2004), pp. 128–29.

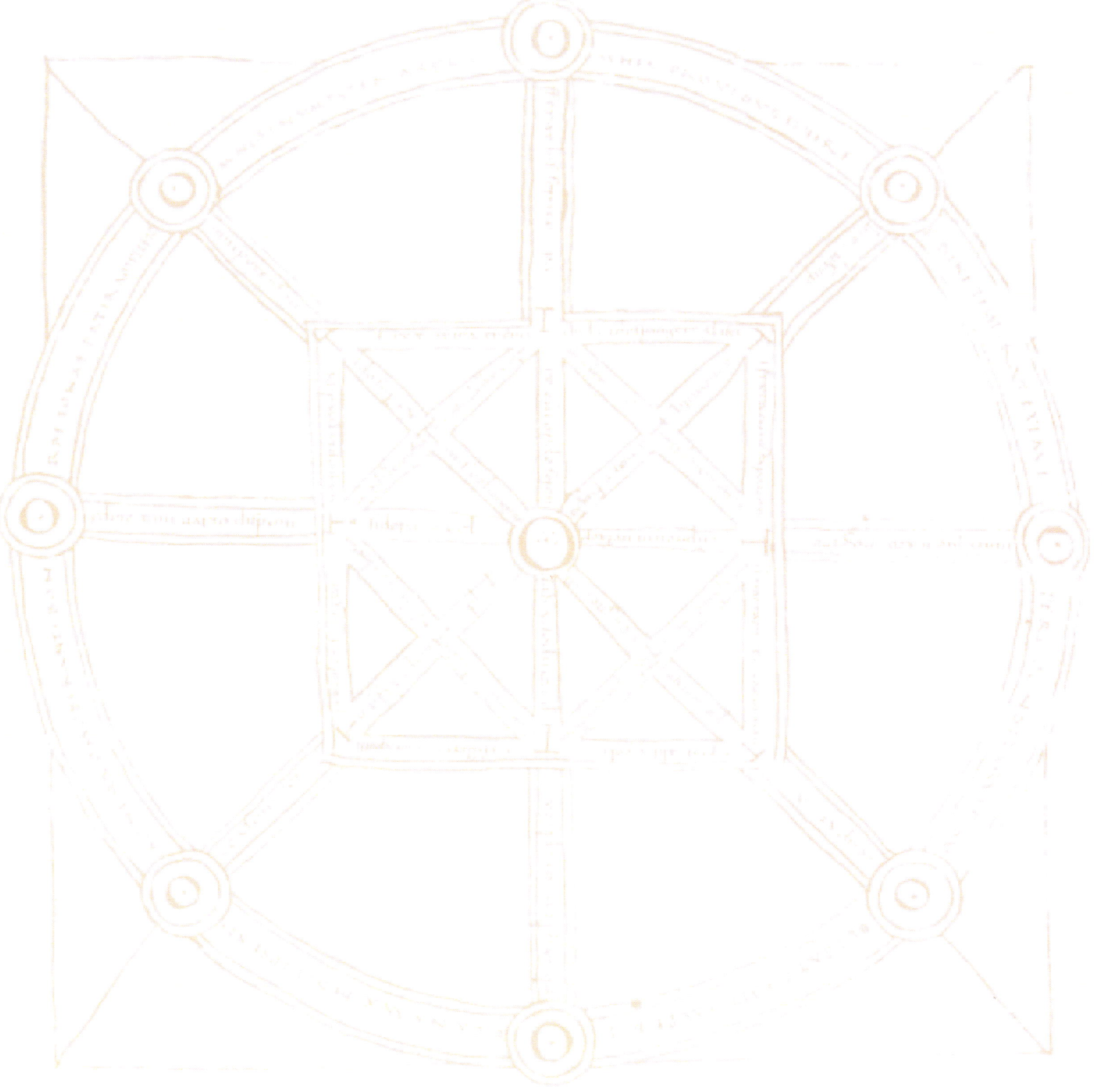

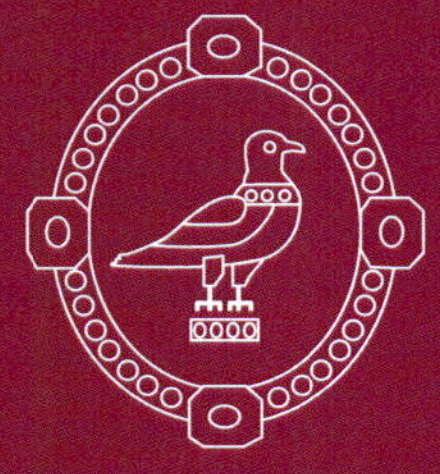

Music Making *the* Invisible Perceptible

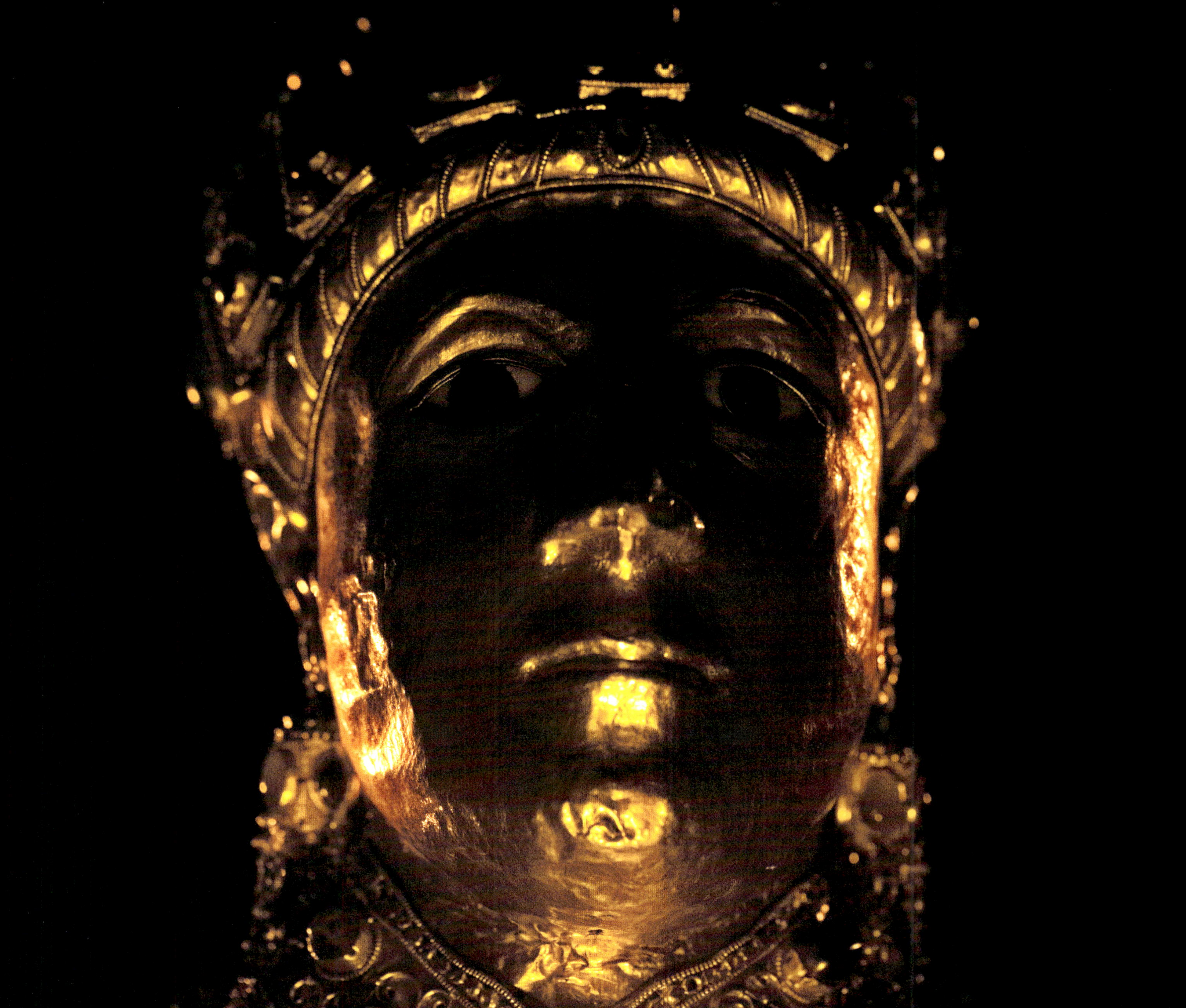

Sainte-Foy, Her Liturgy, and Its Setting

Sainte-Foy (or in Latin, *Santa Fides*, meaning "Holy Faith") was a twelve-year-old virgin who lived during the Roman Empire in the town of Agen, France, at the turn of the third century, when Christianity was still illegal. A Christian from birth, she was persecuted by the state administrators and died a martyr's death, never wavering in her faith when she was arrested, interrogated, tortured, and killed by decapitation. Her relics remained in Agen until 866, when two monks from Conques stole them and carried them about 100 miles northeast to their mother abbey. At Conques, her skull was encased in the wooden core of a gilded statue, now the earliest surviving sculpture in the round in the Latin West (Bousquet 1992; Bousquet 1997; Fricke 2015).

This effigy stands on the altar during the feast day of the saint, October 6, and forms the focus of the liturgy. Candlelight flickers across its golden surface during the night. During the day the statue remains in shadow: a dark silhouette set against the sunlight moving around the sanctuary. At sunset, when the last rays of light touch the golden surface, it suddenly and briefly glows. This sudden illumination inaugurates the beginning of the festal vespers, or evening service (Pentcheva 2023b).

Two liturgies survive for the Feast of Sainte-Foy: an older one, composed in the eleventh century (Huglo 2009; Pentcheva 2021b; Pentcheva 2023a), and a second one, in rhymed poetry, from the late twelfth century (Renner 1997). The eleventh-century music has not been sung for more than a thousand years. Laura Steenberge of the Stanford project "Enchanted Images" has transcribed the eleventh-century Office. We have worked with the mezzo-soprano Argenta Walther to record and to auralize (digitally imprinted) it in the acoustics of the Romanesque church at Conques.

Bringing to life these liturgical songs has made it possible to immerse the contemporary audio-spectator into the reverberant space of Conques and to transform the perception of the golden statue from an object into an actor on the liturgical stage.

This section explores the synergies between the effigy of Sainte-Foy and the music composed for her feast day. Elements that are physically invisible, like the skull hidden in the effigy, are elicited through the music, more specifically in the way the chants place the apex of the melodies on the words for mind (*mens*), face (*species*), and decapitation/amputation (*amputatio*) (Pentcheva 2022a).

Photographs on this page and page 49: Boris Missirkov

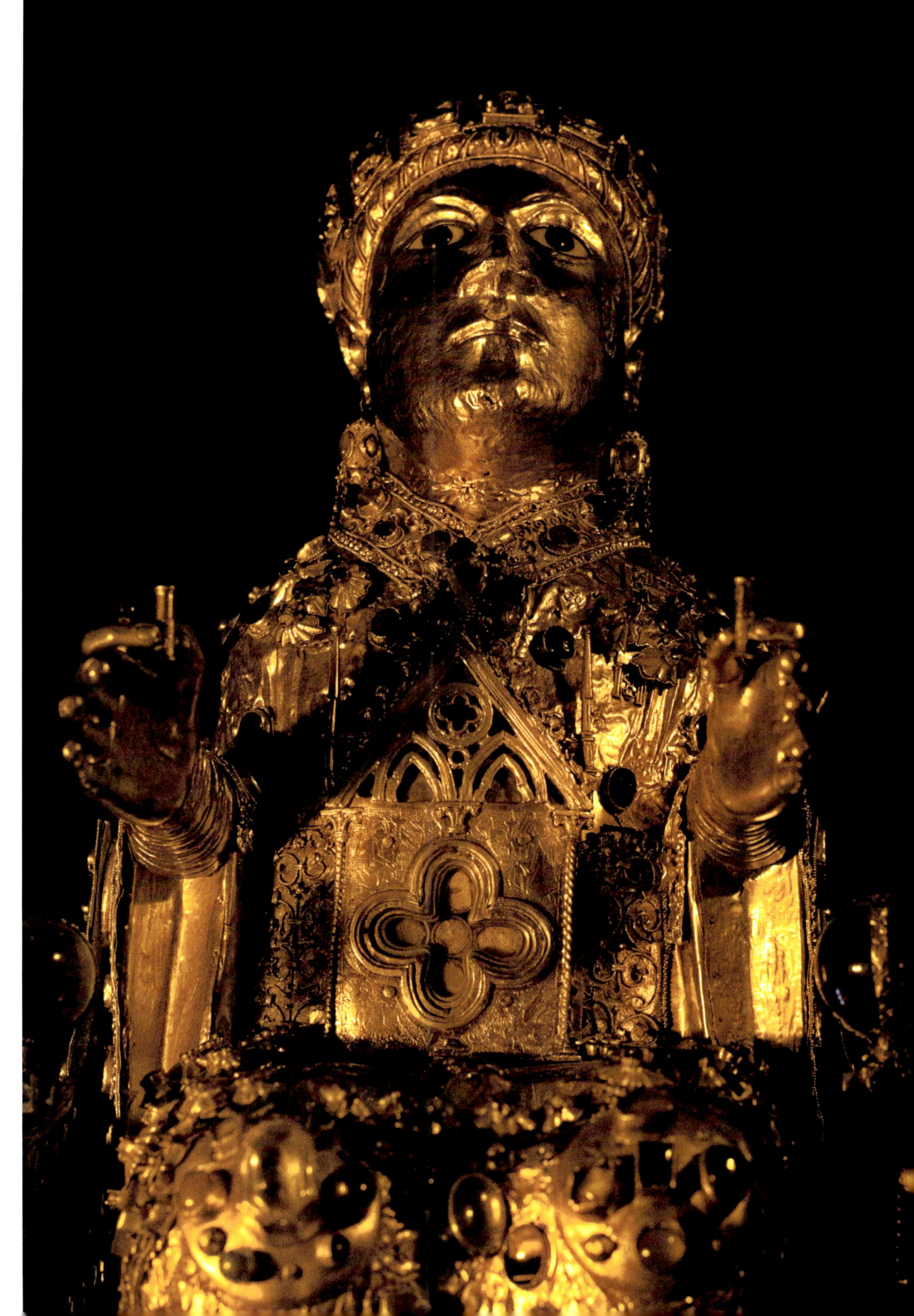

This vespers antiphon *Haec est virgo* (This is the Virgin) is structured to call attention to the mind of the saint. It starts with a stock melody and language (Cantus n.d. chant ID no. 003006), but quickly transforms into a new composition. Only the first three words and accompanying music come from a standard liturgy for female virgin martyr saints. The rest of the antiphon—music and poetry—are newly composed at Conques for Sainte-Foy.

Designed in mode 1 authentic (centered around the pitch *D*), the melodic apex occurs on *mentis* (of [her] mind); it is articulated as a leap to *d*, marking the upper limit of mode 1. The sonic peak draws attention to the head of the statue and, by extension, to the skull concealed in the recesses of the gilded effigy. This antiphon is an example of where hearing the music creates awareness about an energy that remains invisible. Sainte-Foy's skull would not be brought out, yet its energy is marked by the sonic peak of the melody, so its presence is implied in the song (Pentcheva 2022a; Pentcheva 2023ab).

Vespers antiphon, *Haec Est Virgo* (This is the Virgin) (1037–1065)

An antiphon is a short poem sung as a refrain to frame the recitation of a psalm, in this case, Psalm 109 (110). This first antiphon opens the evening liturgy

Paris, BnF, MS Nouv. Acq. Lat. 443, fol. 1

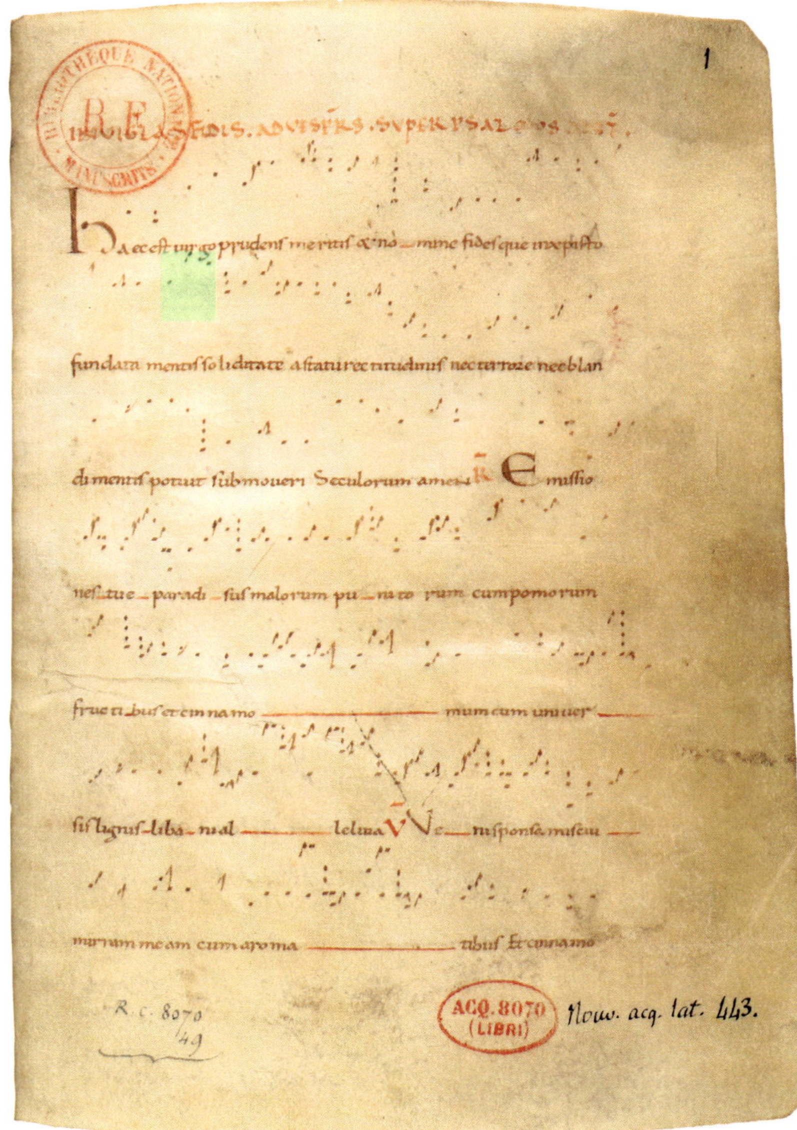

Coloring: Jessica Chen Lee

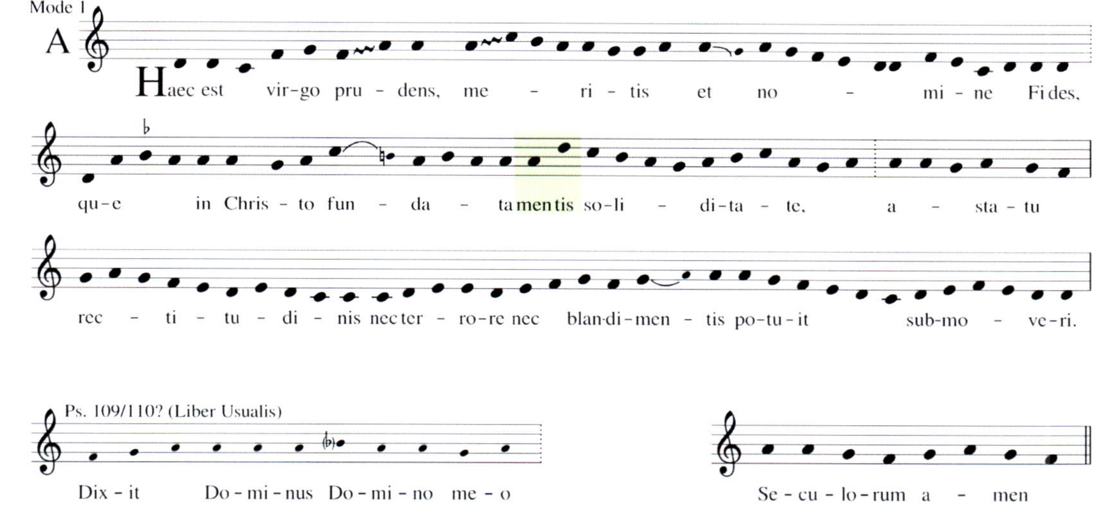

Transcription: Laura Steenberge; coloring: Jessica Chen Lee

Haec est virgo prudens, meritis et nomine Fides, quae in Christo fundata mentis soliditate, a statu rectitudinis nec terrore nec blandimentis potuit submoveri, Seculorum Amen.

"This is the prudent virgin, in merits and in name—Faith—who is rooted in Christ through the resoluteness of her mind in uprightness, which neither fear nor flattery could undermine."

English Translation: Bissera V. Pentcheva

Pairing of Antiphon *Haec est virgo* with Psalm 109 (110) *Dixit Dominus* (The Lord Spoke)

In the liturgy for virgin martyr saints, the antiphon *Haec est virgo* is traditionally paired with the first psalm recitation of vespers: Psalm 109 (110) (Harper 1991, p. 262; Dyer 1989). This psalm narrates how total victory is achieved; the enemies are vanquished; and the scepter of authority is given to the saint, who will shine brightly like the morning star in the luminous ranks of the elect at the end of time. By contrast, the opponent's body is crushed and turned into a footstool for the saint. God smashes the heads of the enemies and then rises victorious his head. The joyfully bright and the bloody macabre come together to mark the power of the saints. But this image of the severed heads also strangely alludes to the martyrdom of Sainte-Foy. The psalm, like the antiphon which frames it, brings the viewer's attention back to the invisible skull that is hidden inside in the statue (Pentcheva 2023a).

1 Dixit Dominus Domino meo sede a dextris meis: donec ponam inimicos tuos scabellum pedum tuorum.

2 Virgam virtutis tuae emittet Dominus ex Sion: dominare in medio inimicorum tuorum.

3 Tecum principium in die virtutis tuae in splendoribus sanctorum: ex utero ante luciferum genui te.

4 Juravit Dominus et non poenitebit eum: Tu es sacerdos in aeternum secundum ordinem Melchisedech.

5 Dominus a dextris tuis confregit in die irae suae reges.

6 Judicabit in nationibus implebit ruinas: conquassabit capita in terra multorum.

7 De torrente in via bibet: propterea exaltabit caput.

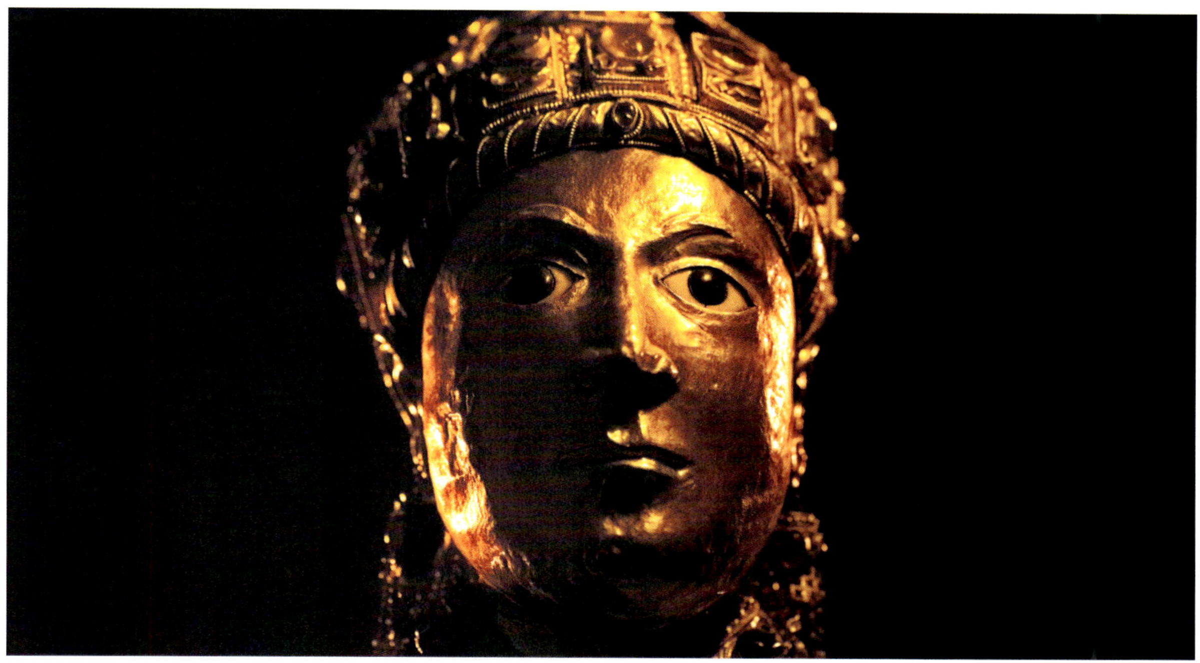

Photograph: Boris Missirkov

1 The Lord said to my Lord: Sit at my right hand until I make your enemies a footstool for you.

2 The Lord will give you a scepter from Sion because of your virtue, so that you would rule in the midst of your enemies.

3 Because of your virtue on the day [of Judgment] you will be among the splendid ranks of the saints, [and will shine] like the morning star begotten before the day.

4 The Lord has sworn, and he will not repent; you are a priest forever according to the order of Melchisedech.

5 The Lord at your right hand has broken kings in the day of His wrath.

6 He shall judge among nations; He shall fill ruins; He shall crush the heads in the land of many.

7 He shall drink of the torrent in the way: therefore, He shall lift up the head.

Latin in *Biblia sacra vulgata*

English translation adapted from *King James Version, Holy Bible*

Illustrated psalters capture how psalm 109 (110) was perceived in medieval culture. Within this decorated initial in the St. Albans Psalter, Christ presides over the cosmos. He sits in the celestial realm, flanked by two angels. Below, in the terrestrial world, the saint climbs a mountain of torrential waters. He holds a scepter. With his free hand he reaches out to touch the knee of Christ. This is a gesture of intercession, pleading on behalf of his congregation, which approaches on the right. The saint's prayer unlocks Christ's mercy. Both the saint and the Lord have the same type of halo, one with a cross inscribed in it. The shared attribute reveals the Christo-mimetic nature of martyrdom, which transforms the saint into a Christ-like figure on earth. The halo with the cross elicits the shape of the martyr's crown: ⊕ (Pentcheva 2023a).

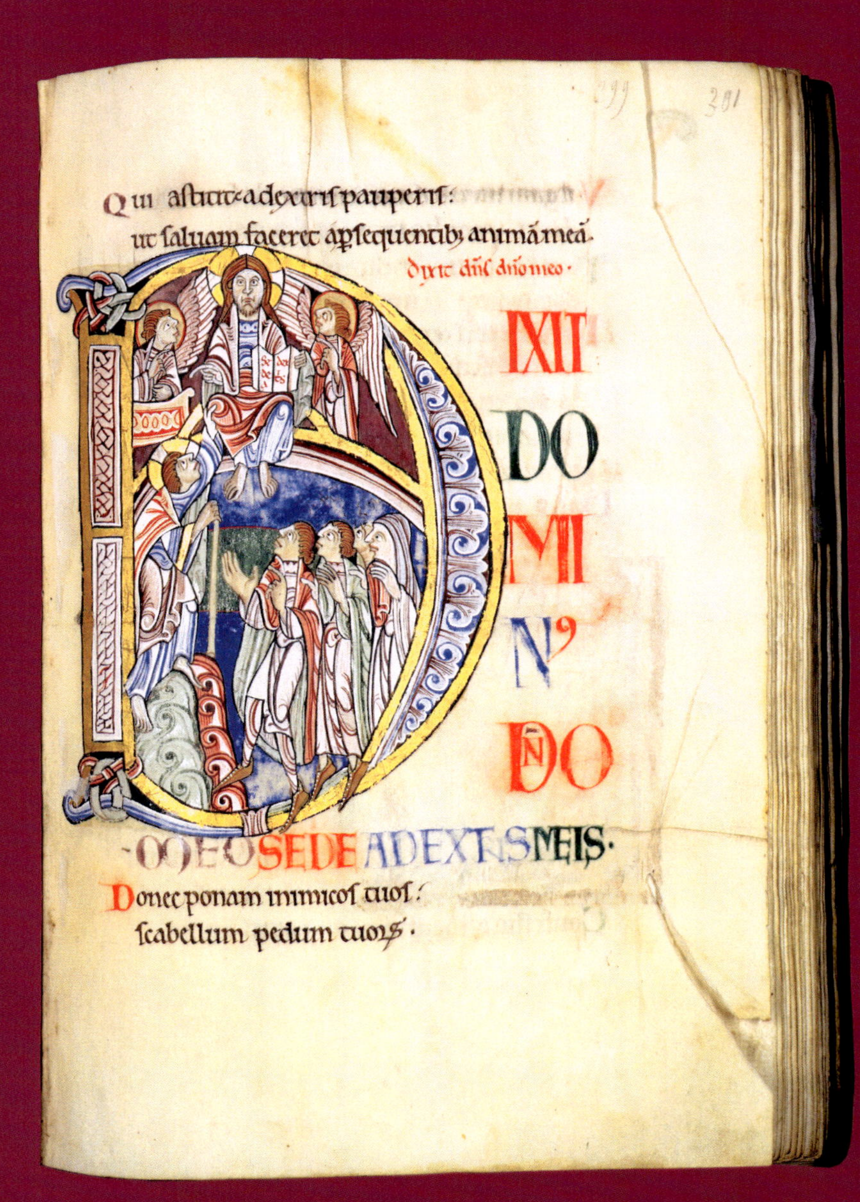

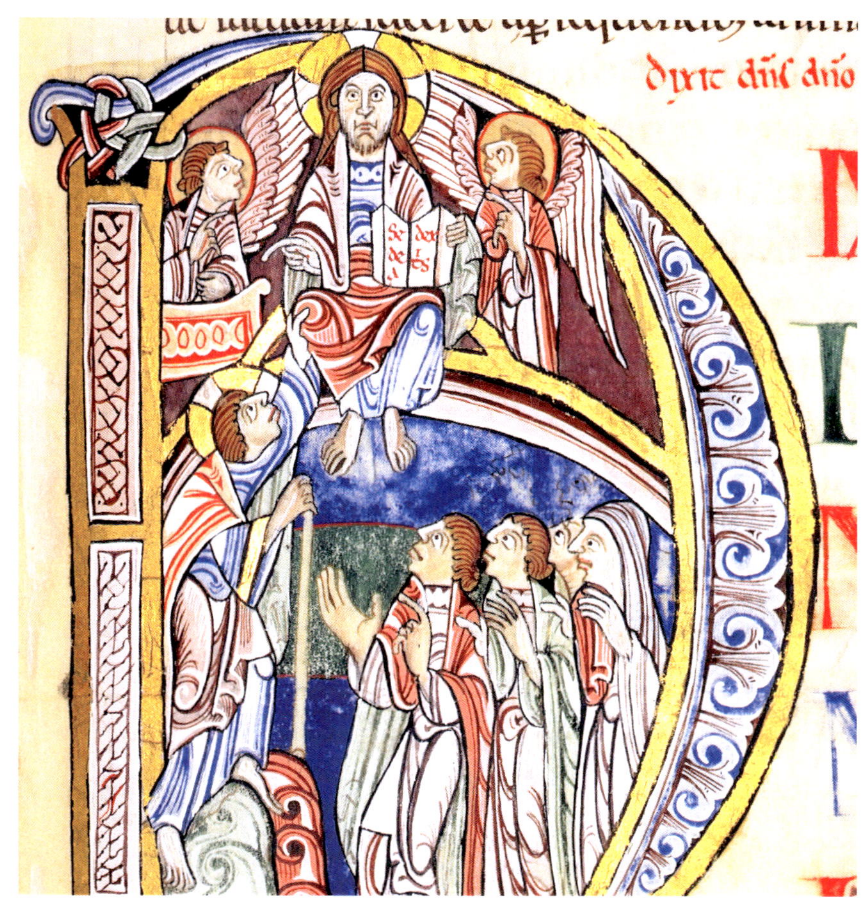

Illumination for Psalm 109 (110)
Dixit Dominus from the St. Albans
Psalter (1120s–1130s)

Psalter associated with the recluse
Christina of Markyate and her patron,
Abbot Geoffrey de Gorham (Gorron)
of St. Albans, England
Hildesheim, Dombibliothek, MS Lat.
St. God. 1/ Cologne, Schnütgen
Museum, Inv. No. M694, p. 299,
Ps. 109 (110)

Antiphon 3, First Nocturn
(1037–1065)

Paris, BnF, MS Nouv. Acq. Lat.
443, fol. 2v

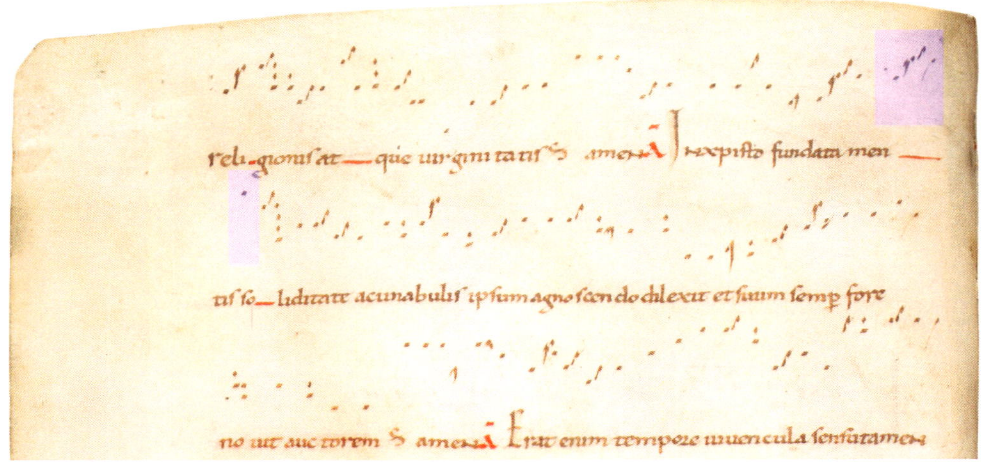

Coloring: Jessica Chen Lee

The fact that the antiphon chant *Haec est virgo prudens* (This is the prudent virgin) opens and closes the recitation of Psalm 109 further draws the attention to the head of Sainte-Foy and the brilliance of her mind. Seeing the statue while listening to this chant subconsciously associates brightness with the word *mens* (mind) of the saint. Besides, the same word also marks the next moment, where the liturgy explores a sonic apex. In antiphon three of the first nocturn *In Christo fundata mentis* (Rooted in Christ through her Unwavering Mind, composed in mode 3, centered around the pitch *E*), the melody reaches the melodic apex, *e*, exactly on the same word, *mens*. The medieval audience would be ready to discern the special meaning of this peak. This is due to the specific structural logic of the composition of the Office. The first nocturn consists of six antiphons, the first is composed in mode 1, the second in mode 2 and this all the way to the sixth antiphon in mode 6 (on modal ordering, Hughes 1983; Harper 1991; Parkes 2020). Not only that, but the very phrase on which the peak on *e* is reached, *in Christo fundata mentis soliditate* (with respect to her mind, she was staunchly anchored in Christ), is the same as the one in the vespers antiphon *Haec est virgo*, where the leap to the first sonic apex, to *d,* was performed. Thus, for a second time, bright sound falls on the concept of Sainte-Foy's mind, drawing attention to the paradox of the invisible relic and the glittering golden face (Pentcheva 2023a).

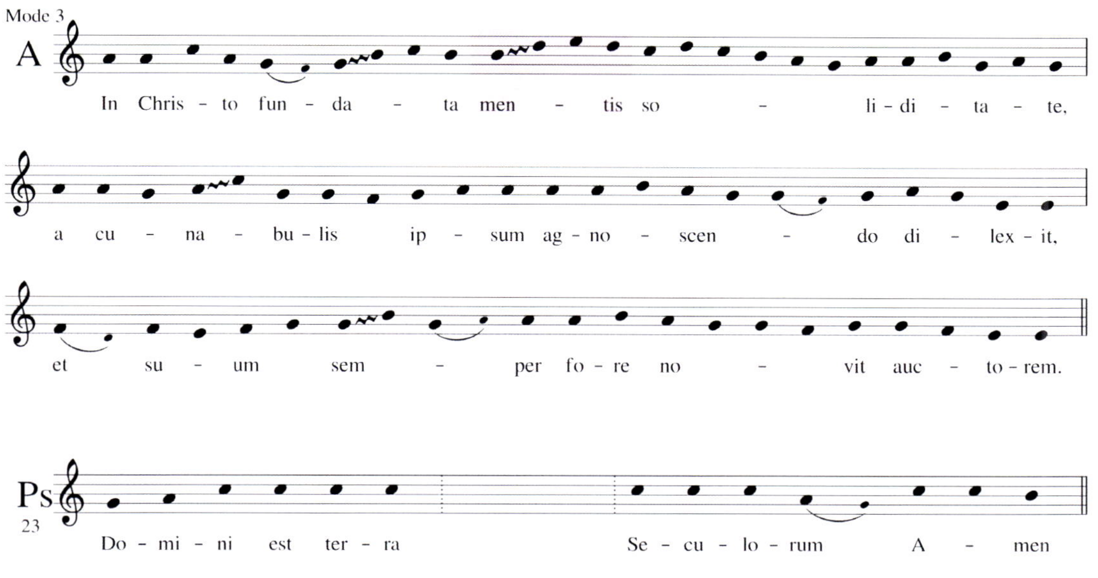

Transcription: Laura Steenberge; coloring: Jessica Chen Lee

In Christo fundata mentis soliditate a cunabulis ipsum agnoscendo dilexit et suum semper fore novit auctorem.

"Rooted in Christ through her unwavering mind, recognizing him from the cradle, she loved him and always from the outset knew him as her creator."

English Translation: Bissera V. Pentcheva

Antiphon 4, First Nocturn
(1037–1065)

Paris, BnF, MS Nouv. Acq. Lat.
443, fol. 2v

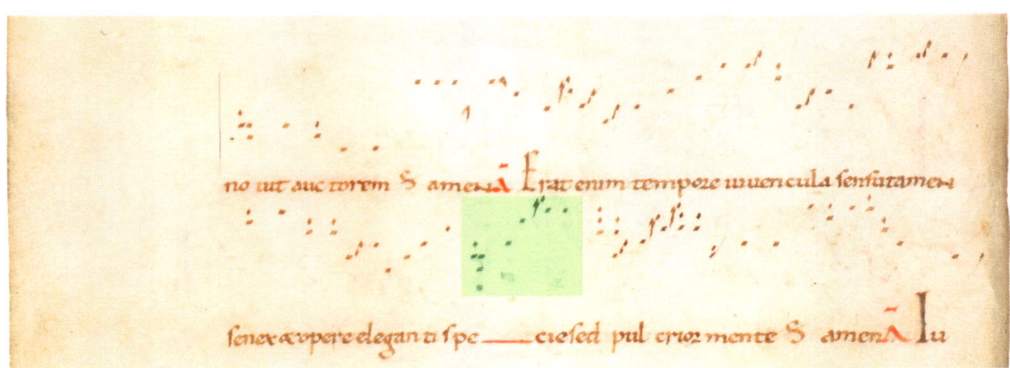

Coloring: Jessica Chen Lee

The golden statue unifies two bodies: the earthly one present in the relics and the heavenly one imagined through the shimmering gold and gems. Both operate in the effigy outside the parameters of mimetic representation, for neither renders a lifelike portrait of a twelve-year-old virgin. On this statue, the face (*species*) is expressionless; the lips and brows are frozen and emotionless. But the music tells the participant in the ritual to imagine this face otherwise.

Antiphon 4 for the first nocturn articulates the saint's countenance with a melodic material that is expansive and dynamic. It sets the word *species* (face) to a melisma that expresses the vividness of the face; at this point, the melodic phrase pushes the *ambitus* (range) of the chant beyond an octave. Written in mode 4 (*E* plagal), the melody descends to a great depth, to *A*, a note below the usual limit for this mode. It then leaps a fifth (*A* to *E*) and continues to rise all the way to a *b*, spanning a distance greater than an octave over the course of a handful of notes. No other word in this entire chant, or even the entire liturgy, experiences the same rapid stretch of material. The ornament at *species* thus draws attention to the face, but it also shapes it as something extraordinary: lively, flexible, pliable, stretchable, extensible. The dissonance between the aural—manifested in the changeable, simultaneously dark (low tones) and bright (high tones)—and the visual (the emotionless golden mask) first stimulates the imagination to envision the vivacity of Sainte-Foy's face and then to project this inner perception onto the impassive mask. Hearing the concept of *species* in the chant thus trains the participant to see more than what is actually rendered in the face of the effigy (Pentcheva 2022a).

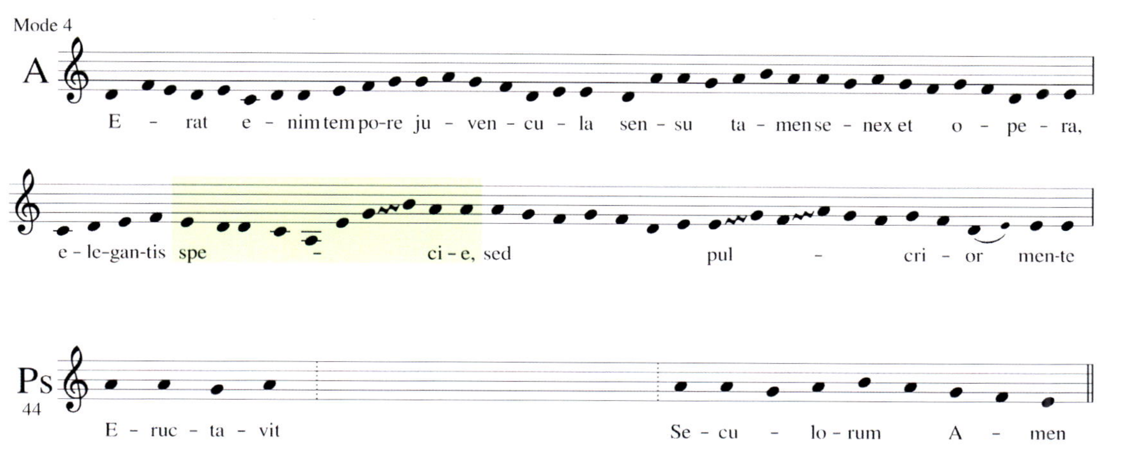

Transcription: Laura Steenberge; coloring: Jessica Chen Lee

Erat enim tempore juvencula sensu tamen senex et opera,
eleganti specie, sed pulcherior mente.

"For at the time she was a young girl, but mature in reason and
deeds, with an elegant face but an even more beautiful soul/mind."

English Translation: Bissera V. Pentcheva

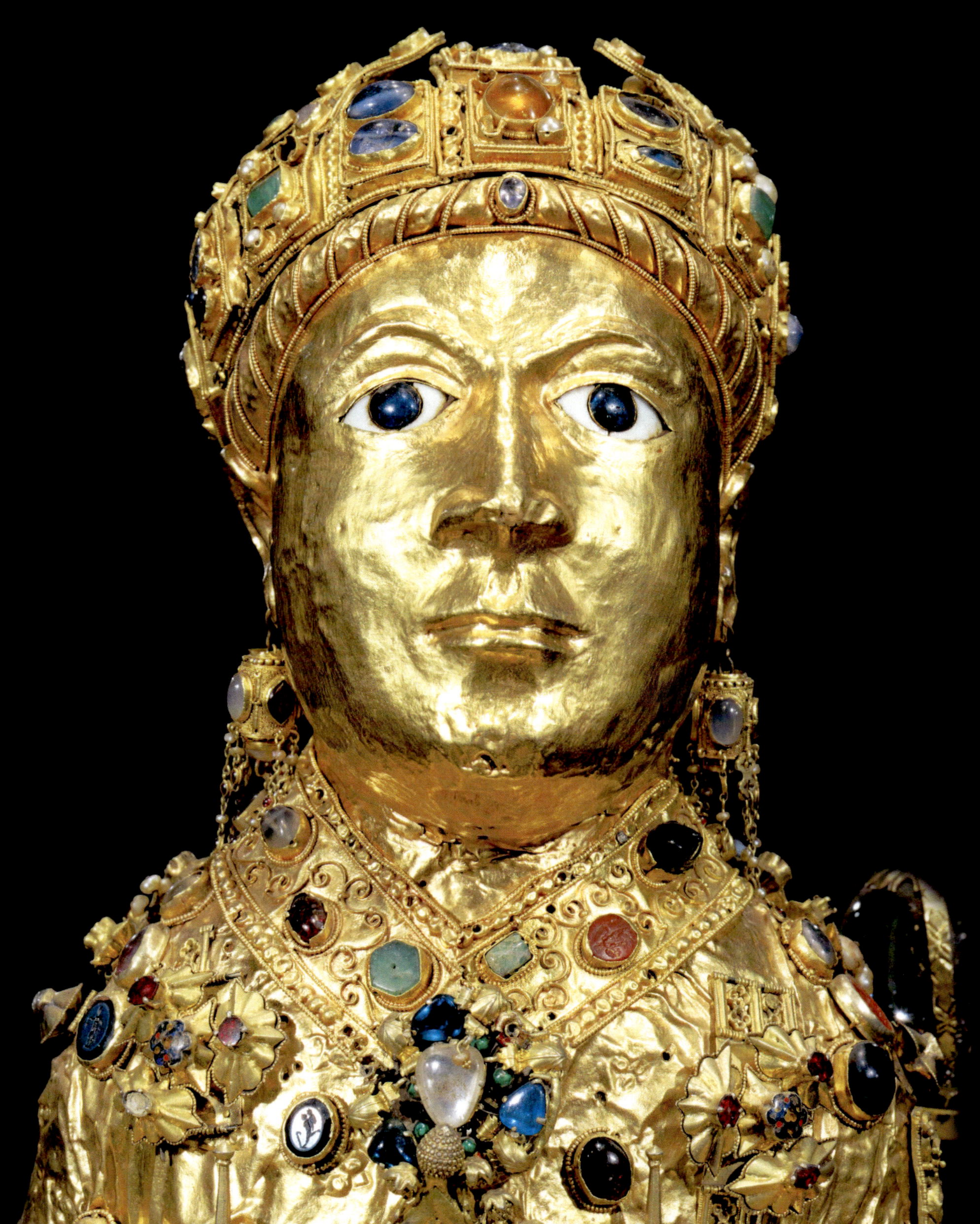

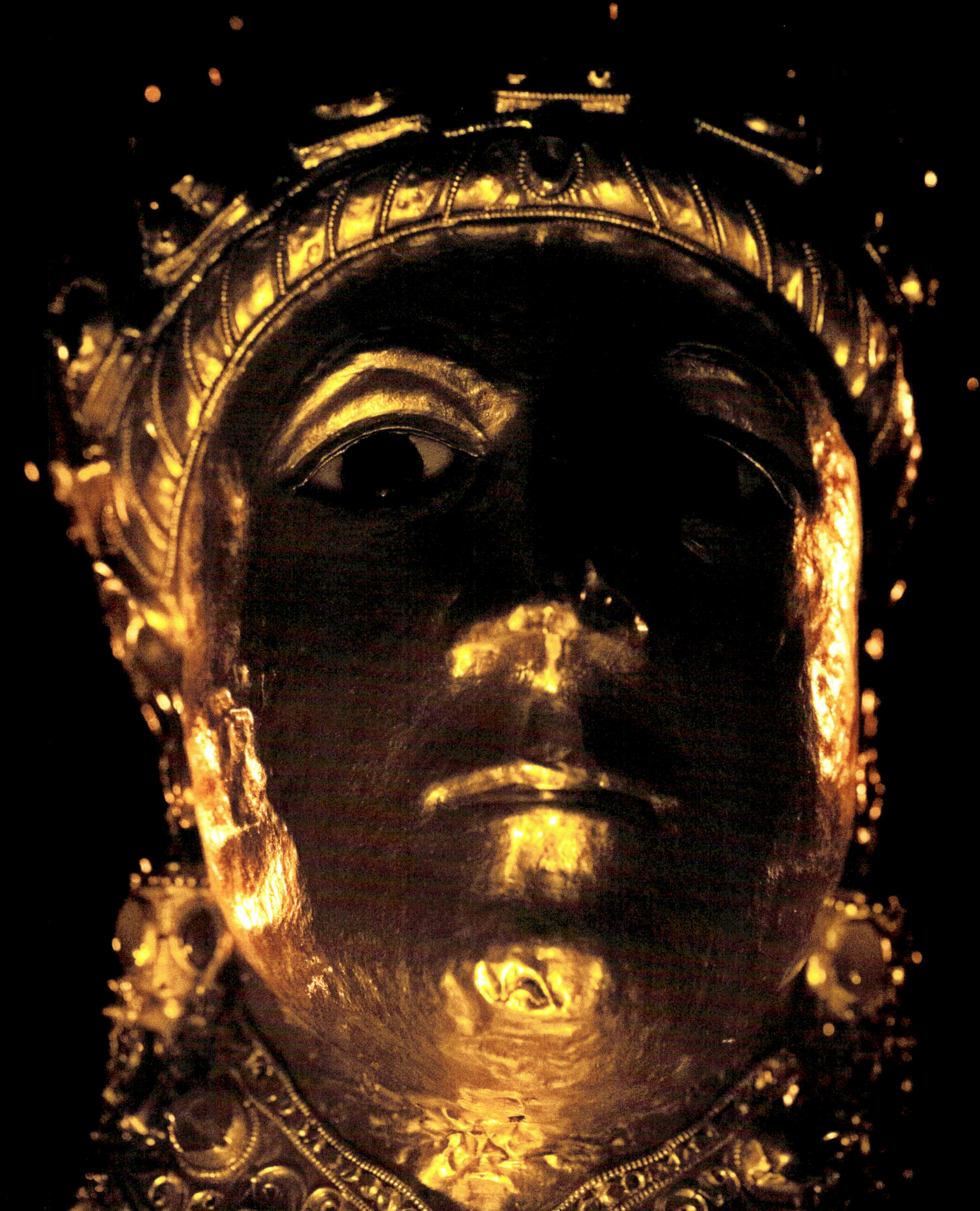

Photograph: Boris Missirkov

Third responsory of the Third Nocturn (1037–1065)

Paris, BnF, MS Nouv. Acq. Lat. 443, fols. 7v and fol. 8r

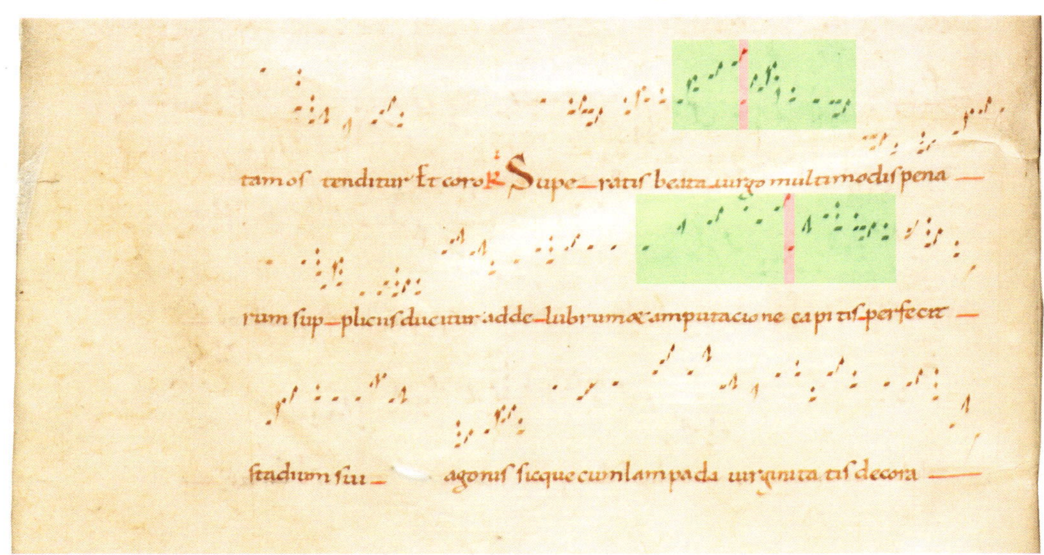

Coloring: Jessica Chen Lee

[**Respond**] Superatis beata virgo multimodis penarum suppliciis ducitur ad delubrum et amputatione capitis perfecit stadium sui agonis, [**Refrain**] *sicque cum lampada virginitatis decoratur gloria passionis*

[**Verse**] Virgo electa a Domino secuta est eum venerando martirii triumpho. [**Refrain**] *Sicque.*

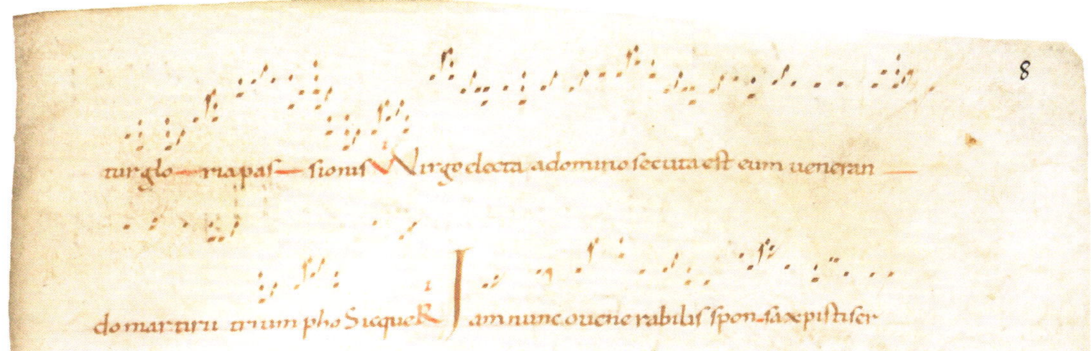

[**Respond**] "After enduring manifold sufferings of punishments the blessed virgin was led to the temple. And with the severing of her head, she completed the course of her struggle; [**Refrain**] *and thus, the light of her virginity was decorated with the glory of her passion.*

[**Verse**] The virgin chosen by the Lord has followed him in the venerable triumph of his sacrifice. [**Refrain**] *and thus…*"

English Translation: Bissera V. Pentcheva

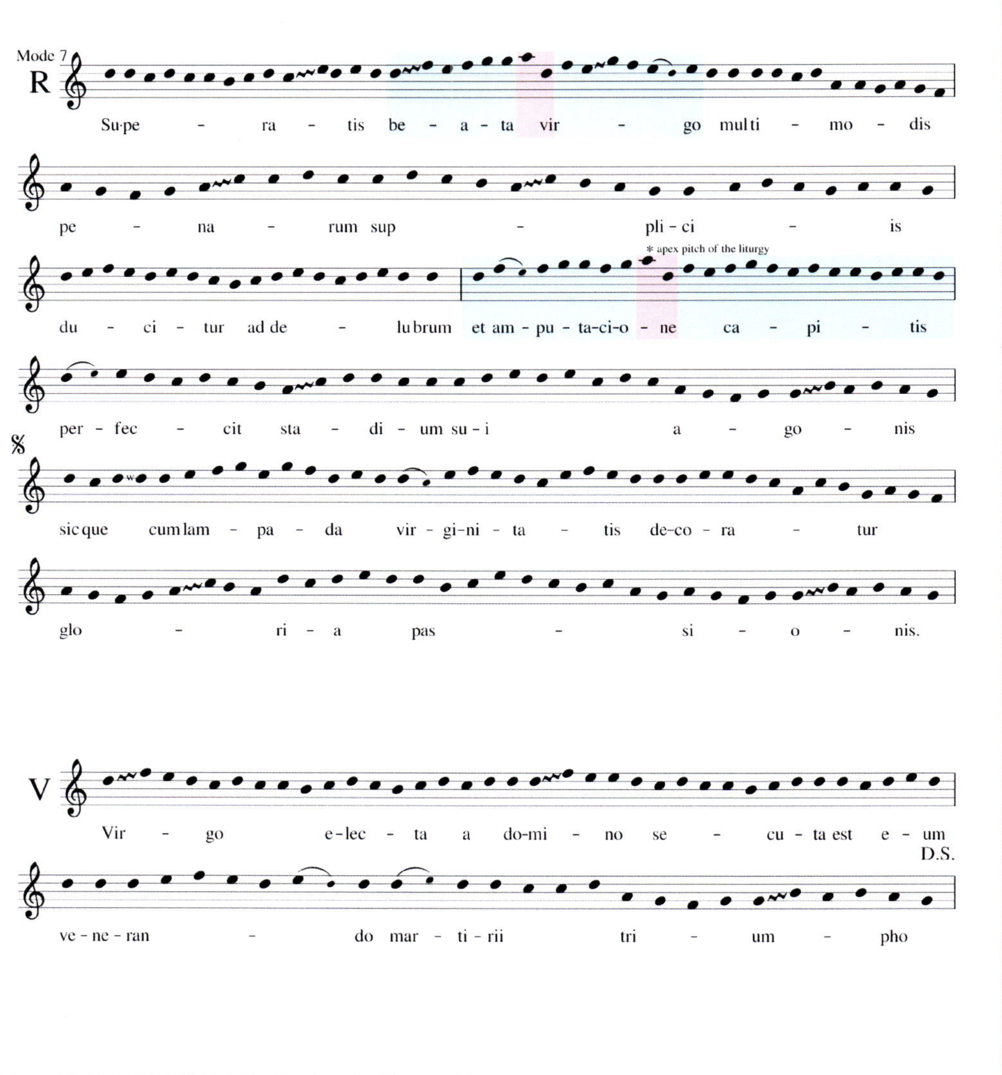

Transcription: Laura Steenberge; coloring: Jessica Chen Lee

The head of Sainte-Foy makes its most dramatic appearance in the chants as it marks the absolute apex of the entire liturgy, high *a*, sung at the word *amputatione* in the penultimate responsory of the Third Nocturn of the night office. It is composed in mode 7 (centered around *G*). As the saint's passion story comes to a close and her martyrdom is achieved, the purposeful play with sonic height to denote her decapitation gives depth to the drama. The spiritual glorification communicated in the melodic brightness — contrasted with the violence of martyrdom enacted in the strain of the voice in its highest register — gives expression to the horror and cruelty done on this child. The vibrancy of this complex moment jolts the memory to recall her martyrdom in the sonic splendor of sainthood and in the human voice of the singer striving to climb to those heights. The liturgy will ascend one last time to the same apex, high *a,* in the second antiphon of lauds close to the end of the festal liturgy on the word *certamine* (battle), followed by the phrase: *coronam celestibus margaritis ornatam* (a crown decorated with celestial pearls) thus, sonically inscribing the glorification of Sainte-Foy (Pentcheva 2023b).

The effigy of Sainte-Foy would command great presence when it was either set on the great altar or on a column behind it. The statue purposefully eschews mimetic representation, because its features are those of an imposing, enthroned man rather than a delicate young virgin (Fricke 2015). Freed from the restraints of lifelikeness (an ideal pursued both earlier and later, in Classical and Renaissance art in the West), this medieval golden image reveals its liveliness in the temporality of shimmering metal (Pentcheva 2010; Pentcheva 2016; Foletti 2019; Pentcheva 2022a). While dissemblant (non-mimetic) in form, the statue possesses unchallenged authenticity because it contains the precious relic of the cranium, the skull of Santa Fides (Pentcheva 2021a).

The golden effigy is a bricolage (assemblage) of parts made at different moments in the life of the statue, revealing both continual concern for preserving the object but also the gradual depletion of resources after the twelfth century. The gilded head was made in the fourth or fifth centuries and thus pre-dates the rest of the statue. The original hands have not survived; the current substitutes were made sometime in the sixteenth century. She grasps two tiny tubular holders, which are used in modern times to place a flower stalk in each, when the statue is decorated for her feast. Similarly, the knee-caps, the Gothic tabernacle on the chest, and the repoussé plaque on the lap were added during the fifteenth and sixteenth centuries. The crystal balls were attached to the throne in the nineteenth century (Gaborit-Chopin 2001).

Gilded Statue-Reliquary of Sainte-Foy, late 9th century

Yew wood core; gold revetment, filigree, gems, and cameos
Height of seated figure, 85cm (33 ½ inches); height of throne, 36 cm (14 inches); depth 24 cm (9 ½ inches)
Abbey Church of Sainte-Foy, Conques, France

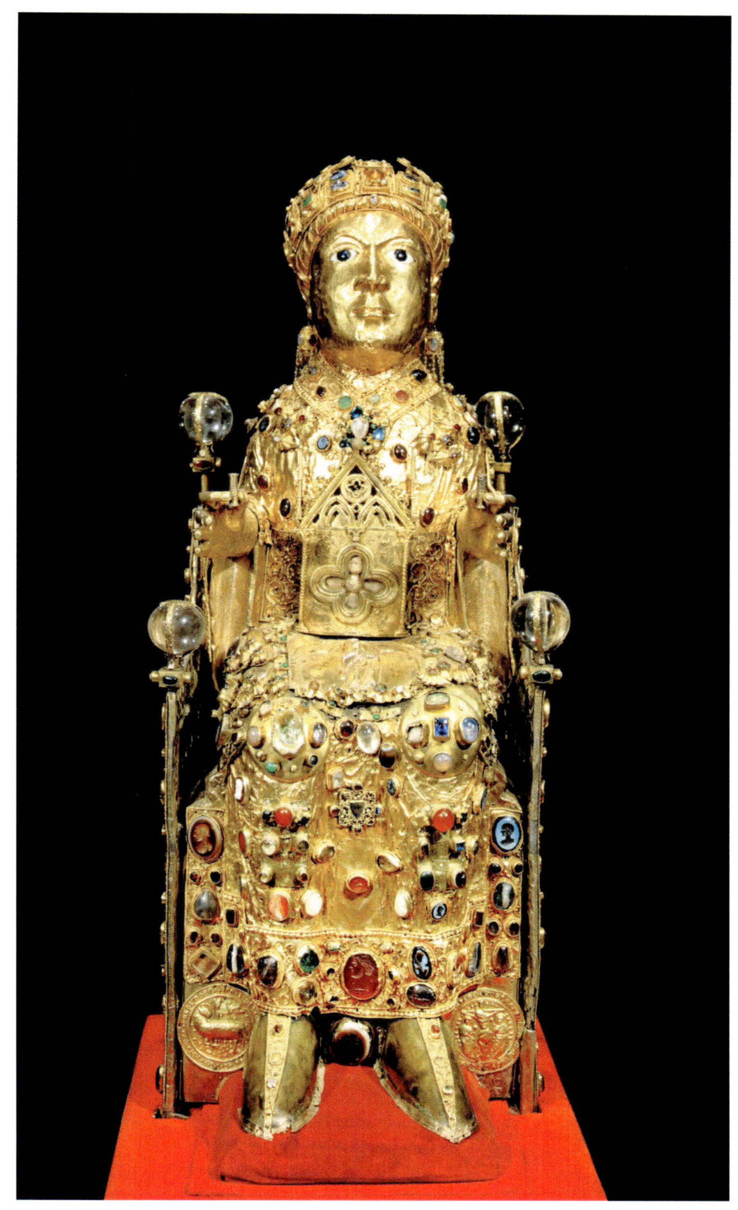
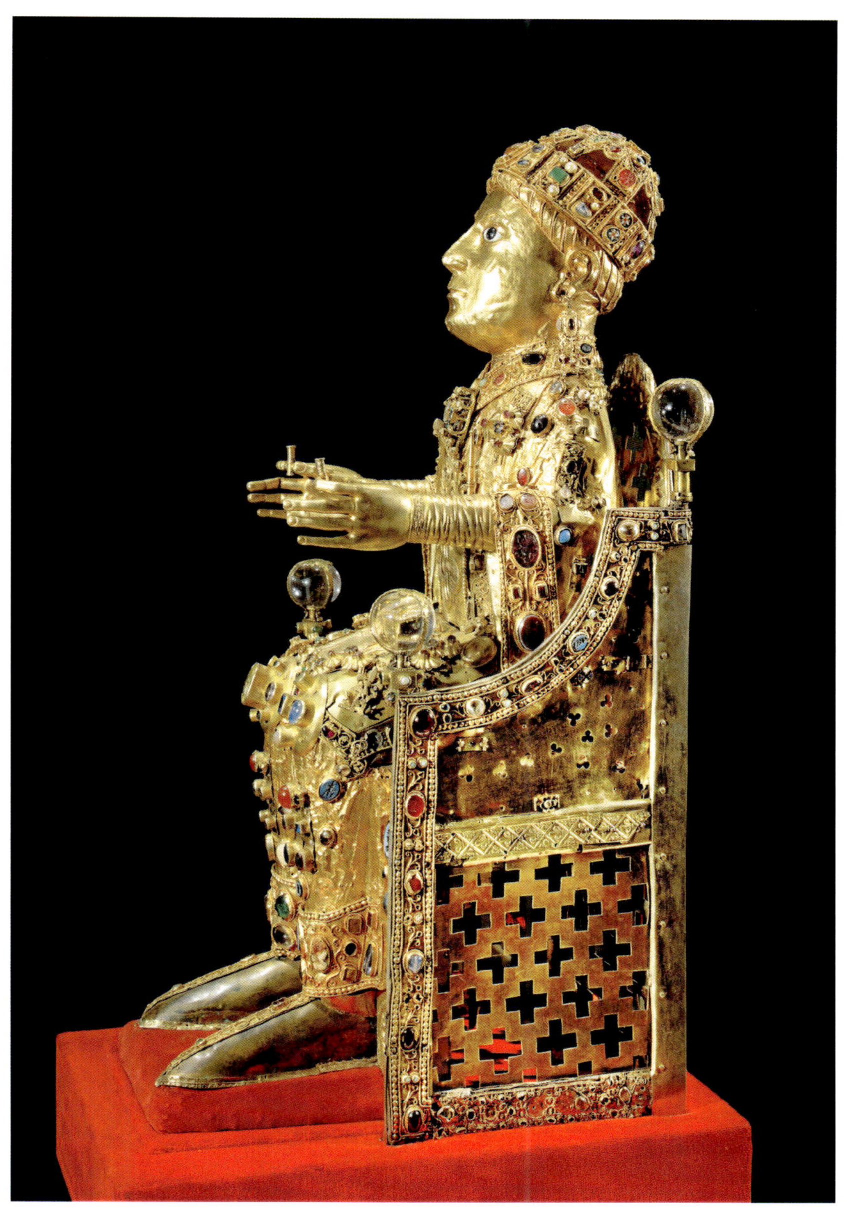

Photographs: Erich Lessing/Art Resource

Photographs of the restoration
of the golden statue by Louis
Balsan (1954)

Reproduced with permission of
La Société des Lettres de l'Aveyron,
Rodez, France

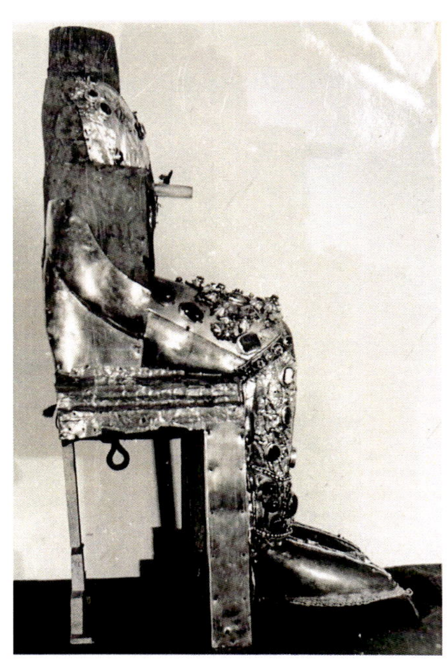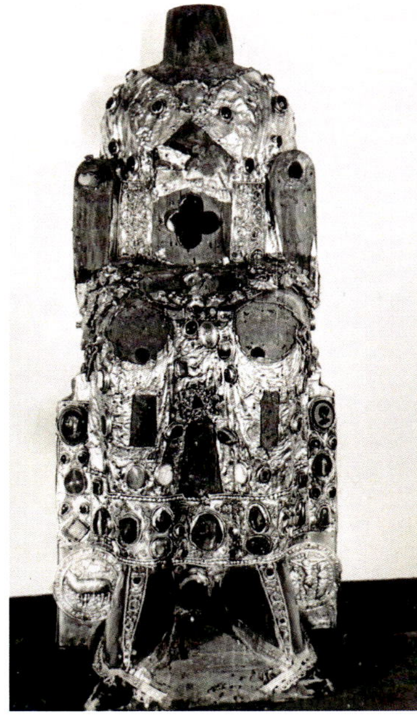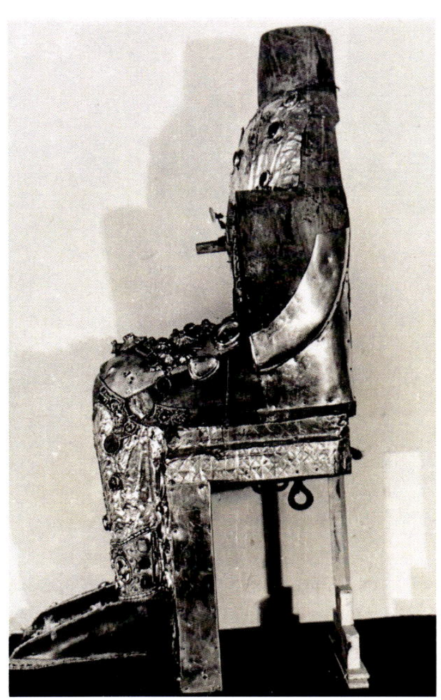

The golden statue of Sainte-Foy was opened only once for restoration in the twentieth century, in 1954. At that time, the metal revetment was removed in order to examine and secure the wooden torso, legs, and throne. The archeologist and photographer, Louis Balsan (1903–1988), took black-and-white photographs of the process. These archival images offer a rare glimpse into the interior of the effigy.

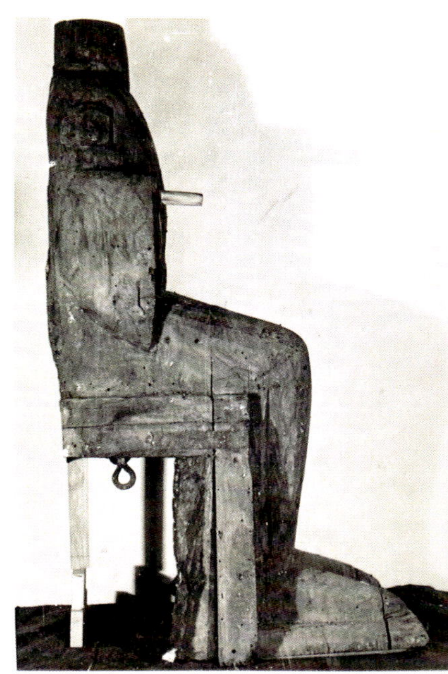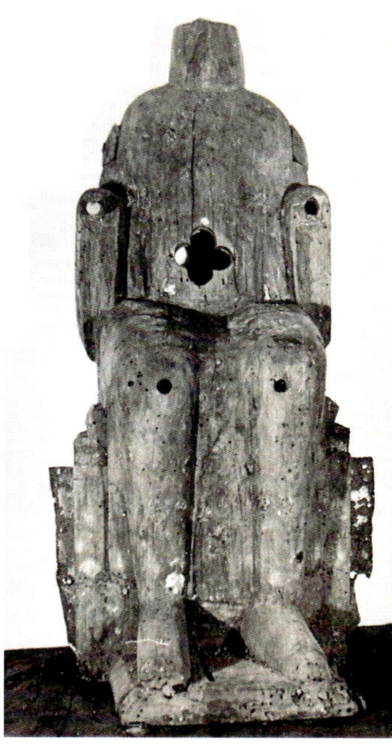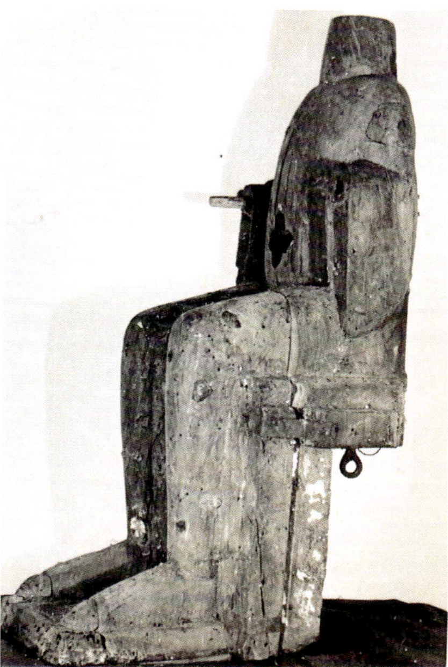

A poignant contrast exists between the glittering gold and gems on the exterior and the rough-hewn wood of the interior. Yew, known as a hard softwood, was used for the torso and legs; it is among the hardest materials to carve, which attests to the minimal articulation of the body (Forsyth 1972). The wooden core offers a stark, primitive representation of a human trunk and legs.

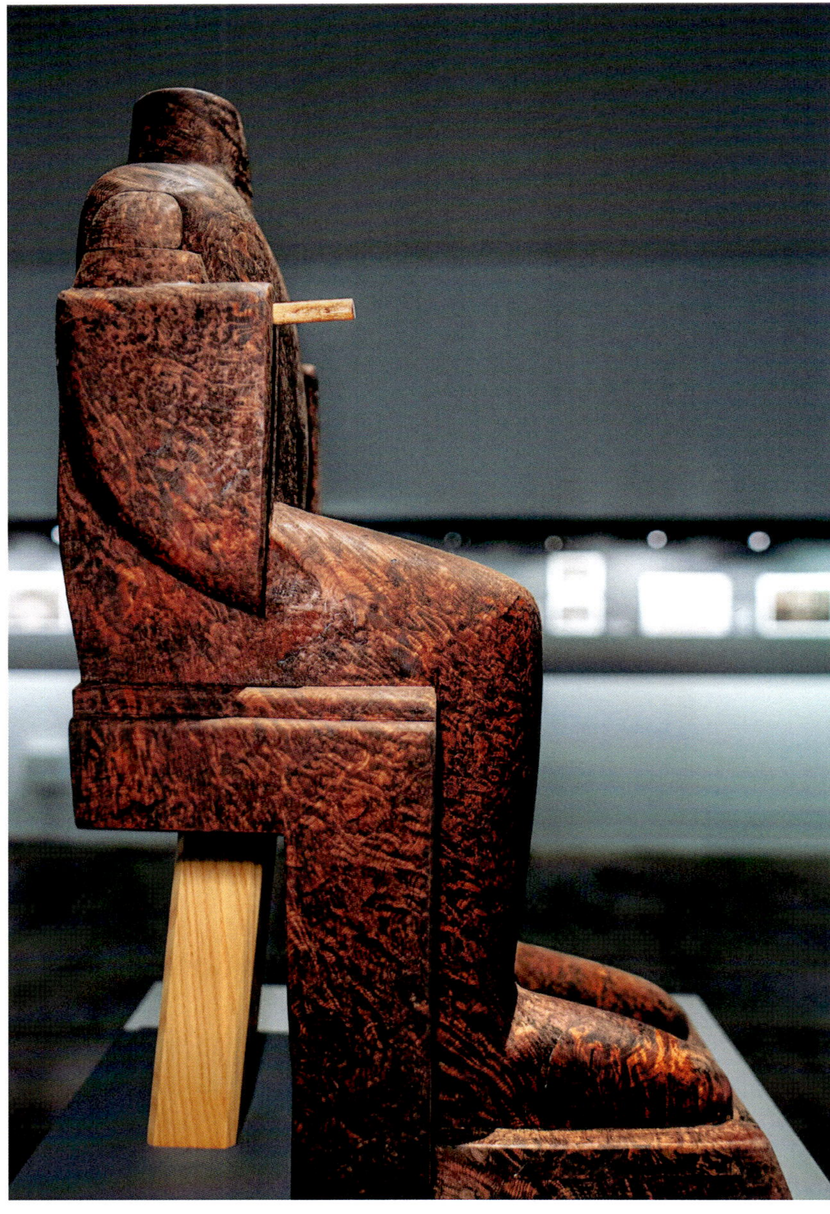

Photograph: Susana Barron

The modern copy of the statue of Sainte-Foy is made in 1:1 scale and is produced on the basis of the black-and-white photographs by Louis Balsan. The original statue at Conques was only once stripped of its gold revetments for a restoration done in 1954. Since then, the interior has been invisible and inaccessible to viewers and scholars. The Stanford exhibition gave modern visitors a unique experience — a peek into the mysterious wooden core — that would be otherwise impossible to achieve even if they go to Conques, France. The modern copy helps the viewer understand the rough and primitive carving of the wooden core and its gaping cavity hollowed out in the back.

It has been a challenge to make this copy as no measurements were done of the original wooden trunk of the effigy of Sainte-Foy in Conques in 1954. Balsan's photographs were our only guide. But these archival documents have never before been published in high resolution. The Société des Lettres de l'Aveyron, Rodez, France, shared with the Stanford project high quality scans of the originals. From them, the sculptor Chris Bell prepared a plaster model in a scale of 1:4. A second sculptor, Royce Johnson, used it to extrapolate the 1:1 scale and carved the statue from a burl of redwood.

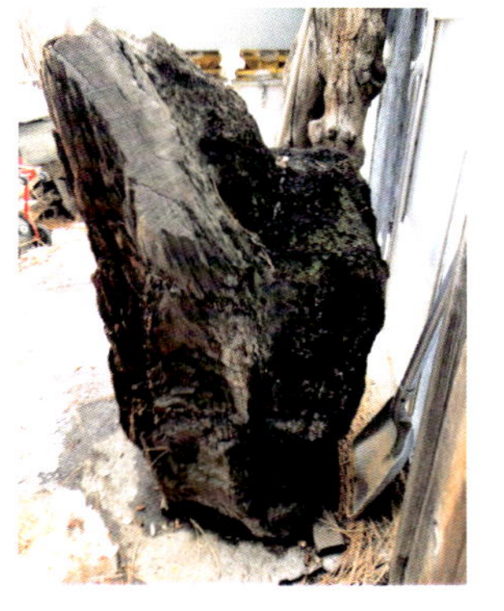 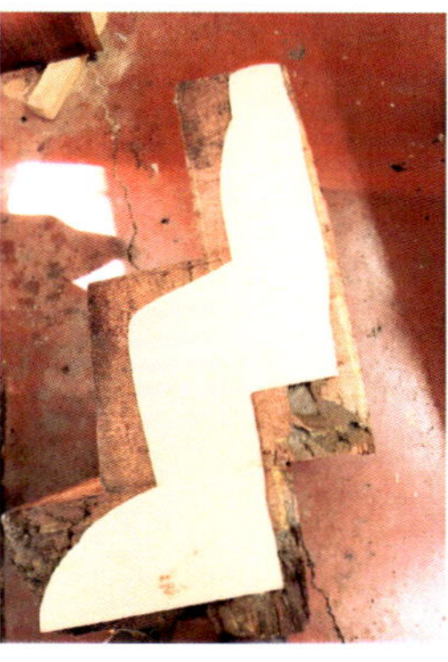 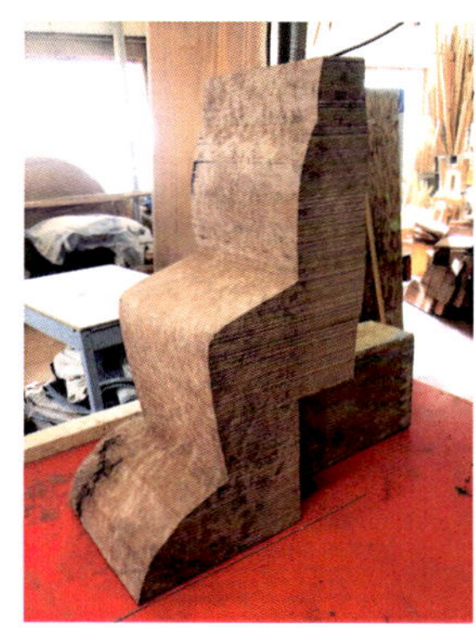 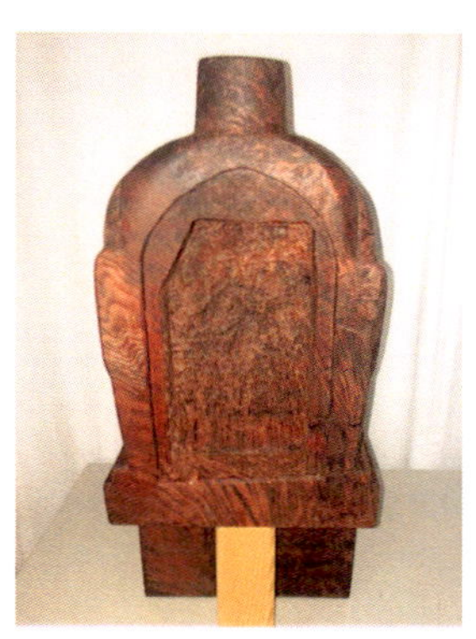

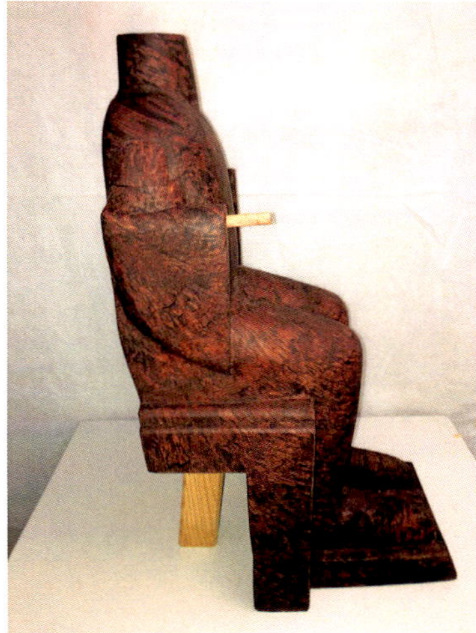 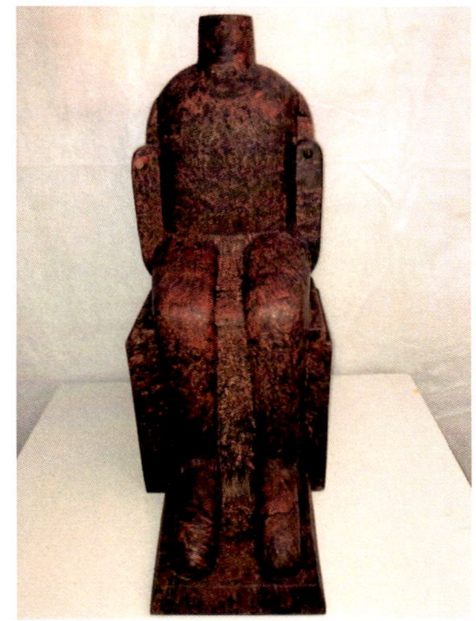 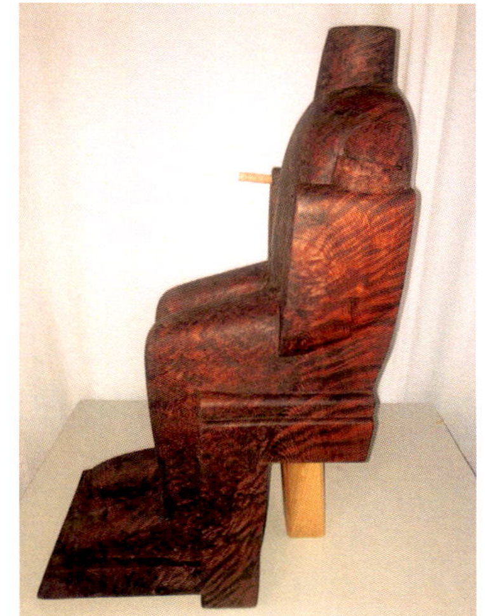

Modern copy of the wooden core of the statue-reliquary of Sainte-Foy (2022)

Redwood burl
Height of the statue 76.2 cm (30 inches); depth 45.72cm (18 inches); width 31.75 cm (12.5 inches)

Royce Johnson, sculptor, Kings Beach, California

Plaster model: Chris Bell, sculptor, Reno, Nevada

A large cavity at the top of the torso has been carved out in the back to hold the skull of Sainte-Foy. The upper section of the cranium rests on a silk cushion and is wrapped in another Eastern luxury textile. The inscription on a metal band affixed to the skull certifies the authenticity of the relic; it was placed there in 1878, on the orders of the cardinal and bishop of Rodez, Joseph Christian Ernest Bourret (1827–1896) (Gaborit-Chopin 2001).

Photographs: Louis Balsan

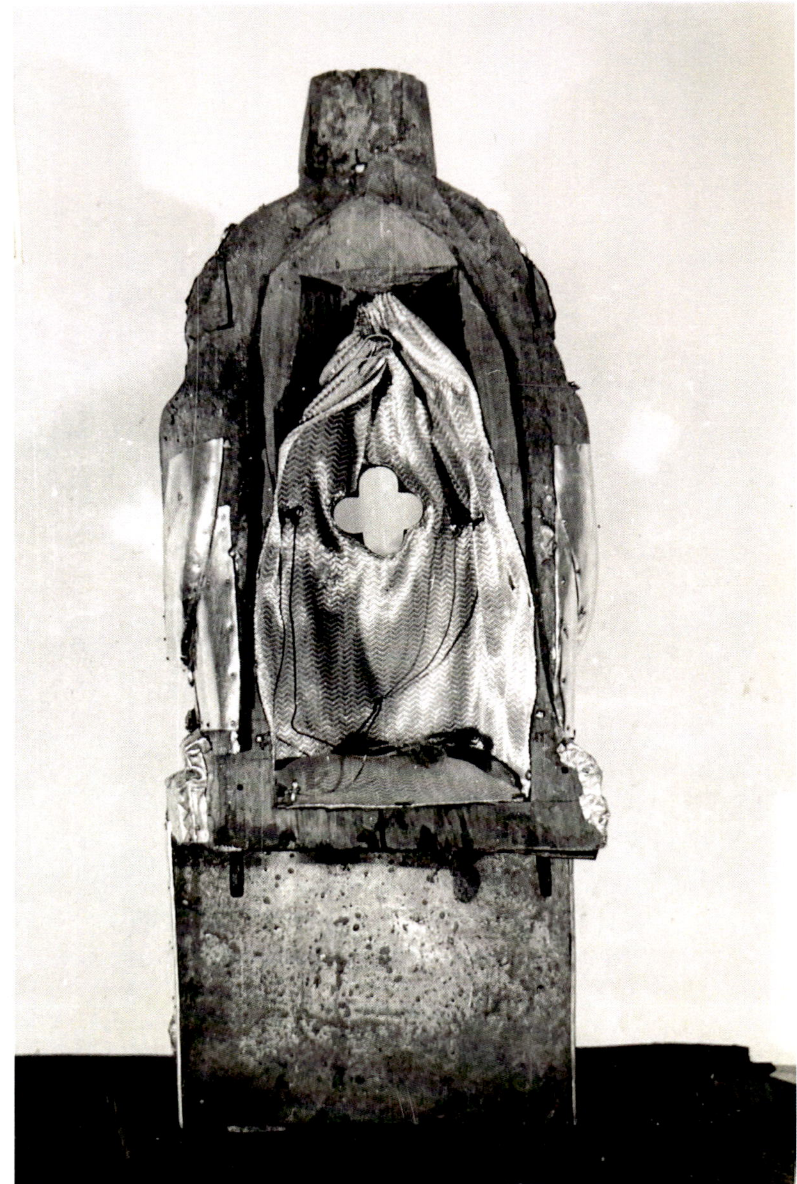

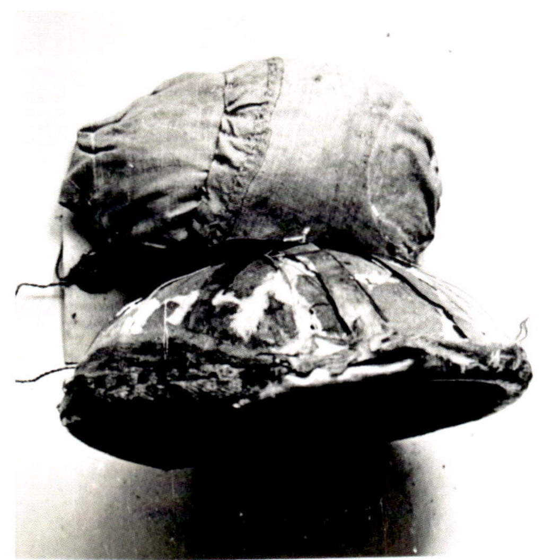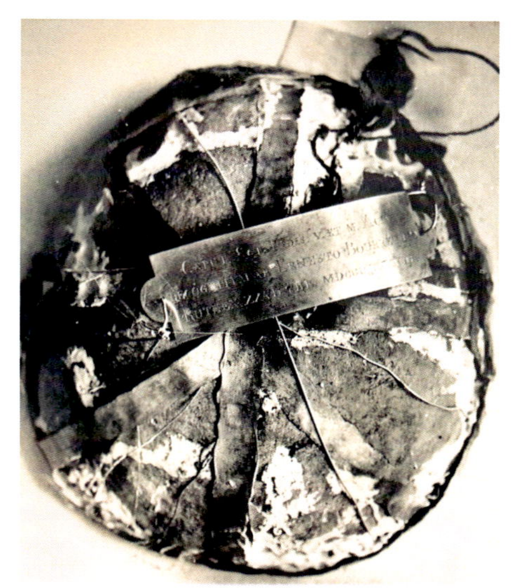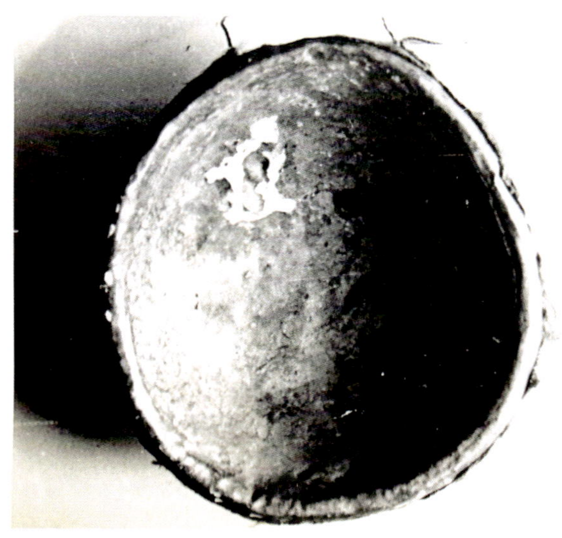

Skull of Sainte-Foy

Reproduced with permission of La Société des Lettres de l'Aveyron, Rodez, France

A lush silk of a deep wine-red color wraps the skull (Gaborit-Chopin 2001). Roundels envelop birds and leafy crowns. Each circlet in this network is composed of strings of pearls tied with gems. The overall composition elicits the image of a crown. The repeated motif of the diadem should recall the flowers and stars in the chants for Sainte-Foy. The glorified saint has ascended to heaven. The celestial court is imagined in the splendor of gold, silks, gems, and eternally blooming flowers. The star power of this vision is sustained by the luxury objects brought in contact with the relics of the saint.

The silk used to wrap the skull came from the East, possibly Byzantium. Its wine-red color suggests a product of the imperial workshops. The emperor had a monopoly over the production of purple silk; no one could weave, trade, or wear this material outside the palace or imperial gifts. Byzantine diplomacy wielded power through elite gifts of *porphyreos* silk. We may never know exactly how this luxury textile ended up at Conques. It could have come in the ninth century as a Carolingian imperial gift. Two kings of Aquitaine made donations to Conques: Louis the Pious (778–840) in 819, and Pippin (817–838) in 838 (Desjardins 1879; Bousquet 1992; Remensnyder 1995). The imperial exclusivity of silk bestows a Byzantine aura to the relics and the cult of Sainte-Foy at Conques. Before the twelfth century, the splendor of the Byzantine court defined how the celestial realm was imagined in the West.

Silk, Byzantine, 9th century

Weft-faced compound twill (*samit*) technique

Photograph: Erich Lessing/AKG Images

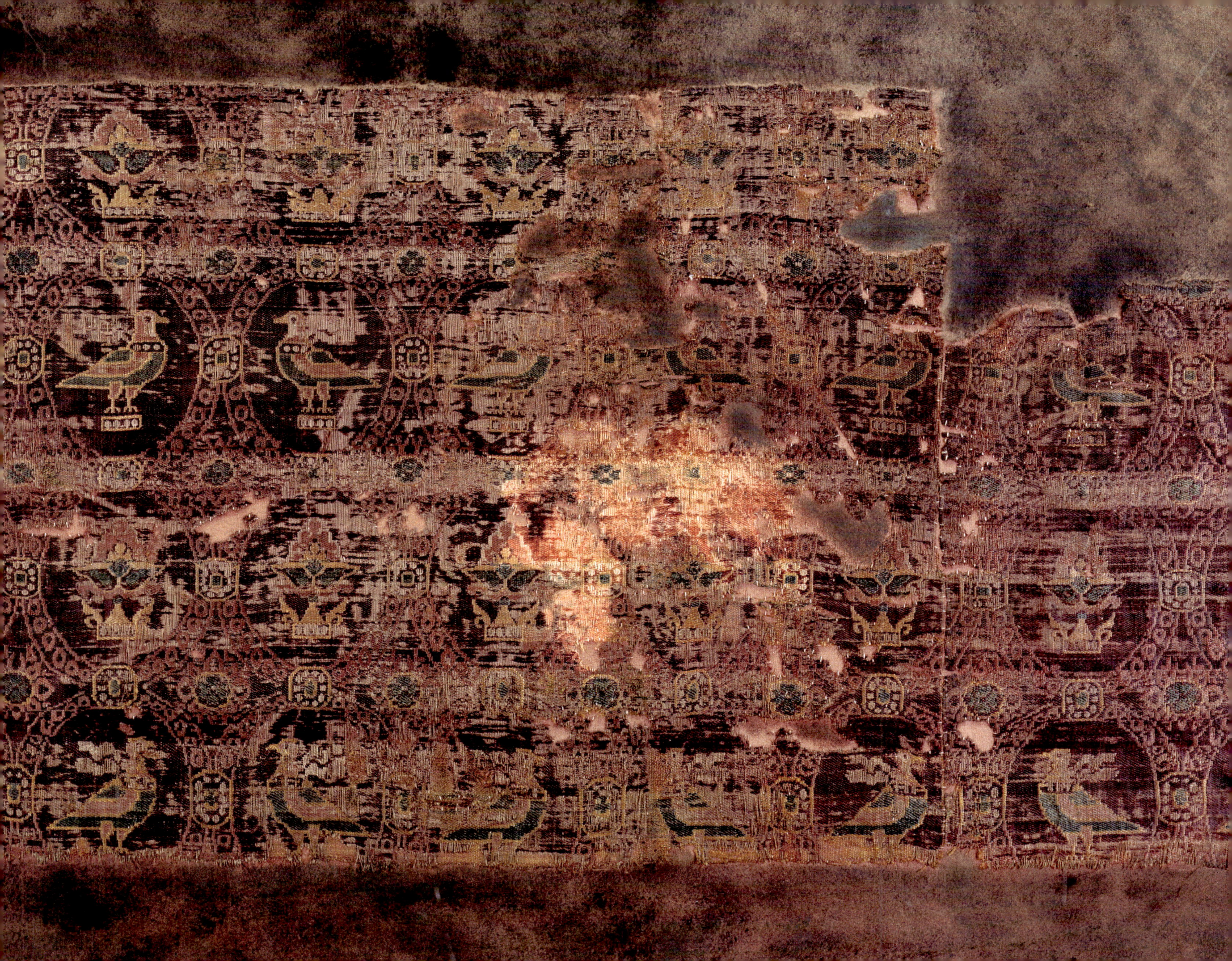

Body as Water, Martyrdom as Purple Silk, Sainthood as Pearl

Although recent studies have shown that this textile is not dyed using murex, its purple color still elicits images triggered by Byzantine *prophyreos* (Berthod 2019). Purple silk's wine-dark hue brings about associations with water and sacrifice (Constas 2014). The dye comes from sea murex, a type of mollusk. When crushed, these creatures release a substance used for coloring. Christian theologians have described the human body as a silk woven from the sea and dyed in the murex's vital liquids. And while the color purple suggests blood and sacrifice, its origins in water also call to mind associations with the pearl. In medieval times, people believed that when a bolt of lightning strikes the sea, it makes the oyster conceive its precious gem. The resulting opalescent, spherical bead never ceases to emit the luminous energy that engendered it. The Byzantine silk that wraps the relics with its color and its pearl designs entertain concepts of sacrifice and vesseling of the divine. Sainte-Foy is both a pearl and a shell; her martyrdom transforms her into a luminous gem and a container of Christ, the spiritual *margarita* (pearl) (Pentcheva 2023b).

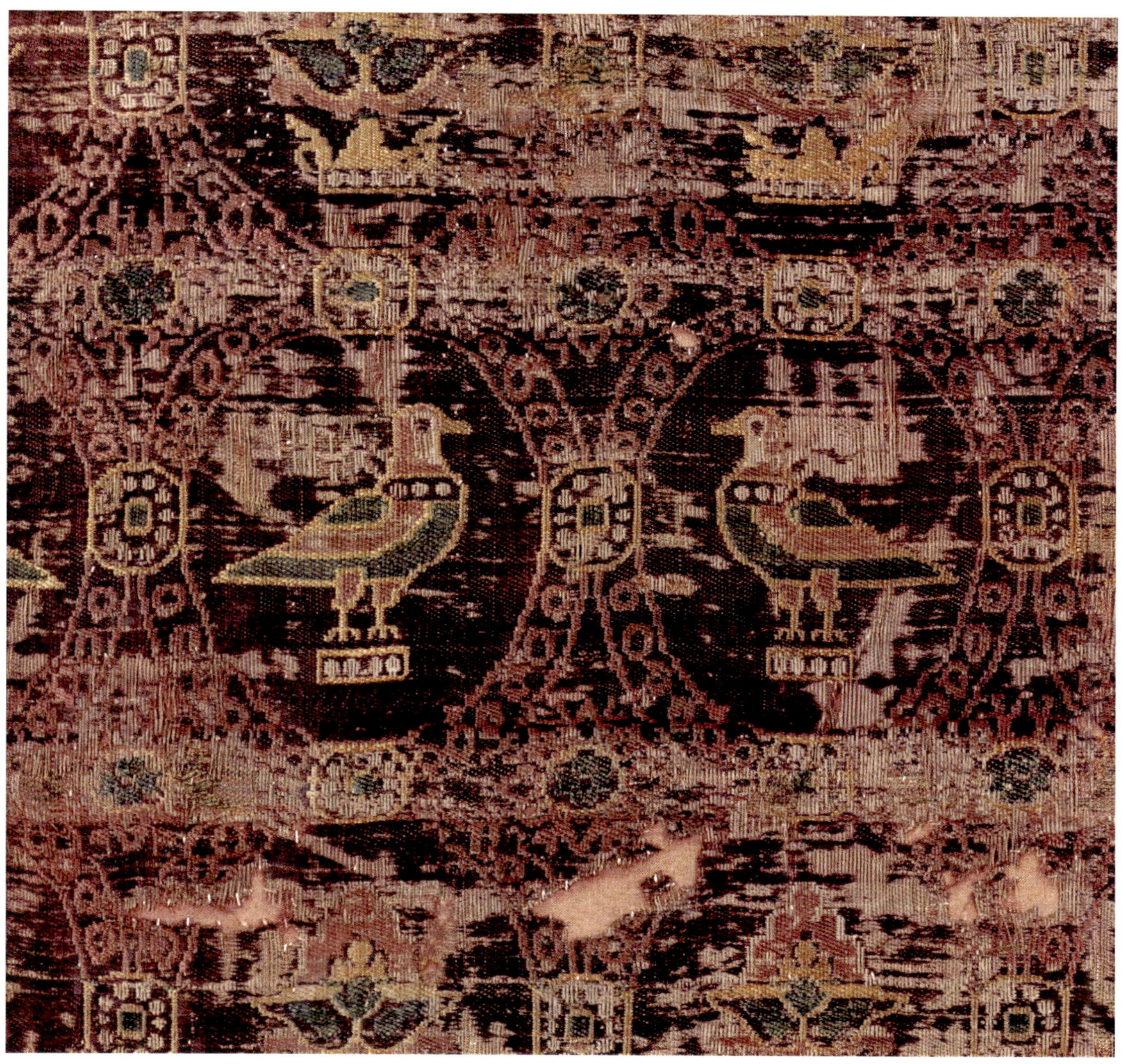

Detail, Silk, Byzantine,
9th century

Weft-faced compound twill
(*samit*) technique

Photograph: Erich Lessing/AKG Images

Imagining Flowers

The statue's gems, ancient cameos, and gold filigree give vibrancy to its metal surface. The clustering of these glittering materials parallels the rich metaphors in the poetry of the chants such as *Emissiones Tue* (Your aromas) of the vespers responsory, where *Fides* is compared to flowers, stars, and gems. All are small, vivid objects that can easily be conjured up in one's imagination (Scarry 1990). The liveliness of the saturated color of the flowers, the luminosity of the gems, and the brightness of the stars elicit the very energy of life that propels the faithful to come to Conques and seek access to it through Sainte-Foy (Cox-Miller 2009; Hahn 2012; Pentcheva 2023a).

Photograph: Miguel Novelo

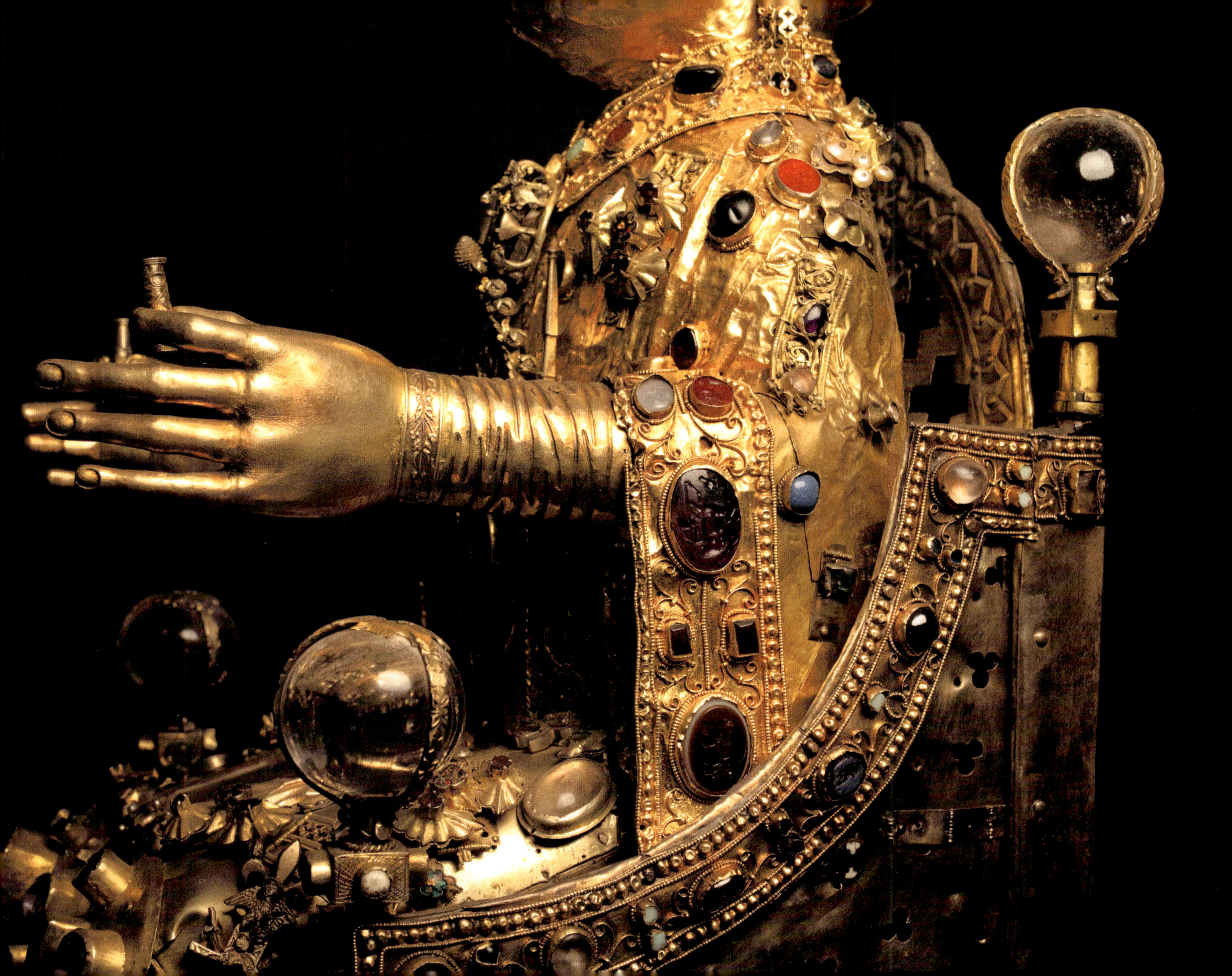

Scrim with the Projection of the Gilded Effigy of Sainte-Foy

The computer-generated model of the statue of Sainte-Foy was done using photogrammetry. A vast number of photos were taken using a mirrorless camera set on a gimbal to capture every inch of the sculpture. Cross-polarizing lighting minimized the reflections off the metal surface. A combination of software (Adobe Lightroom, Photo Catch with Apple's Object Capture API, and Autodesk Maya) was used to post-process and stitch the photographs to create the digital model. Projecting it on a semi-transparent scrim as opposed to a high-resolution video screen achieves a floating, ethereal effect, as if the statue hovers in thin air. This impression is reminiscent of the medieval *Book of Miracles*, which described Sainte-Foy as drifting invisibly along with the drafts of air.

Scrim projection of the
golden statue of Sainte-Foy

AudioVision in the Middle Ages
Exhibition at the Stanford Art Gallery

Model and projection: Miguel Novelo
Photograph: Susana Barron

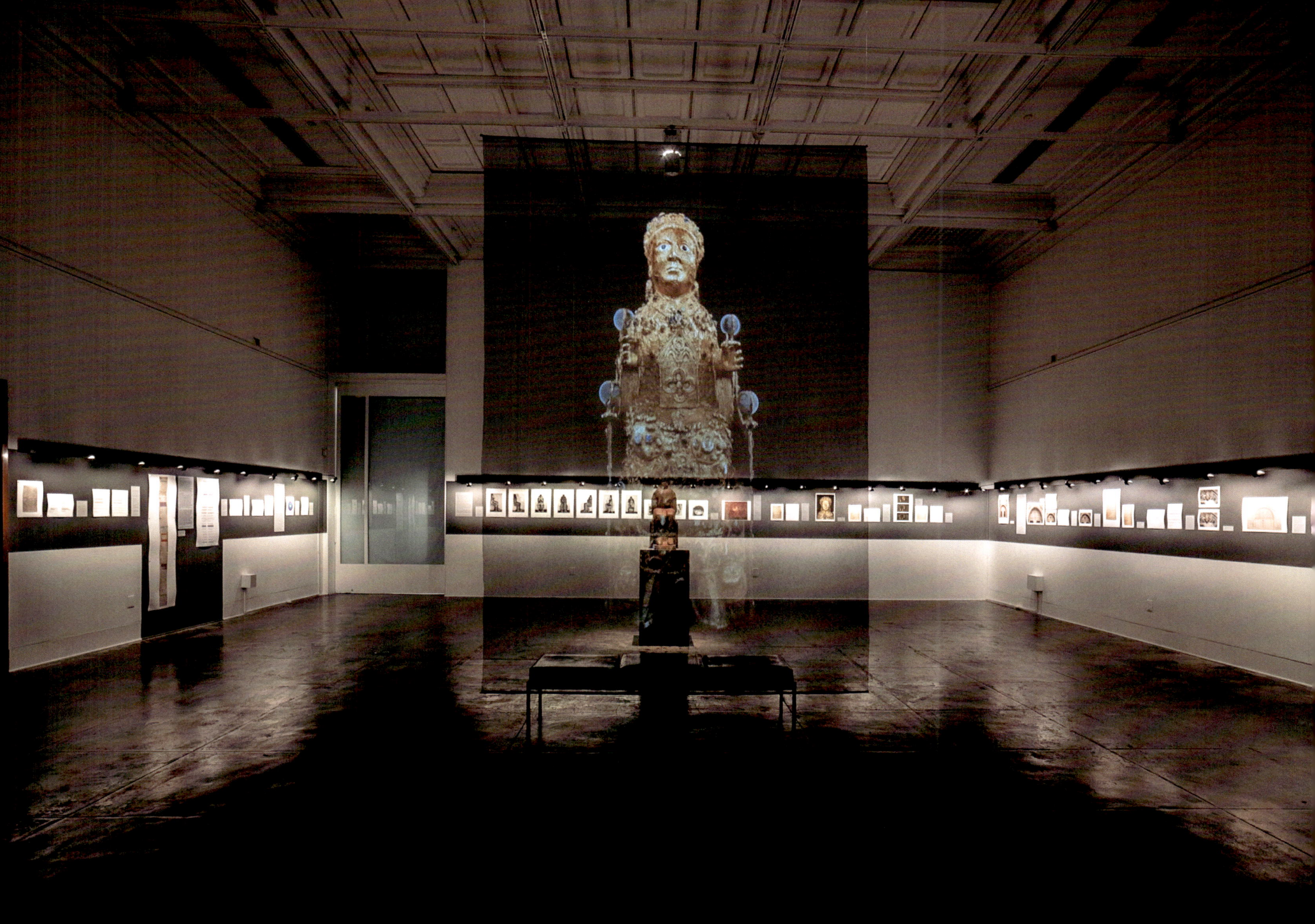

Multimedia Interlace

The *libellus* with the Office of Sainte-Foy groups together all of the responsories for the three nocturns in one place. The decorated initial "B" announces their start. Notably, this is the only ornamented letter in the entire manuscript. The interlacings in this miniature express the affinity among music, word, and imagination (Bonne 2012; on materiality, Bynum, 2011). The vegetal loops and circles (*choroi*) visually correlate to the sonic ring structures that take place in the singing of the responsories with elaborate refrains and *prosae* (*sequentiae*). The excess materiality — words, notes, visual figuration — forms the décor in which the metaphysical becomes perceptible, be it as sound, color, or design (Pentcheva 2023b).

Libellus of the *Office of Sainte-Foy* (1037–1065)

Paris, BnF, MS Nouv. Acq. Lat. 443, fol. 4.

specie sed pulchrior fide AD CANT. A Multenum uenientes

adspectaculum passionis sancte fidis et uidentes constanciam eius ere

diderunt indominum ihesum xpistum S amen & Iuuenili etate florens

Magnorum martirum tirocinio uirtuti

B EATISSI RESPONSORIA

ME — VIRginis fidis —

natalis diem sollempniter

recurren — tem deuotissi me excipi — amus que nodum comple —

te certaminis in cursu cho — rona celitus immissa adeo —

Poetry and melody support each other to stir maximum sensorial effect. The responsory is an elaborate chant sung after the readings at vespers and during the night service. This example, *Emissiones tue* (Your aromas) starts by describing the fragrance of a garden full of fruits and spices. By means of these verbal suggestions, the imagination is drawn to the sense of smell. Then the melody amplifies this olfactory sensation in the refrain, where it specifically loads the word "cinnamon." This is sung to an extensive *melisma* (the singing of many notes on one syllable). Such a concentration of sonic energy on the word for a spice, achieved by the melisma, creates a form of aural décor. The melisma gives prominence to *cinnamomum* while, at the same time, it obscures the meaning of the word by stretching its utterance with musical ornaments. Sonic amplification through melodic ornament activates the memory of smell and recalls the numerous visual interlacing of flower and vegetal images in the manuscripts, in the golden statue of Sainte-Foy, and in the relief sculptures in the church. Audio-spectators are thus invited to dwell in the imagined space of the lush vegetation of Paradise, filled with aromas and pleasant, repeating sounds (Pentcheva 2023a).

Visual and aural décor in the evening (vespers) responsory *Emissiones Tue* at Conques

Paris, BnF, MS Nouv. Acq. Lat. 443, fols 1rv

Coloring: Jessica Chen Lee

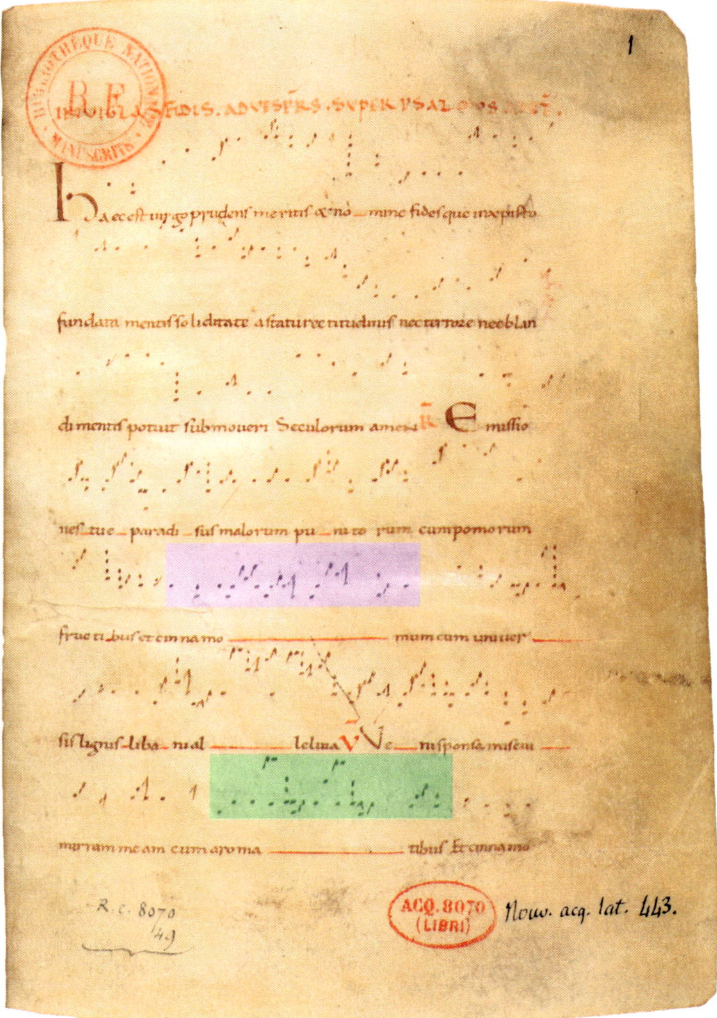

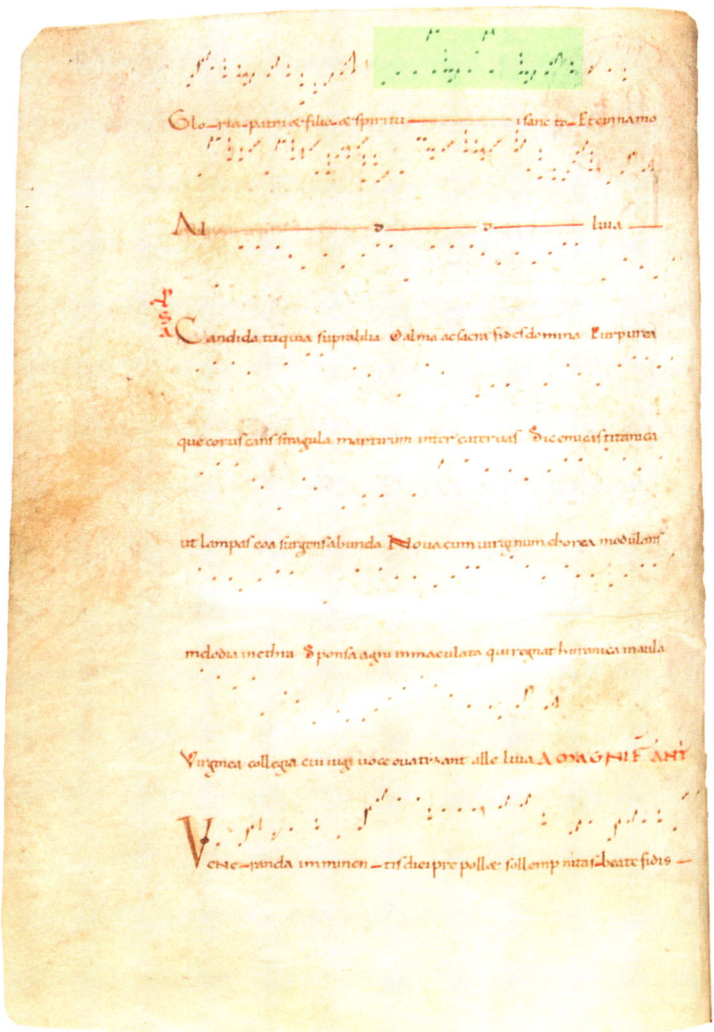

Melismas, poetry, perfume, and smoke all come together at vespers, because incense is most intensively burned right before the singing of the hymn of praise to Mary: the Magnificat. The responsory *Emissiones tue* (Your Aromas) precedes this hymn and prepares the stage for the sensual encounter with the divine. The first melisma on *cinnamonum* is then echoed in two other melismas — on *aromatibus* (with fragrances) and *Spiritui Sancto* (to the Holy Spirit) — in the verse *Veni sponsa* (Come, My Bride) and the doxology (the singing of "Glory to the Father, Son, and Holy Spirit"). They help sustain the participants' focus on the sense of smell. The repeated melismas prompt the listener to imagine the spirit in the wisps of perfume issuing from the burning incense (Pentcheva 2023a; on word painting in music, Mahrt 1990; Treitler 2003). The sonic ornament elicits the olfactory memory of incense, especially in the way its fragrance-releasing vapors are visually interlaced. Song and smell tease the desire to sense the invisible divine in the scent drifting in the air and in the sonic energy arising from breath exhaled in chant.

Animation of the Interior of the Abbey Church of Sainte-Foy at Conques

Two animations for day and night, respectively, show a movement to the altar and then a tilt up to the dome of the transept tower, and a return back to the floor, where the image of the rotating wheel of the *musica mundana* (music of the spheres, as shown in the diagram of Paris, BnF, MS Lat. 776, fol. 1v) appears (Pentcheva 2020ab). A third animation — a time lapse — explores the movement of the sunlight in the church interior on the feast-day of Sainte-Foy, October 6.

The architectural model was created through photogrammetry. A vast number of photos taken in situ in 360° rotation in the nave and sanctuary were then used to assemble the model. The renderings of the interior were then done using V-Ray® 3D Max software.

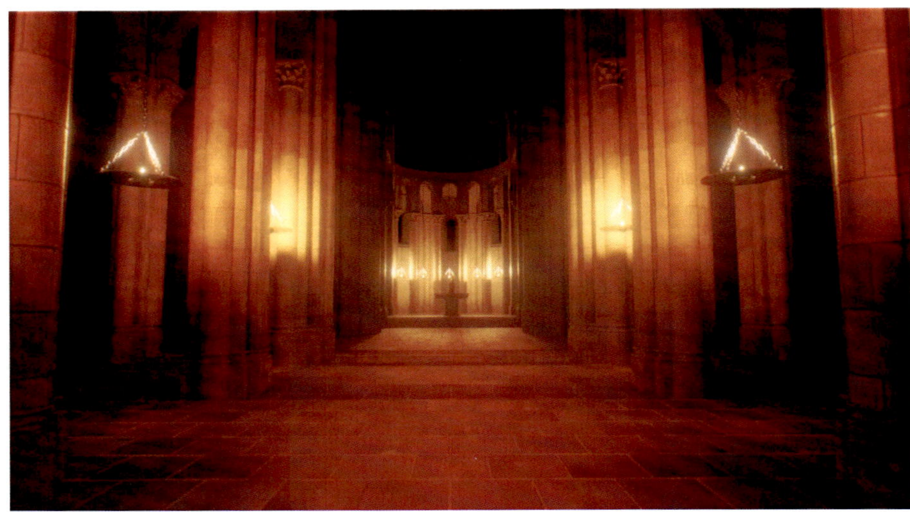

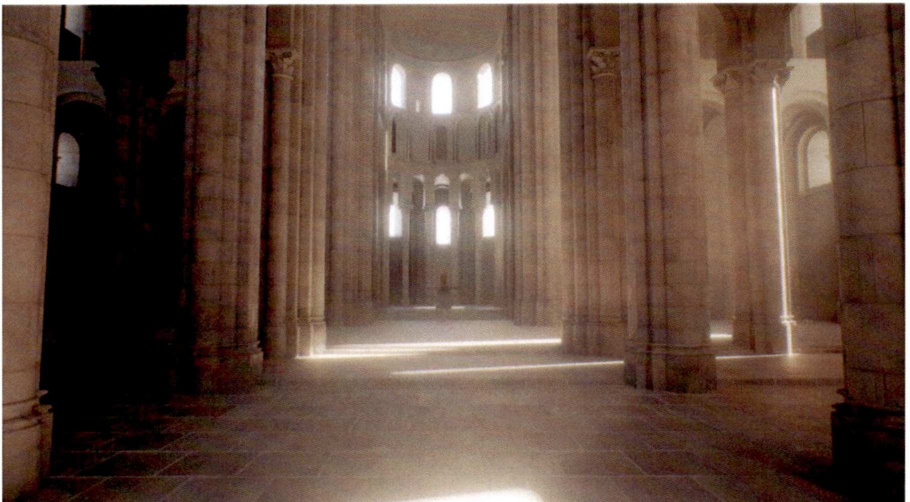

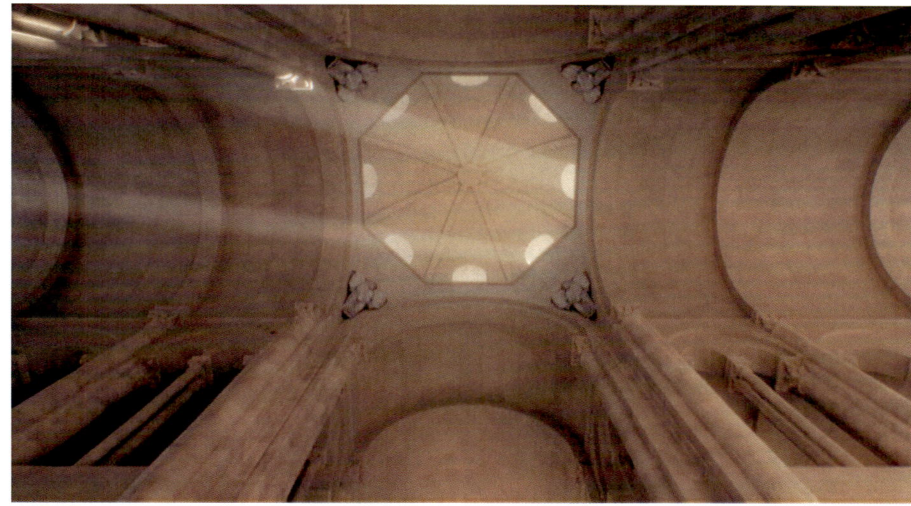

A major insight that came from the time-lapse exploring how sunlight travels in the sanctuary on the day of the feast (October 6) is that the golden statue persistently remains in shadow. Only at sunset, the last rays coming from the rose and two lancet windows on the West facade frame the effigy in two luminous bands of light. As these rays continue on their course, the left one touches and briefly bathes in light the golden surface of the image. This miraculous and ephemeral splendor coincides with the beginning of the vespers service and inaugurates the festivities. Once again, the design of the architecture, the position and appearance of the statue, and the composition of the music show that they are carefully coordinated in order to create a maximum sensorial effect.

Animations

A fly through the nave and sanctuary at Conques during the day; a fly through the nave and sanctuary at Conques during the night

Animation: Blagoy Kostov, Illusion Box Studio, Sofia, Bulgaria, for Stanford's "Enchanted Images" Project

A Time-Lapse on October 6
(Feast day of Sainte-Foy)

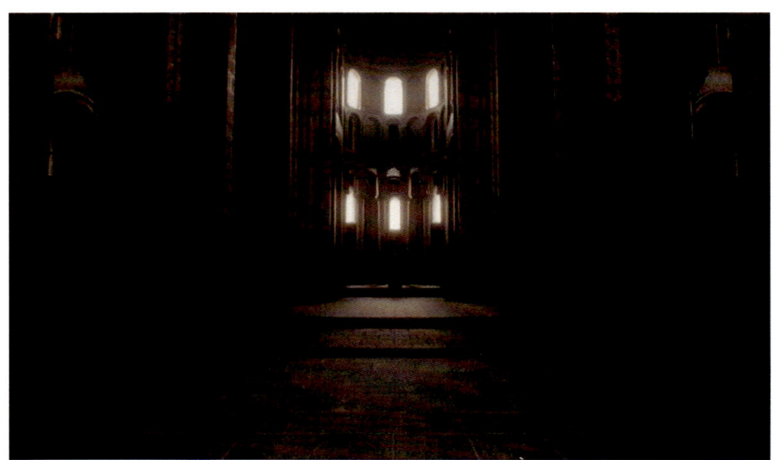

First light

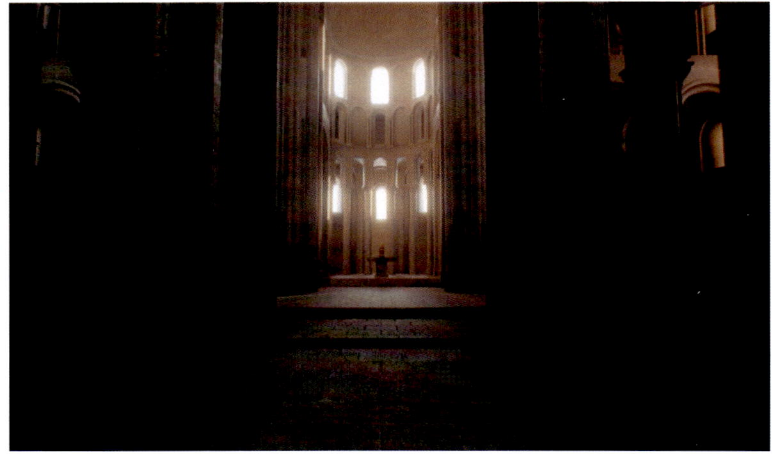

First sunrays

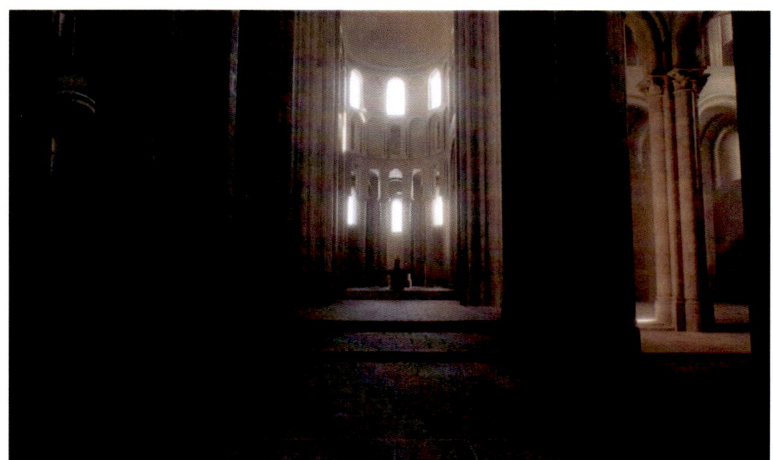

Noon

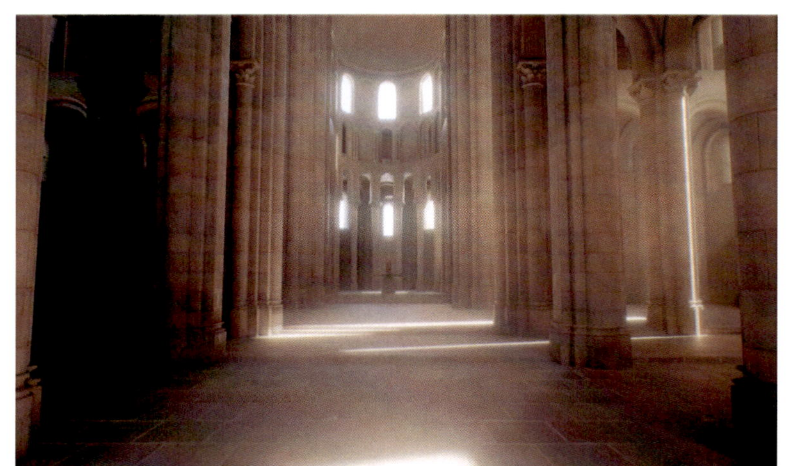

Afternoon

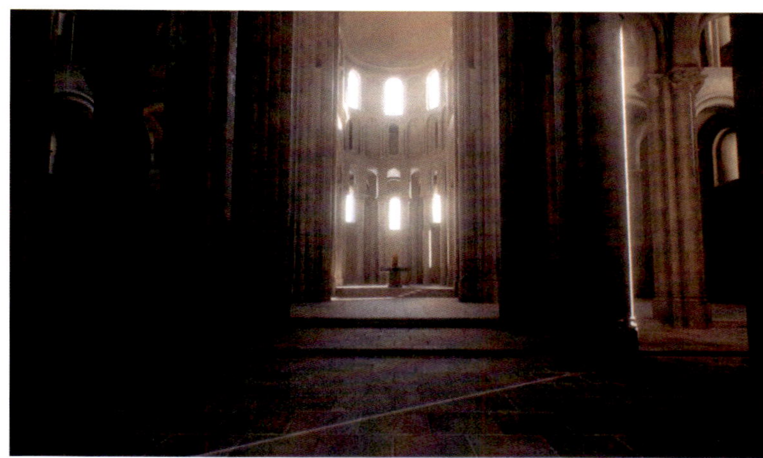

Early morning

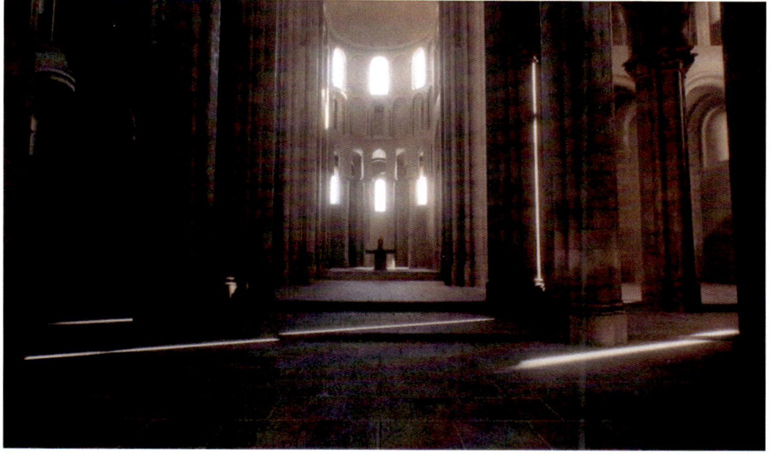

Late morning

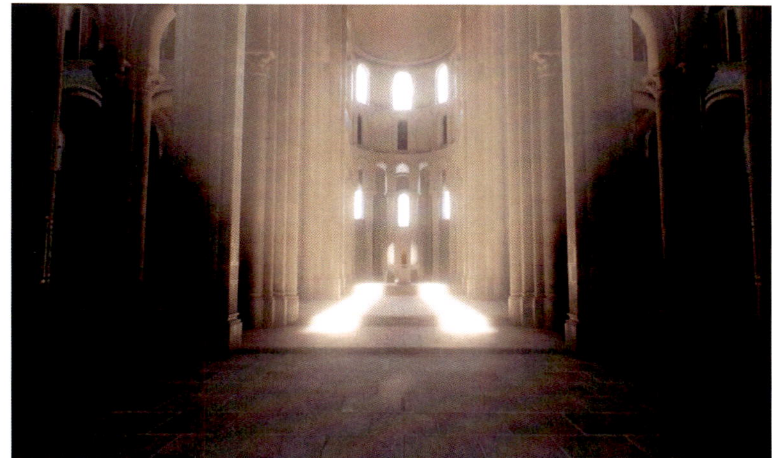

Sunset

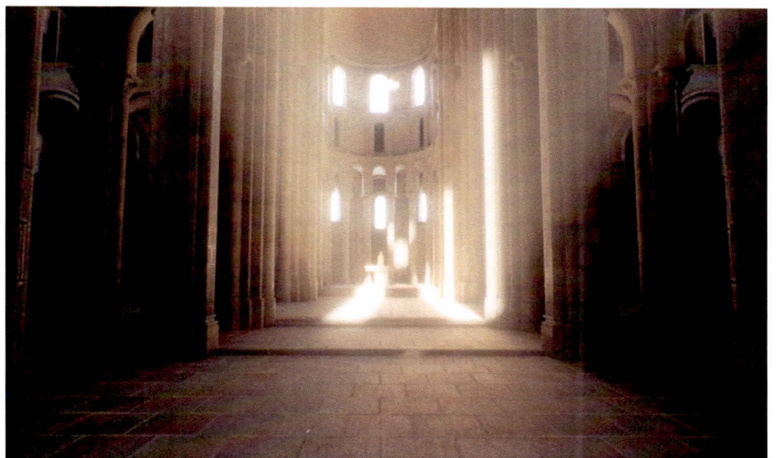

Sunset with light coming from the rose window and the two gates
of the West façade

Animation:
Blagoy Kostov,
Illusion Box Studio,
Sofia, Bulgaria, for
Stanford's "Enchanted
Images" Project

PART THREE

AudioVision: Synergy of Chant *and* Image *on the* West Façade *at* Conques

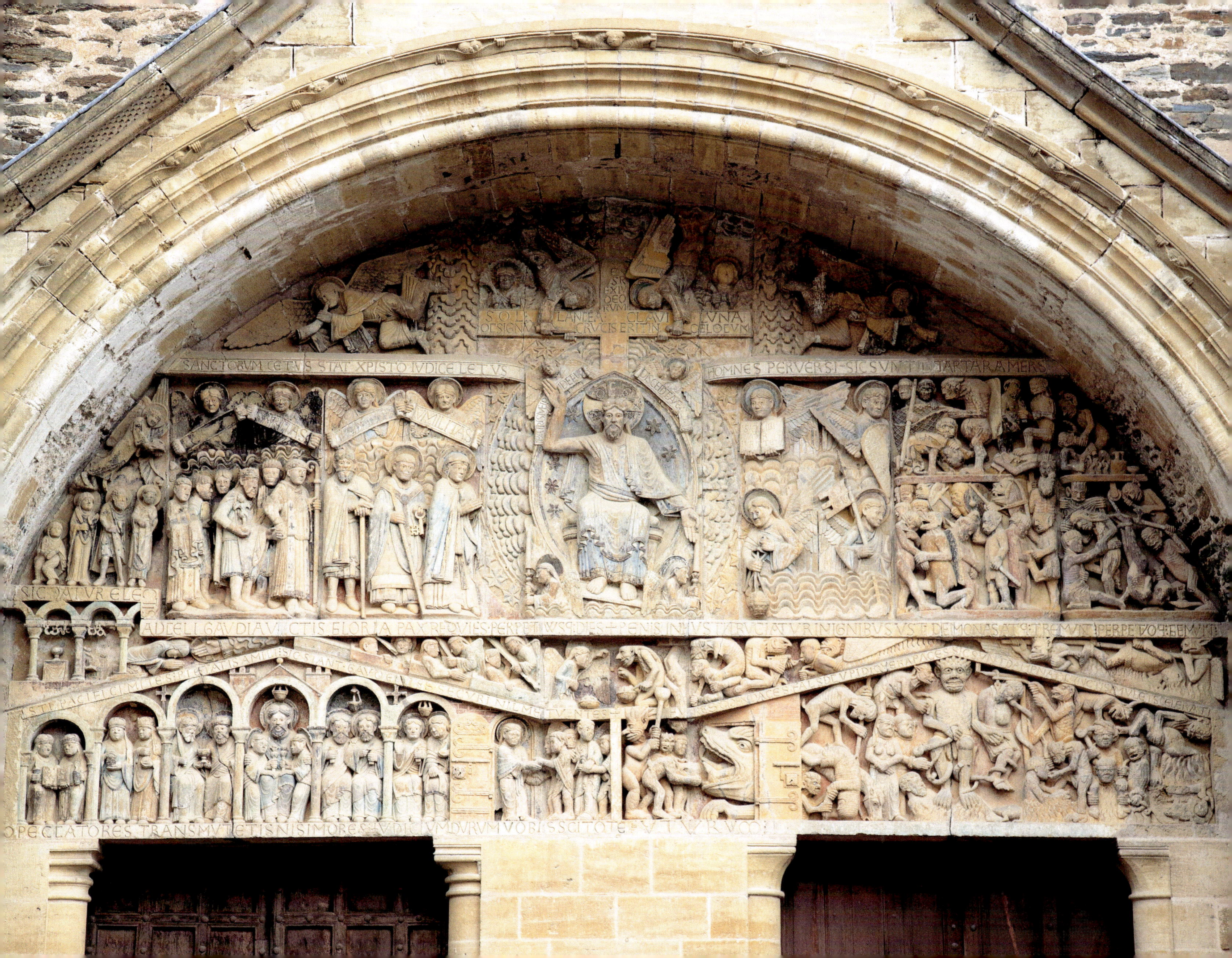
SOL
DESIGNA
LANCEA · CLAVI
CRVCIS ERIT IN
LVNA
CELOEVM
SANCTORVM CETVS STAT XPISTO IVDICE LETVS
HOMNES PERVERSI SIC SVNT IN TARTARA MERSI
SIC DATVR ELEC
AD CELI GAVDIA VICTIS GLORIA PAX REQVIES PERPETVVSQ DIES + PENIS INIVSTI CRVCIATVR IGNIBVS VSTI DEMONAS ATQ TREMVNT PERPETVO
TATIS AMICIS SIC SANT GAV
O PECCATORES TRANSMVTETIS NISI MORES IVDICIVM DVRVM VOBIS SCITOTE FVTVRVM

AudioVision: Reliefs, Inscriptions, Chants

The Last Judgment on the west façade of the church of Sainte-Foy at Conques presents the most complex figural program (Bonne 1984). The inscriptions on the horizontal bands spell out the rewards and punishments that the blessed and the sinful, respectively, will receive at the end of time (Kendall 1989; Kendall 1998). Other featured texts are direct quotes from chants (Bouché 2006; Pentcheva 2022ab). These special music-souvenirs stimulate the audio-viewer to recall certain melodies associated with important liturgical feasts. These chant-quotes have enabled this project to restore the images at the bottom part of the façade. In modern times this wall between the two doors is blank. But more likely it originally held a relief that is currently displayed in the church's interior.

The facade is divided vertically into two parts seen from the point of view of Christ in the center of the composition in the role of the Judge (Bonne 1984). His proper right-hand side (to the viewer's left) is dedicated to the faithful. His proper left-hand side (to the viewer's right) is allotted to the

sinful, vividly depicting their numerous tortures. The horizontal bands present another set of contrasts: the ascent of the faithful versus the fall of the sinful. The Virgin Mary and Saint Peter in the middle register lead the blessed in a procession toward Christ. Sainte-Foy appears in the register below, tucked into a wedge-like compartment that reveals the sanctuary and the throne in the interior of the church at Conques. Here, Sainte-Foy has stepped away from her majesty/seat and kneels in prayer. She beseeches the Judge on behalf of her servants.

Powerful energy bursts out from this exchange between Sainte-Foy and the Lord. The dead begin to rise from their tombs, as each successive lid peaks higher, allowing bodies to emerge and to stand in judgment. At the center right, beneath the feet of Christ, the Archangel Michael holds the balance. The Devil tries to weigh down one of the pans by pushing it with his finger, as human fate hangs in the balance. The tilted line disrupts the uniformity of parallel lines and signals the precarious state between judgment and salvation. If the

Archangel is not vigilant, the devil will cheat. This suspense also emanates from the inscription on the bottom horizontal register, covering only half of the span. The text addresses and arrests the viewer, warning of the dire consequences resulting from the lack of forethought and repentance.

This section of the exhibition explores *AudioVision* as synergy between chant and monumental sculpture. It shows how many of the inscriptions in the relief sculpture at Conques are quotations from chants. These excerpts serve as prompts stirring the memory to recall the melodies (Carruthers 1990; Busse-Berger 2005; Bouché 2006). In addition, the structure of some of these inscriptions echoes the poetic form of the genre of songs known as *prosae* or *sequentiae* (Pentcheva 2022ab).

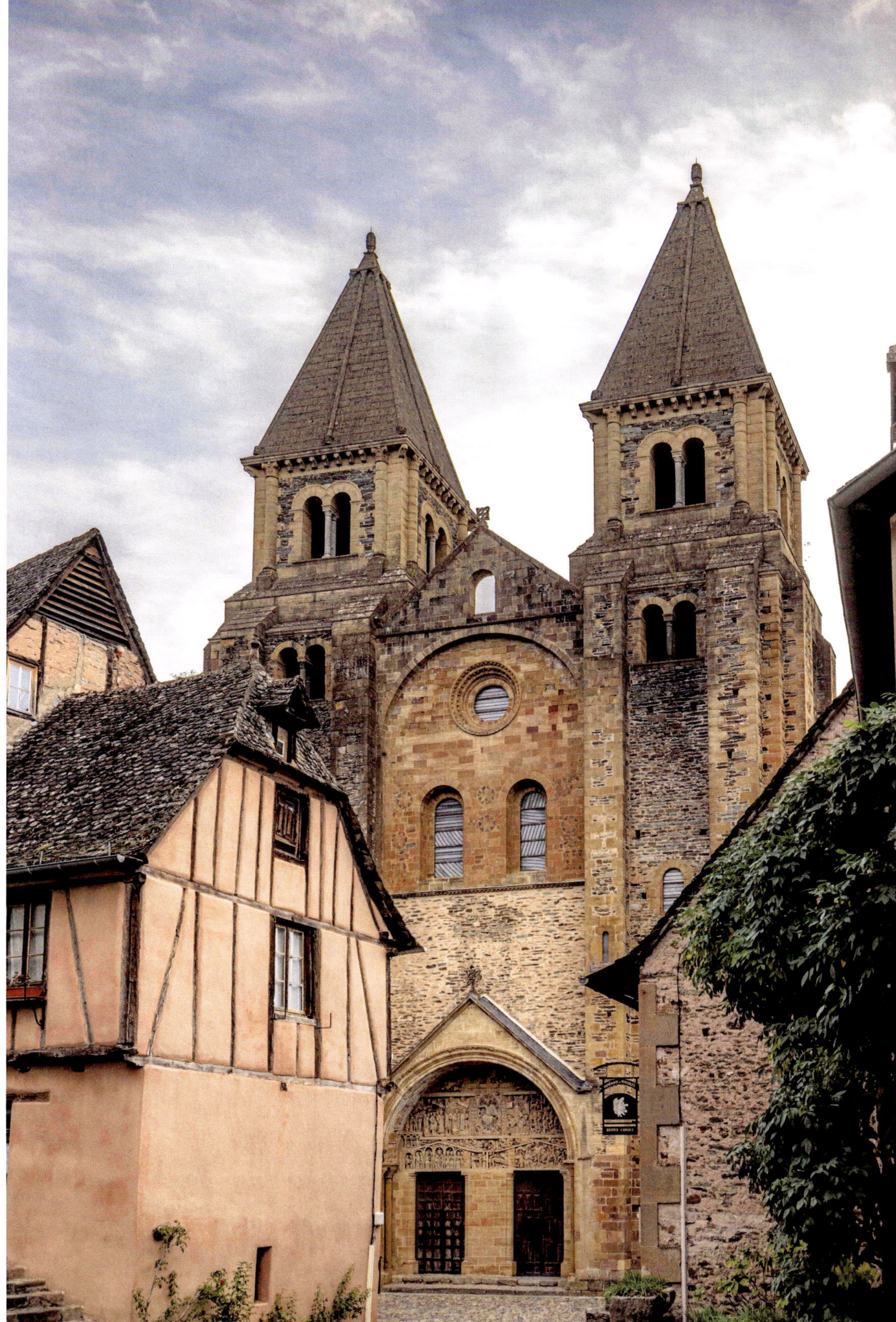

The structure of this inscription with its pairing of lines resembles the "double cursus" (where the same melody will be sung to two lines of poetry) of the genre of chants known as *prosa/sequentia* as for instance in this exhibition *Candida tu quia* or *Almiphona iam gaudia* (on *prosa/sequentia*, see Roederer 1974; Crocker 1977; Kelly 1974; Kelly 1977; Kelly 2011; Iversen 2007; Iversen 2010; Fassler 1993; Fassler 2019). The *prosa* has a single line at the beginning and end and in between — several pairs of double cursus. In a similar way, the verses on the tympanum at Conques are arranged in such a way that a single line is set at the top (here the line from Matt. 24:30 *Hoc signum curcis*) and at the bottom, while paired lines in what resembles a double cursus appear in between. This evocation of the structure of chant is significant. It suggests that the rise of monumental relief sculpture over the course of the eleventh and early twelfth centuries shares origins with certain genres of music. *Sequentiae* and *tropes* appear as the sonic equivalents of narrative bas-reliefs and historiated capitals (Iversen 2010; Pentcheva 2022ab). These new creations in art and music expand beyond the texts of Scripture and elicit stronger affect from the audience.

Inscription (1105–1115)

West Façade, Abbey Church of Sainte-Foy, Conques, France

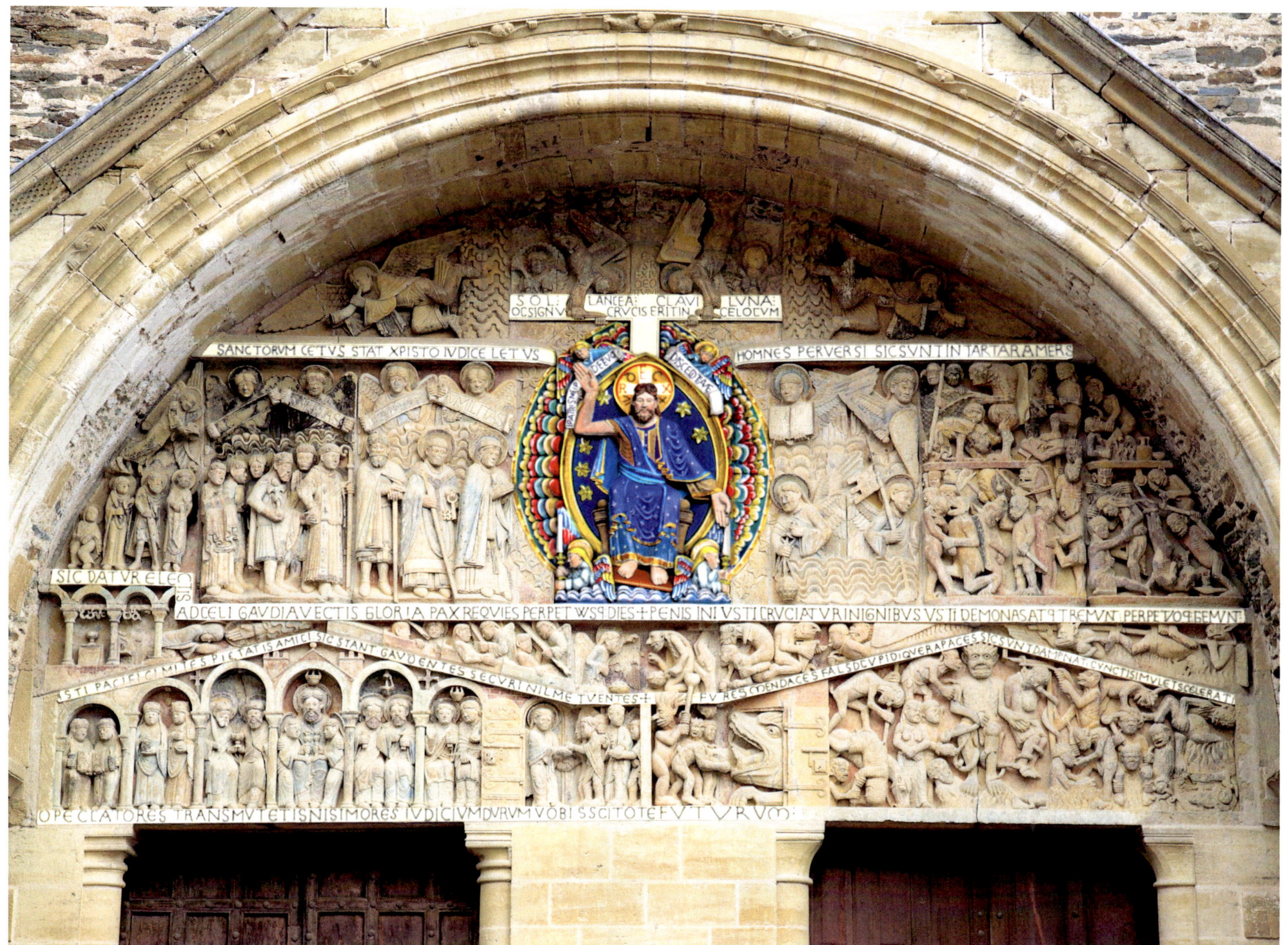

Photograph: Boris Missirkov; coloring: Jessica Chen Lee

The Latin inscription on the Tympanum

1 HOC SIGNUM CRUCIS ERIT IN COELO CUM (Matthew 24:30)

2a SANCTORUM CETUS STAT XPISTO IUDICE LETUS

2b HOMINES PERUERSI SIC SUNT IN TARTARA MERSI

3a SIC DATUR ELECTIS AD CELI GAUDIA UECTIS GLORIA PAX REQUIES PERPETUUSQUE DIES

3b PENIS INIUSTI CRUCIATUR IN IGNIBUS USTI DEMONAS ATQUE TREMUNT PERPETUOSQUE GEMUNT

4a CASTI PACIFICI MITES PIETATIS AMICI SIC STANT GAUDENTES SECURI NIL METUENTES

4b FURES MENDACES FALSI CUPIDIQUE RAPACES SIC SUNT DAMPNATI CUNCTI SIMUL ET SCELERATI.

5 O PECCATORES TRANSMUTETIS NISI MORES: IUDICUM DURUM UOBIS SCITOTE FUTURUM

SOL: LANCEA: CLAVI LUNA:
HOC SIGNUM CRUCIS ERIT IN CELOCUM

SANCTORUM CETUS STAT XPISTO IVDICE LETVS   HOMINES PERVERSI SIC SVNT IN TARTARA MERSI

SIC DATUR ELECTIS
AD CELI GAUDIA VECTIS GLORIA PAX REQUIES. PERPETVVSQVE DIES + PENIS INIVSTI CRVCIATVR IN IGNIBVS VSTI DEMONAS ATQVE TREMVNT : PERPETVOSQVE GEMVNT :

CASTI PACIFICI MITES PIETATIS AMICI SIC STANT GAUDENTES. SECURI NIL ME TUENTES + FURES MENDACES FALSI CUPIDIQUE RAPACES SIC SUNT DAMPNATI CUNCTI SIMUL ET SCELERATI.

O PECCATORES TRANSMUTETIS NISI MORES : JUDICUM DURUM VOBIS SCITOTE FUTURUM :

1 This sign of the cross shall be in heaven when (Matthew 24:30)

2a The assembly of the saints stands joyfully before Christ the Judge

2b [while] wicked men are thus plunged into Hell.

3a Thus to the elect transported in heaven are given joy, glory, rest and perpetual days.

3b The unjust, burned in fires, are tormented by punishments, they shudder at the demons and groan endlessly.

4a The chaste, the peace-loving, the gentle, the lovers of piety stand rejoicing and secure, without fear.

4b Thieves, liars, hypocrites, and the rapaciously avaricious are thus simultaneously condemned and defiled.

5 Sinners, unless you do not change your ways, know that a harsh judgment will be upon you in the future!

Translation (lines 2-5): Kendall 1989, pp. 165–69

The inscription *Hoc Signum Crucis erit in coelo cum* (This Sign of the Cross will be in Heaven When) is written on the horizontal cross-bar. While it derives from Matthew 24:30, it is also a quote from the first line of a famous responsory (an elaborate chant sung after the readings) for the Feasts of the Invention (i.e., finding) and the Exaltation of the Cross, celebrated on May 3 and September 14 respectively (Bouché 2006). The inscription thus activates *AudioVision*; it jolts the memory to recall the signature song of the Feast of the Cross. But there is an added significance to commemorating September 14 at Conques. This date falls twenty days before the feast of the patron saint on October 6, and thus it inaugurates the festal season of Sainte-Foy at Conques (Bouché 2006).

The inscription *Hoc Signum Crucis erit in coelo cum* (This Sign of the Cross will be in Heaven When) (1105–1115) as the incipit of a responsory for the Feast of the Cross

Horizontal bar of the cross, West Façade, Abbey Church of Sainte-Foy, Conques, France

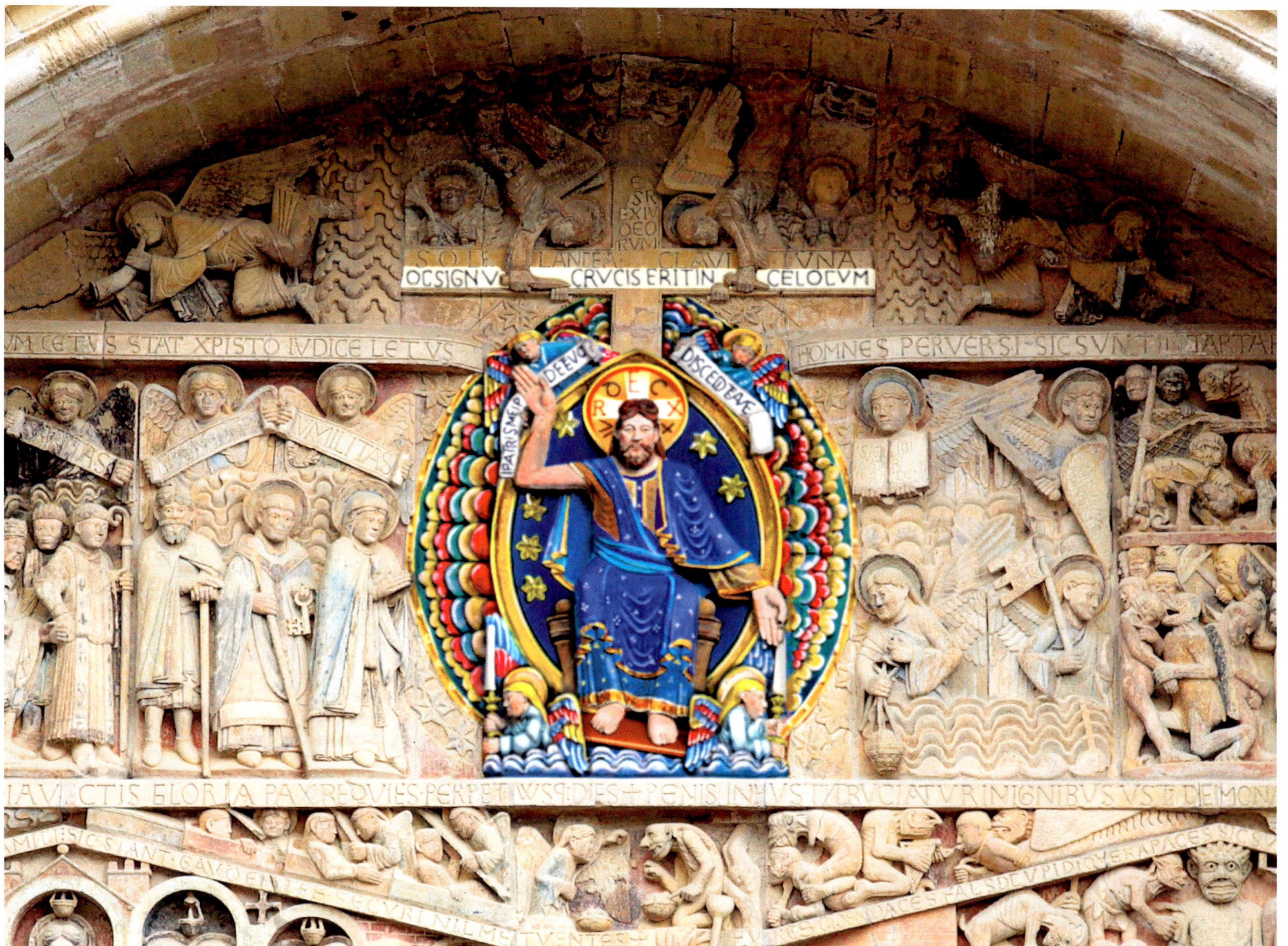

Photograph: Boris Missirkov; coloring: Jessica Chen Lee

The Responsory *Hoc signum crucis* whose opening
line appears on the façade

Opening Line: Hoc signum crucis erit in coelo, cum Dominus ad iudicandum venerit.

Refrain: *Tunc manifesta erunt abscondita cordis nostri, Alleluia*

Verse: Cum sederit filius hominis in sede maiestatis suae et coeperit iudicare saeculum per ignem.

Refrain: *Tunc manifesta erunt abscondita cordis nostri, Alleluia*

Doxology: Gloria Patri, et Filio, et Spiritui Sancto

Refrain: *Tunc manifesta erunt abscondita cordis nostri, Alleluia*

Opening Line: This sign of the Cross shall be in Heaven when the Lord comes in Judgment.

Refrain: *Then shall be revealed the things hidden in our hearts. Alleluia.*

Verse: When the Son of Man shall sit on his glorious throne and shall begin to judge the world with fire.

Refrain: *Then shall be revealed the things hidden in our hearts. Alleluia.*

Doxology: Glory be to the Father, the Son, and the Holy Spirit.

Refrain: *Then shall be revealed the things hidden in our hearts. Alleluia.*

Translation: Bissera V. Pentcheva

The music of this responsory is special in how the refrain mirrors the second half of the opening line. Usually, refrains have their own separate melody. See, for instance, *Emissiones tue* (Your aromas) of the vespers responsory for Sainte-Foy. The sonic mirroring in the *Hoc signum* responsory insists on the linkage of two actions: that when God shall sit on the throne to judge, then all the secrets in our heart will be revealed. The aural linkage sharpens the semantics of the sentence, emphasizing how the power of the Judge will permeate the universe and no one will escape His piercing gaze. The music thus enhances the effect of the metal-infilled eyes of the Christ sculpted on the tympanum. Originally, his gaze would have been set on fire by the rays of the setting sun. Today, the lead infill is lost, and the eye sockets are empty, having lost the power of the piercing gaze of the Judge (Pentcheva 2022a).

Responsory *Hoc signum Crucis* for the Feast of the Cross on September 14 (12th century)

From the liturgical manuscript of
Saint-Maur-des-Fossés, Northern France
Paris, BnF, MS Lat. 12044, fol. 113v.

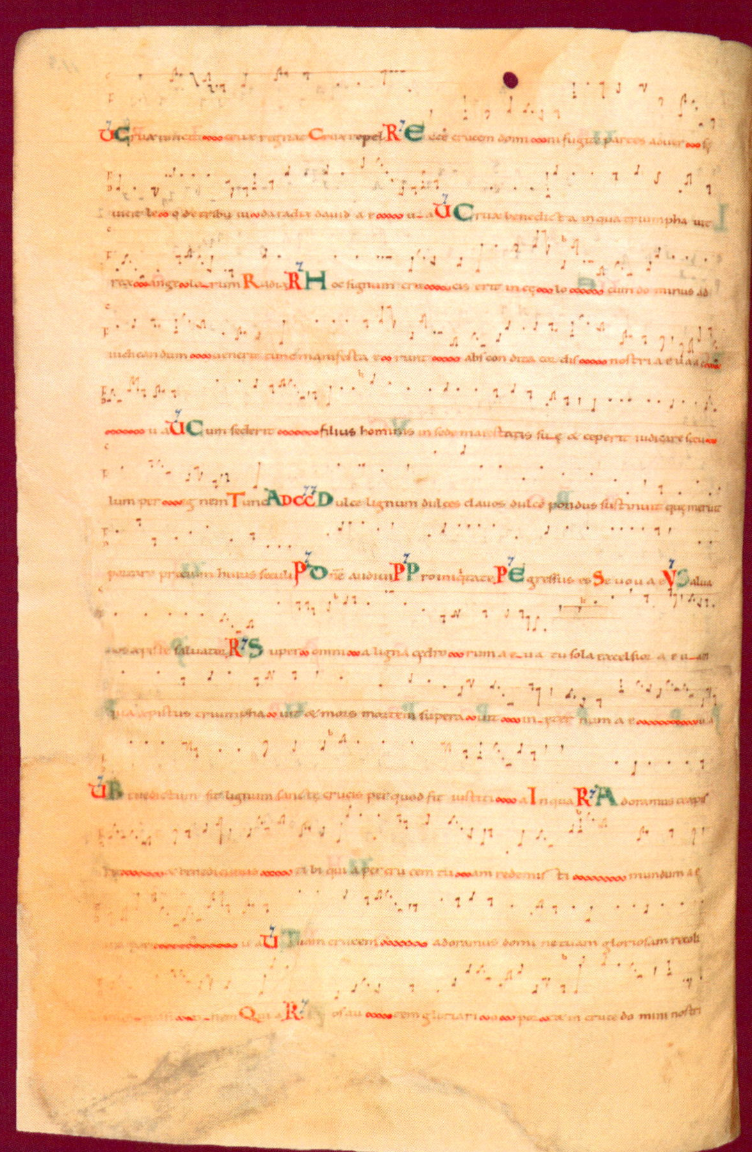

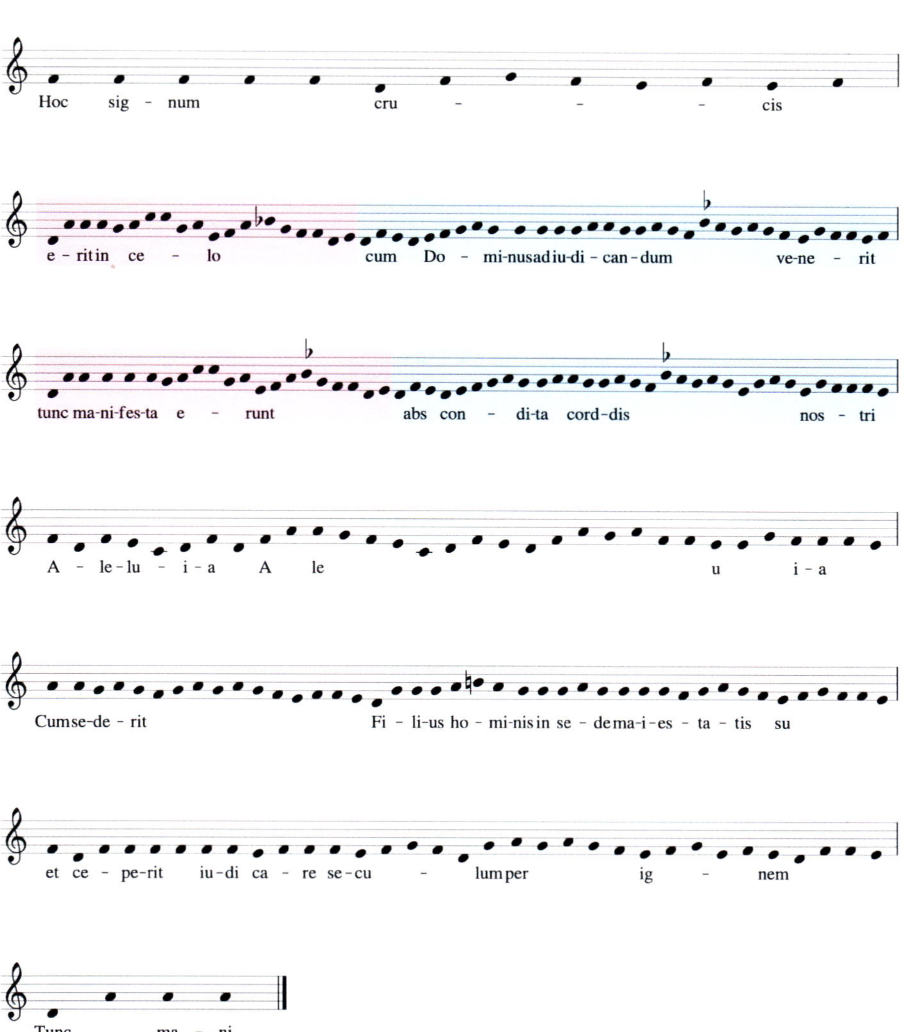

The Melody of the Responsory
Hoc Signum Crucis

(Cantus n.d., chant ID no. 006845)

Transcription: *Bissera V. Pentcheva; coloring: Jessica Chen Lee*

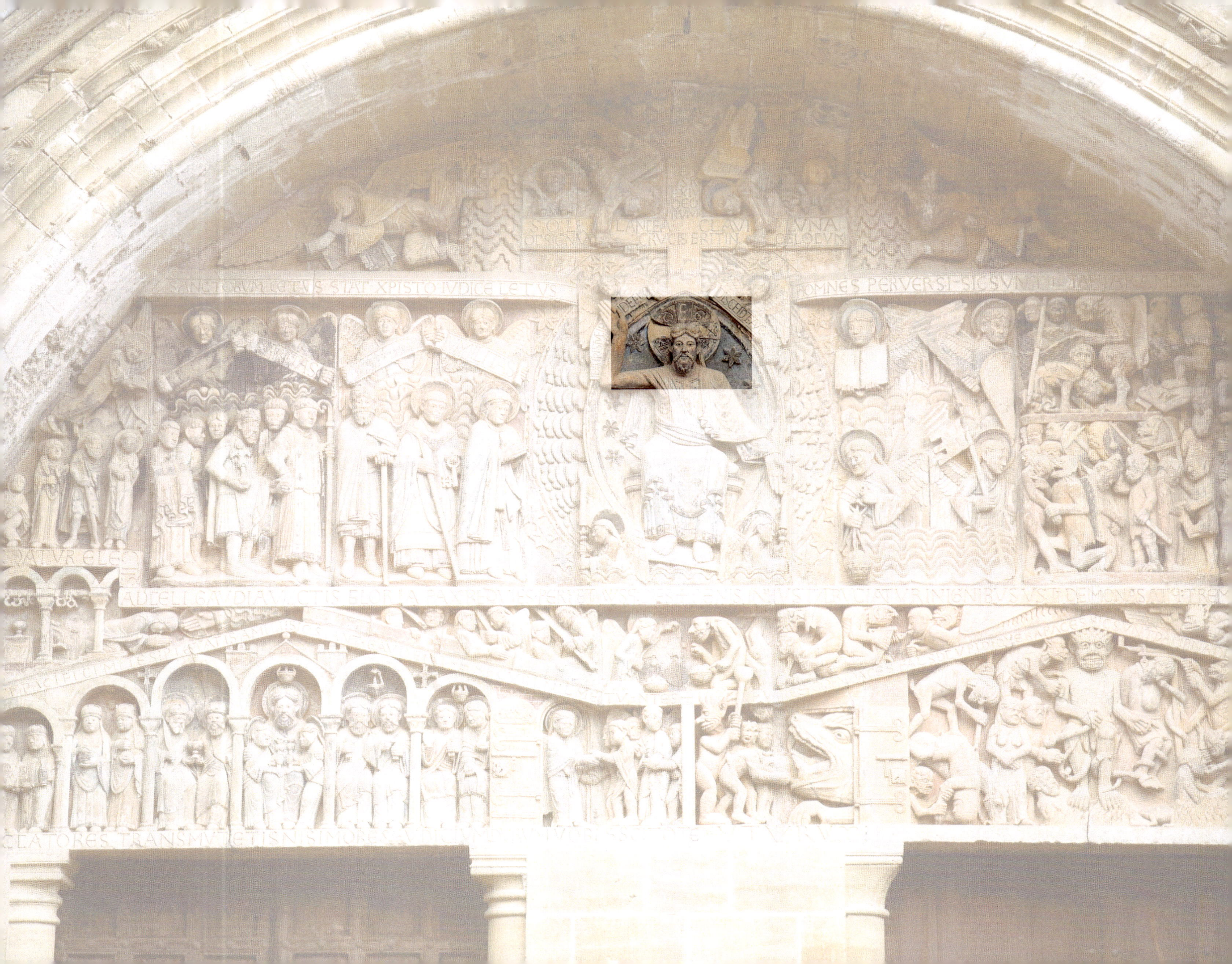
SOL LANCEA CLAVI LVNA
DESIGNA CRVCIS ERIT IN GELORVM
SANCTORVM CETVS STAT XPISTO IVDICE LETVS
OMNES PERVERSI SIC SVNT
ATVR ELE
ADDELTI GAVDIA CTIS ELORIA PAX REQVIES ATVR IN IGNIBVS VST DEM
CEATORES TRANSMVTETIS NISI MORES

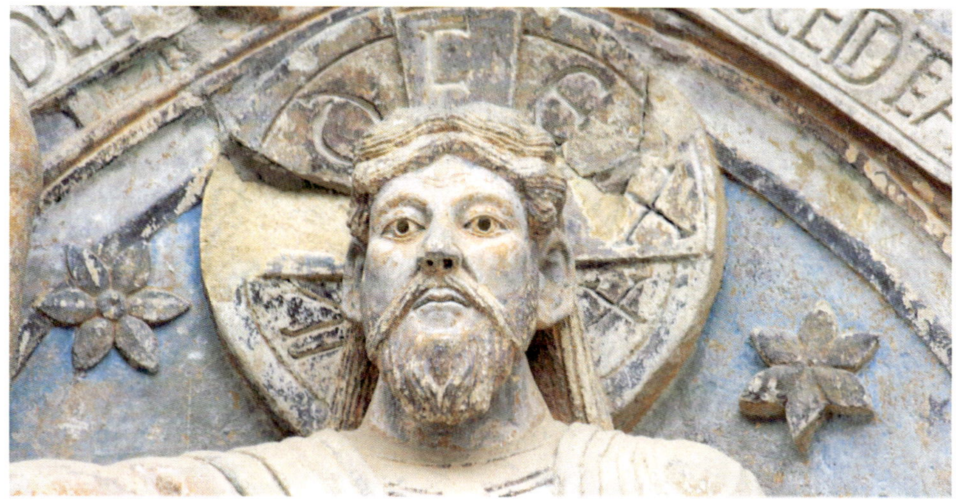

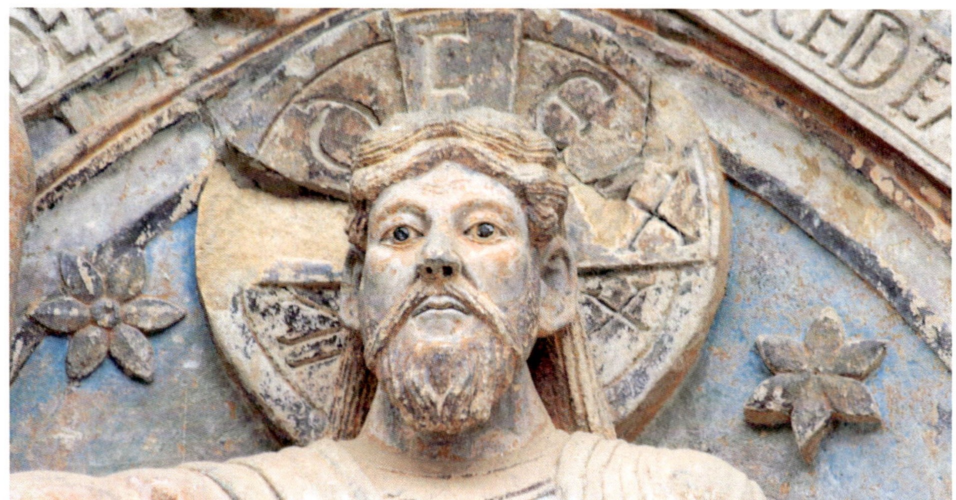

Photograph: Boris Missirkov; digital reconstruction of lead-infill in the eyes of Christ: Jessica Chen Lee

Above: Detail from the Tympanum of the west façade

Below: Digital reconstruction of lead-infill in the eyes of Christ

As illustrated in this nineteenth-century litho-graph, a high-relief sculpture of Sainte-Foy was once located on the trumeau (the verti-cal space between the two doors) on the west façade of the church. This image clearly articulates the identity of the patron saint. The statue was removed in the nineteenth-century reconstruction, apparently because it postdated the Romanesque period. But, as a result, there are currently no clear signs on the façade to indicate that the church is dedicated to Sainte-Foy.

West Façade, Abbey of Sainte-Foy,
Conques (1105-1115)

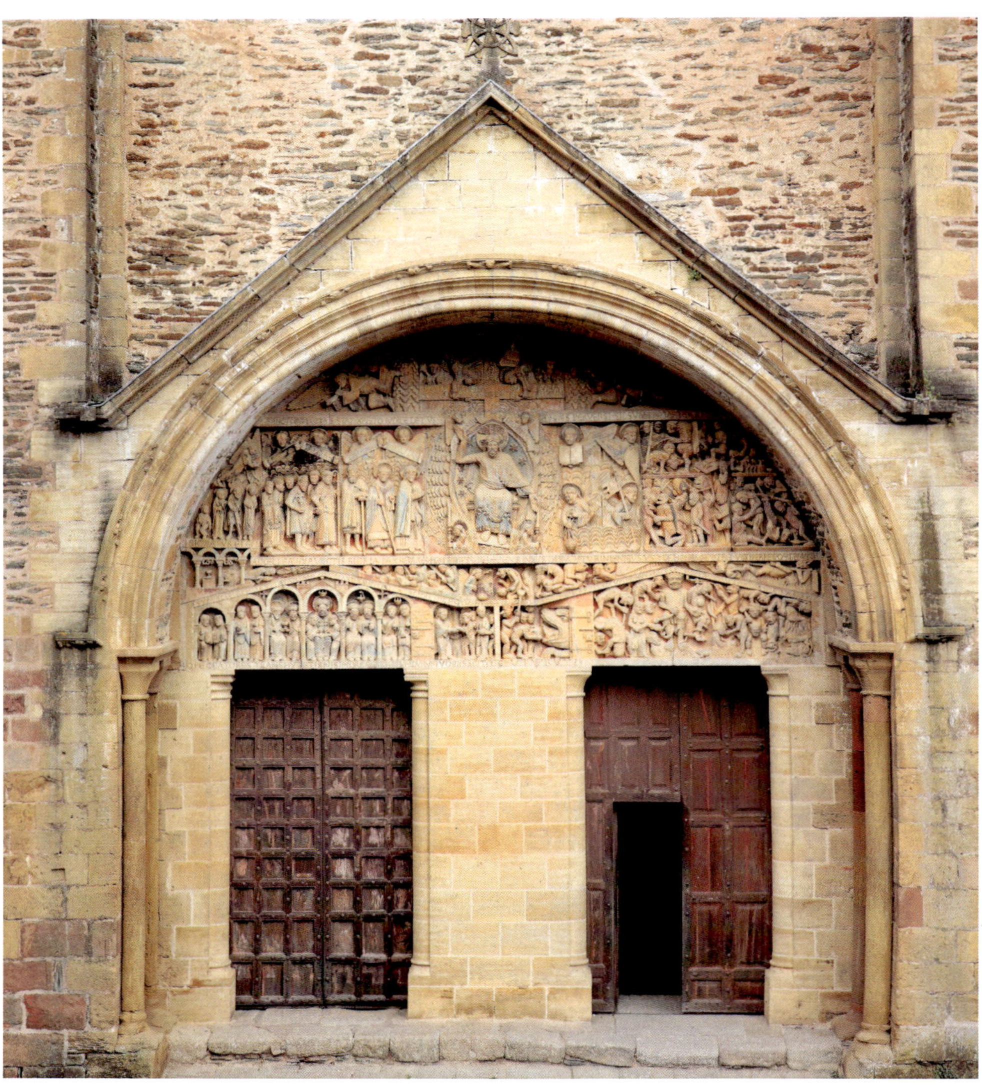

Photograph: Manuel Cohen

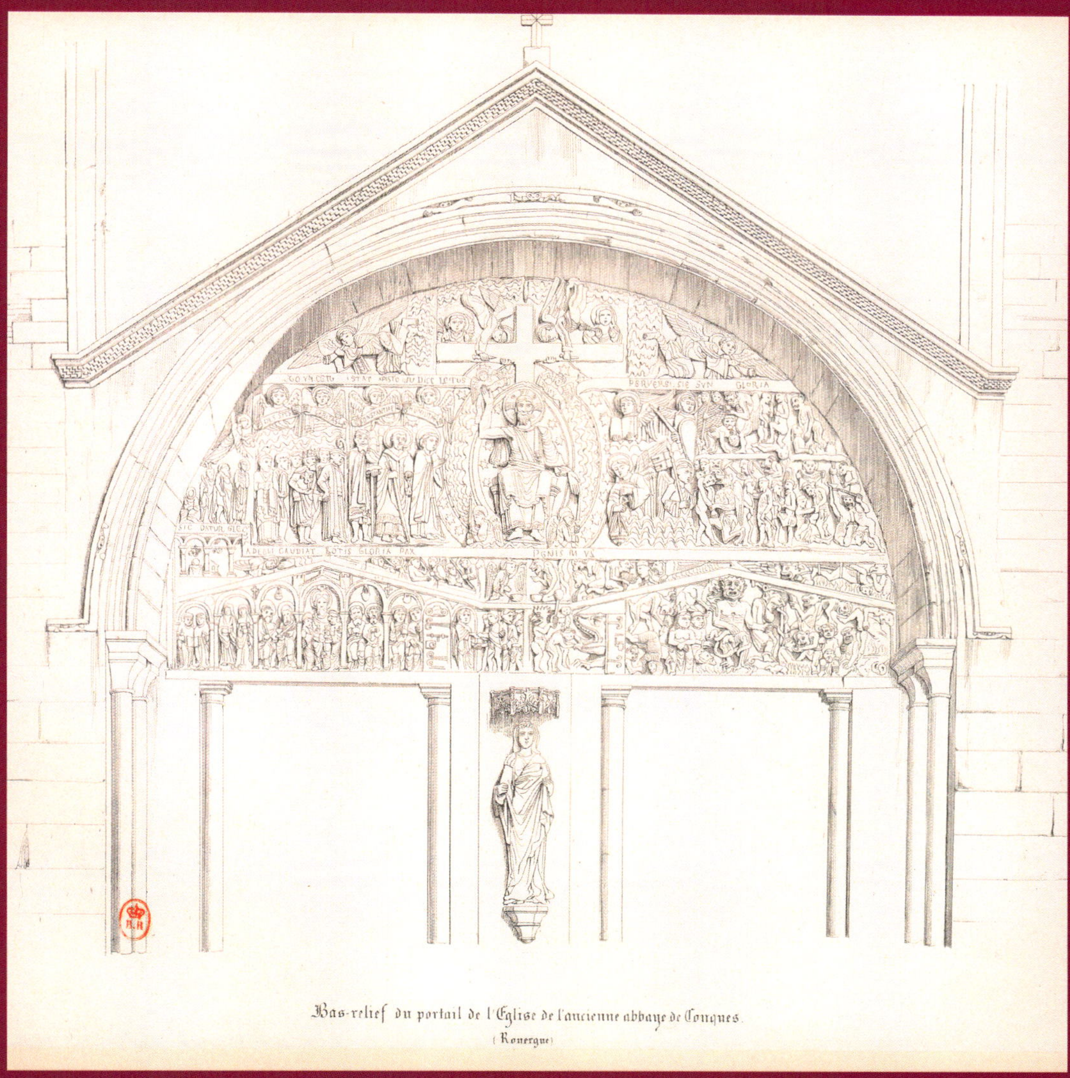

Illustration of a Gothic Relief on
the Trumeau, Abbey Church of
Sainte-Foy, Conques, France

Lithograph after Charles Nodier,
Isidore-Justin-Séverin Taylor, and Alphonse
de Cailleux, *Voyages pittoresques et
romantiques dans l'ancienne France*, 18 vols.
(Paris: P. Didot, 1833–1837), *Languedoc*, 2
vols. (Paris: P. Didot, 1835). Vol. 1, part 2,
p. 268

lthough no sculpture currently decorates the exterior wall between the two doors (known as the *trumeau*) on the west façade of the Abbey Church of Sainte-Foy, this space traditionally features the patron saint in examples from other buildings. Did the façade originally have a relief of the patron saint in the twelfth-century? A different panel, with a scene of the Annunciation, exists on the north wall of the transept in the church's interior. Based on its dimensions, it would fit perfectly the trumeau of the west façade. Two scholars in the early twentieth century suggested this possibility (Rascol 1942–45; Bousquet 1947). Restoring this panel back to the exterior would be logical, because it introduces the beginning of the plan of Salvation, which is then fulfilled in the image of the Last Judgment in the tympanum above. Further evidence that the Annunciation carving was likely designed for the exterior comes from the excerpt of a chant inscribed on the unfurled scroll carried by the Archangel Gabriel (Pentcheva 2022b).

High-relief sculpture, *The Annunciation*
(1105–1115)

North wall, transept, Abbey Church of Sainte-Foy, Conques, France

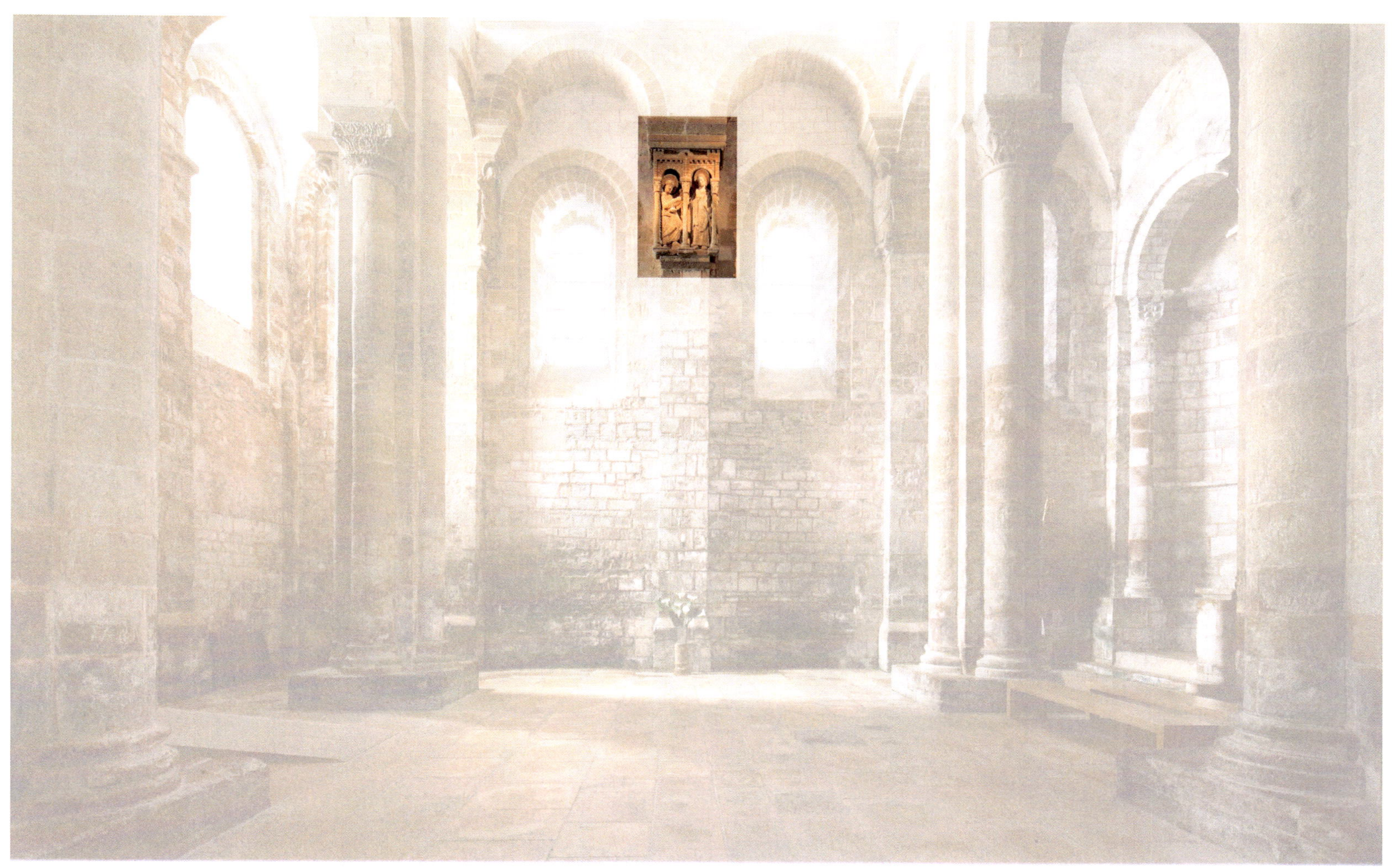

Photograph: Manuel Cohen

The words of this inscription are quoted from the poetry of a famous sequence *Salve porta perpetua lucis* (Hail gate of perpetual light) performed on the Marian feasts of the Annunciation, Advent, Purification (Presentation in the Temple), Dormition, and Assumption (Cantus n.d., chant ID no. ah53108, Fassler 2010, p. 394). Sequence (also referred to in medieval sources as *prosa* or *prosula*) is a genre of chants that expand the narrative of Scripture with new poetry and use the model melodies of untexted melismatic alleluias (Kelly 1974, Kelly 1977, Kelly 2011; Fassler 1993, Fassler 2019). *Candida tu quia* and *Almiphona iam gaudia* are two other examples of sequences featured in this exhibition.

Inscription, *"[missus] e[st] Gabriel angelus a D[eo]"* (The angel Gabriel has been sent by God) (Luke 1:26) written on the scroll

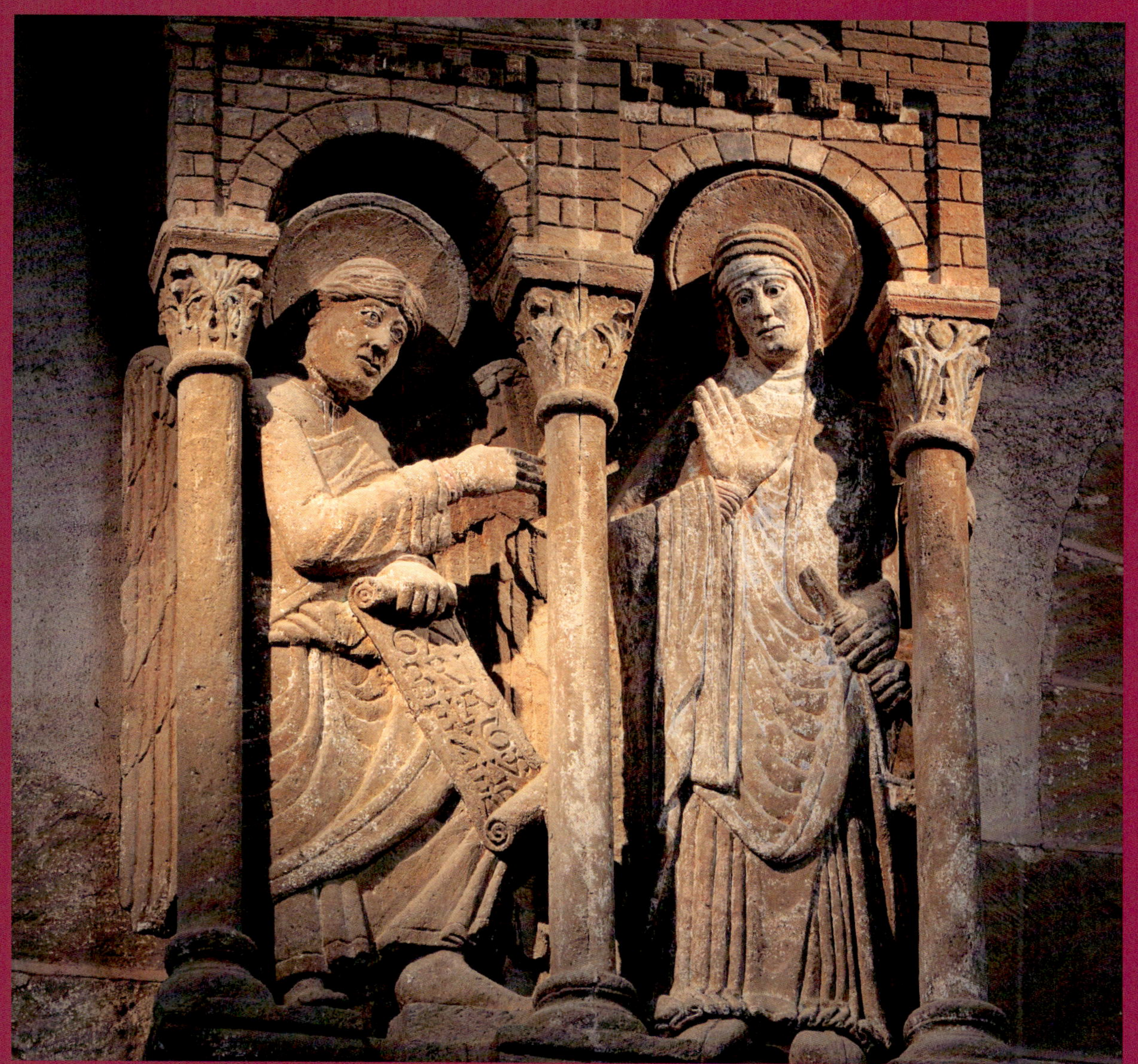

Photograph: Manuel Cohen

Text of the Sequence (*Prosa*) *Salve Porta*

1 Salve porta perpetua lucis fulgida,

2a mari stella inclita domina, virgo materque Dei Maria

2b pre-electa ipsius gracia ante secularia tempora

3a **cui missus Gabriel archangelus** miram retulit **a Deo** femina mundo nunquam audita.

3b Aveto tu Maria quae totius plena muneris effulgens gracia est nam te cum Dominus

4a qua propter es tu sola inter cunctas mulieres mater benedicta,

4b ne paveas divina quia letaberis te fore gravida.

5a Magnus hic erit Ihesus filius summi ac throni davidis gloria et regi meta ipsius non erit aliqua

5b mox ad haec dicta parans credula corda concipis dominum sabaot sic verbum caro factum est ex te virgo sacrata.

6 Te ergo petimus ut pro nobis Deum rogites/salve ut nos per omnia saeclam, amen.

1 Greetings, gleaming eternal gate of light,

2a Star of the sea, renowned mistress, virgin and mother to God, Mary

2b You were pre-selected before the times for His [God's] grace.

3a **The Archangel Gabriel, sent by God**, surprised this chaste woman with what she now heard:

3b 'Hail, you Mary, who are filled with all gifts, and who shines with grace, for God is now with you.

4a You and only you among all women are now a blessed mother,

4b Do not be afraid, for you will rejoice in being divinely pregnant,

5a For your son will be the great Christ of the Davidic throne, there would be no one of such glory and authority after Him.

5b As the [Virgin] was presently taking heart in what he was saying, he added further: 'you would conceive the Lord Sabaoth, so the logos will become incarnate in your body, O hallowed virgin.'

6 You, indeed, we beseech so that you would intercede with the Lord on our behalf, save us, so that we [can live] in eternity, Amen!

Translation: Bissera V. Pentcheva

Salve Porta Sequence (elaborate chant sung to the melody of a text-less Alleluia) (987–996)

Paris, BnF, MS Lat. 1118, fol. 167rv Monastery of Sant Sadurní de Tavèrnoles, Catalonia

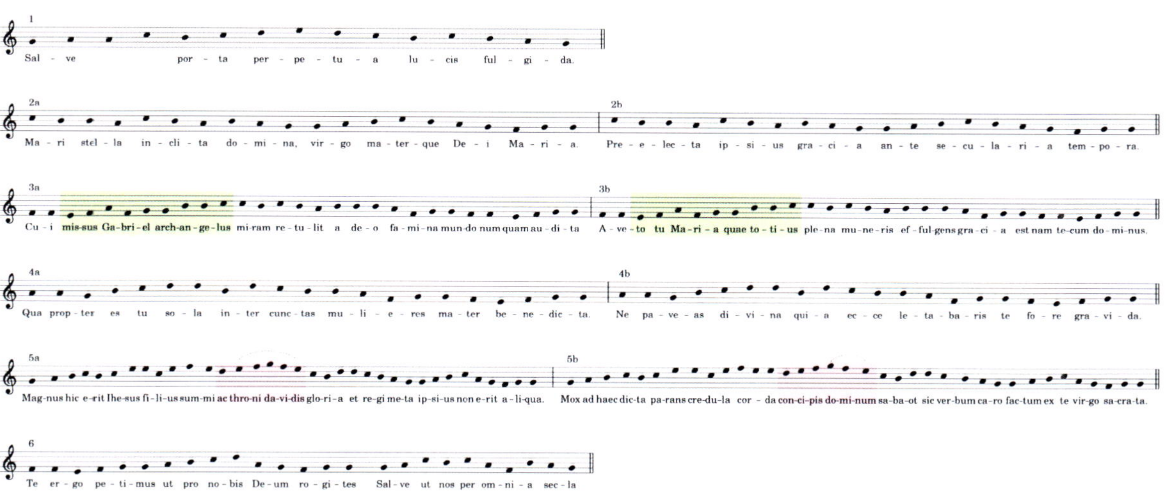

Transcription: Laura Steenberge; coloring: Jessica Chen Lee

High-relief, Sainte-Foy
standing behind the Virgin
(1105 – 1115)

North wall, transept, Abbey Church
of Sainte-Foy, Conques, France

Photograph: Manuel Cohen

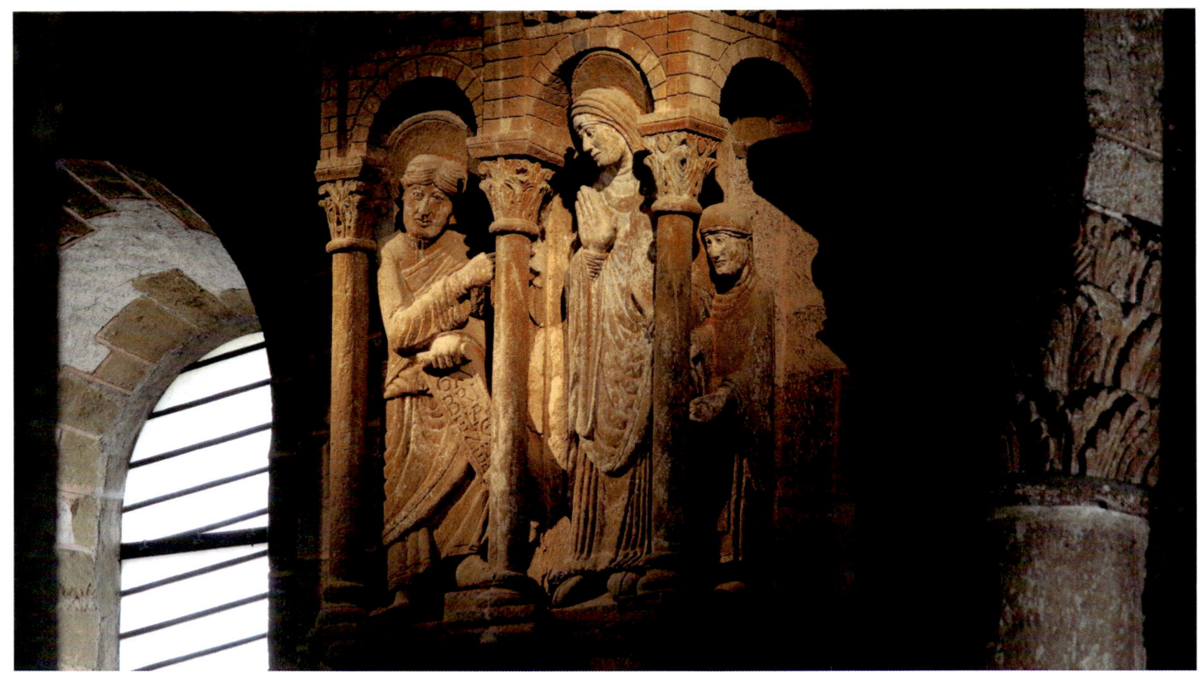

One might ask what is the benefit of linking the Annunciation with the Last Judgment on the west façade? The answer lies in recognizing the presence of Sainte-Foy. A female figure, huddled behind Mary's left in the Annunciation panel, presses a ball into the hand of the Virgin. In the past, this figure has been viewed as a servant. The object she places into Mary's hand suggests it is a precious gift: a ball of wool or of incense. A valuable present such as this reveals the identity of this figure as Sainte-Foy. By forcing the incense into the Virgin's hand, Sainte-Foy's stance suggests that she is asking the Queen of Heaven to look leniently on her faithful. The patron saint, hidden in Mary's shadow, works continuously and tirelessly to secure the salvation of her loyal servants. If the Annunciation panel were to be restored back onto the trumeau, it would become more evident that the patron Sainte-Foy is both close to her subjects at the gates and also high up in the heavenly realm, praying for the salvation of her servants at the end of time on the tympanum above (Pentcheva 2022b).

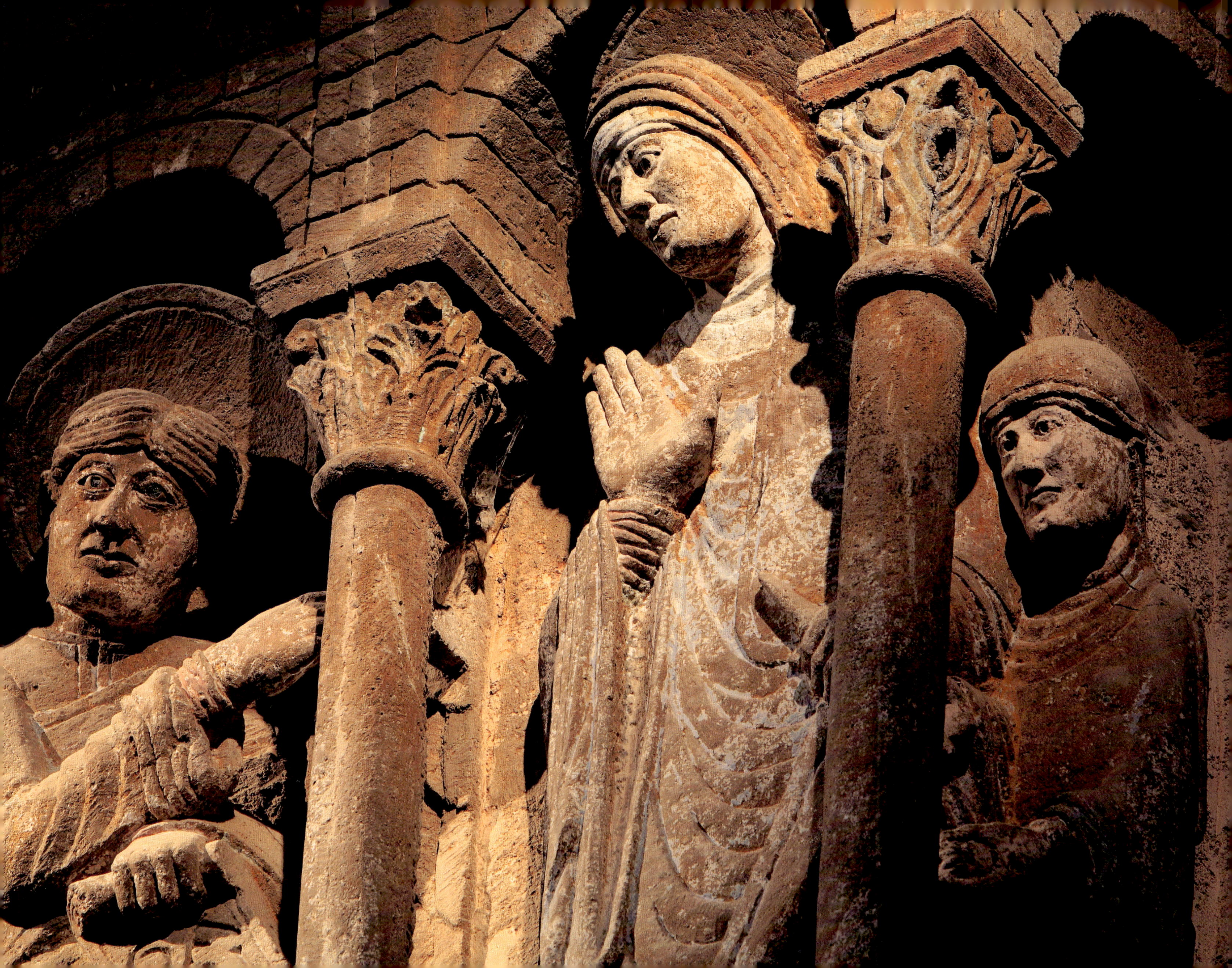

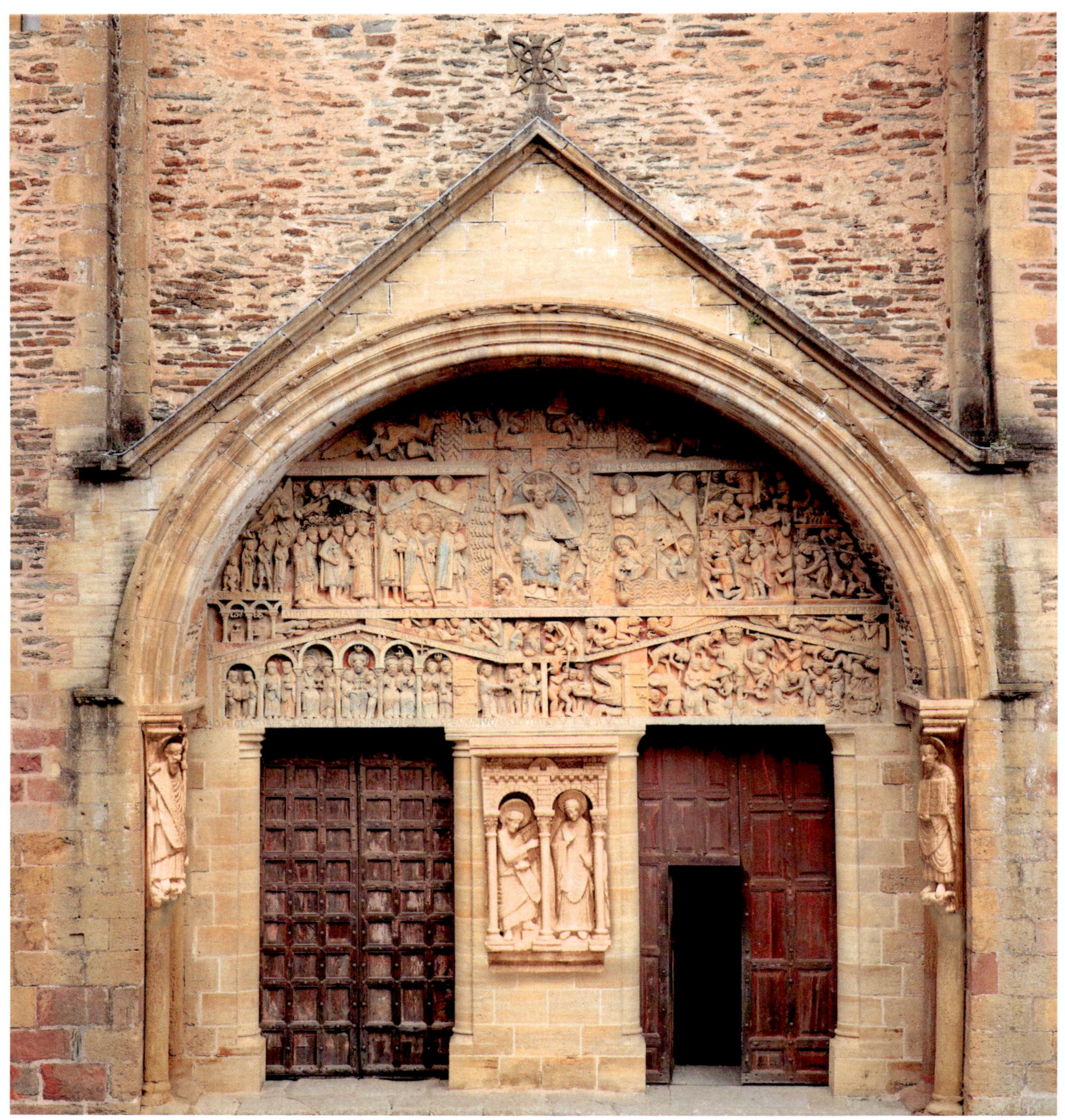

Reconstruction of the
West Façade, Abbey
Church of Sainte-Foy,
Conques, France
(1105 – 1115)

Photograph: Manuel Cohen; reconstruction: Bissera V. Pentcheva

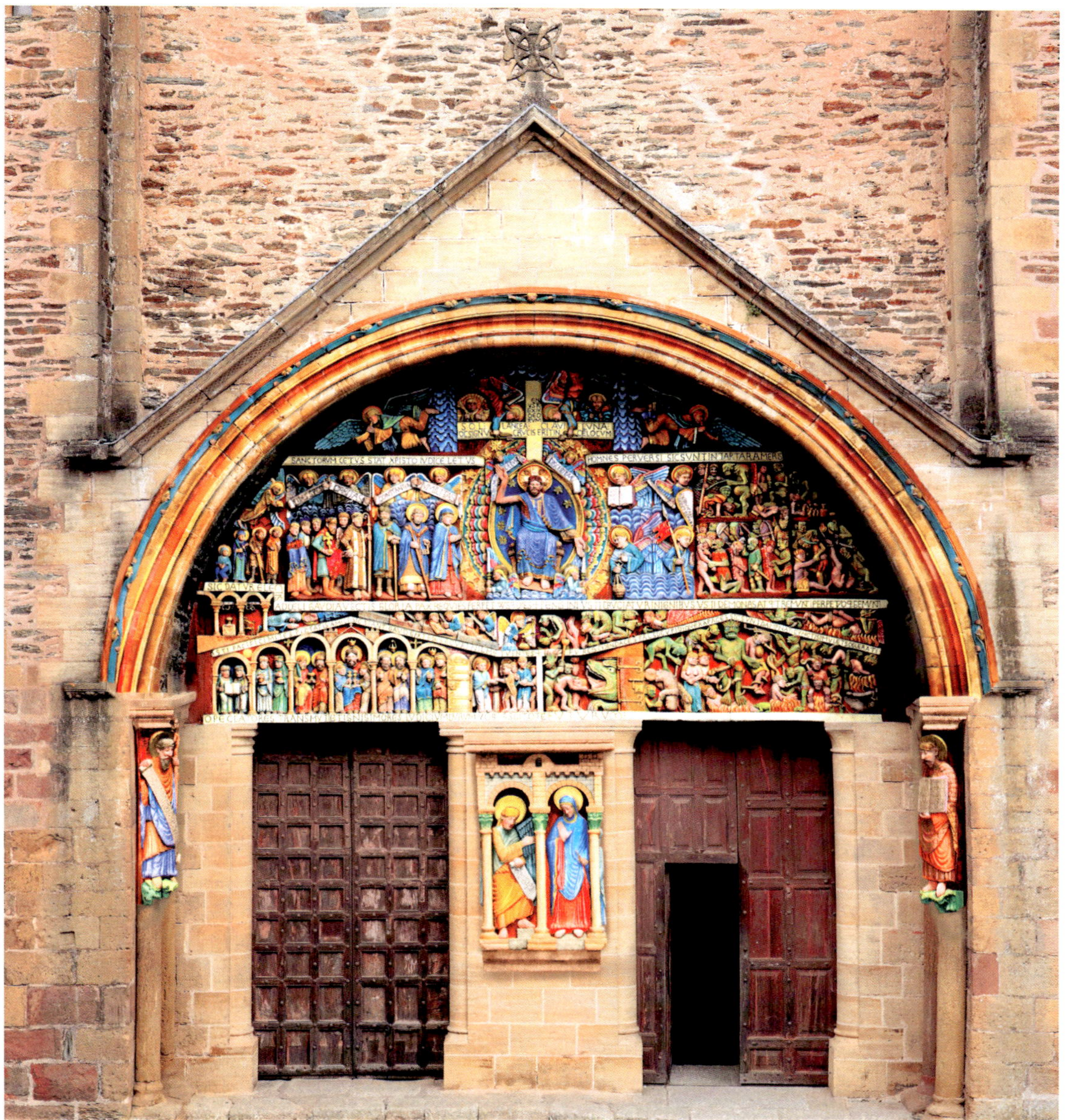

Coloring: Jessica Chen Lee

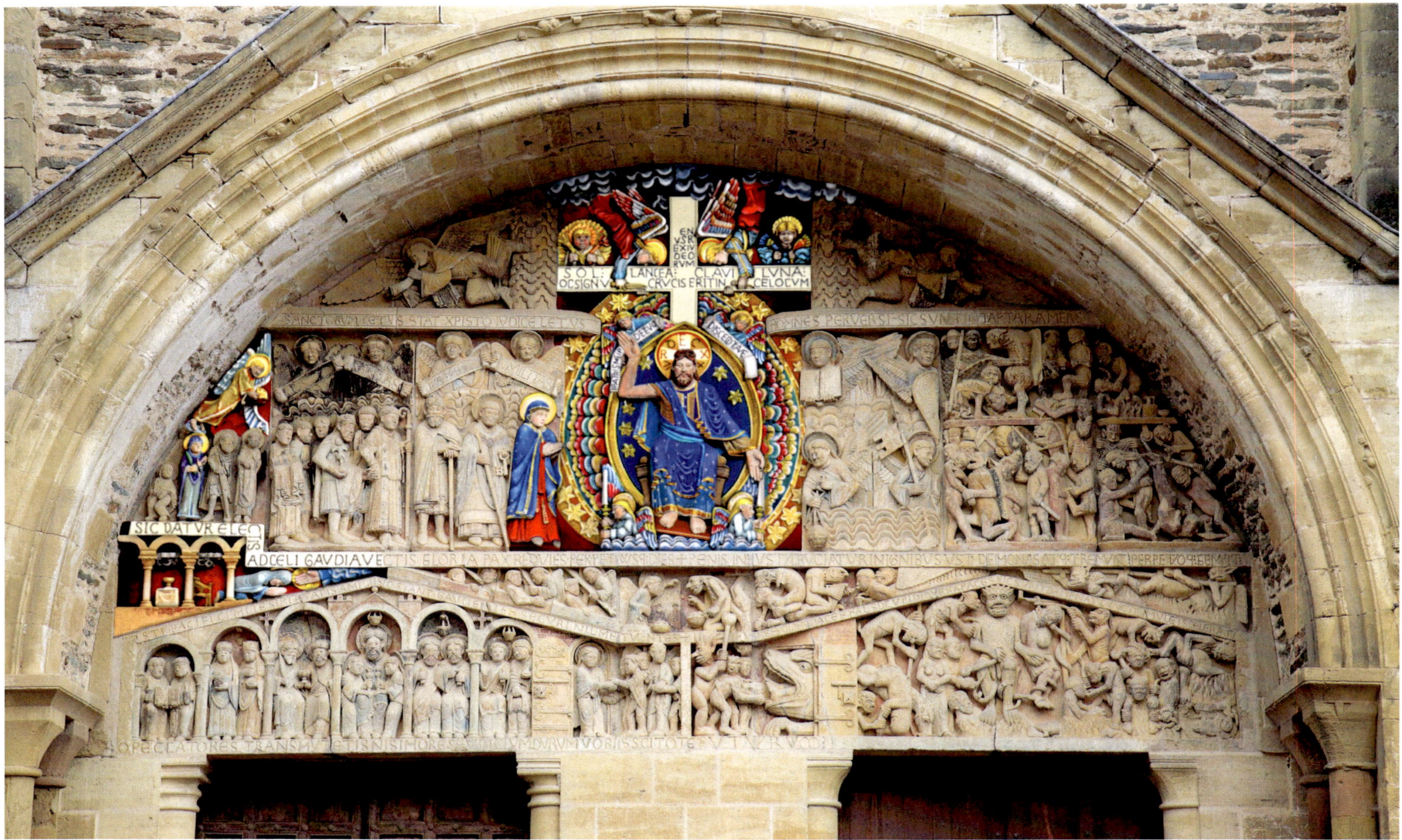

Photograph: Boris Missirkov; coloring: Jessica Chen Lee

Sculptures on the West Façade at Conques (1105 –1115)

The application of color traces the main characters: Sainte-Foy, the angel proffering
the crown, and the intercession of the Virgin in front of Christ the Judge

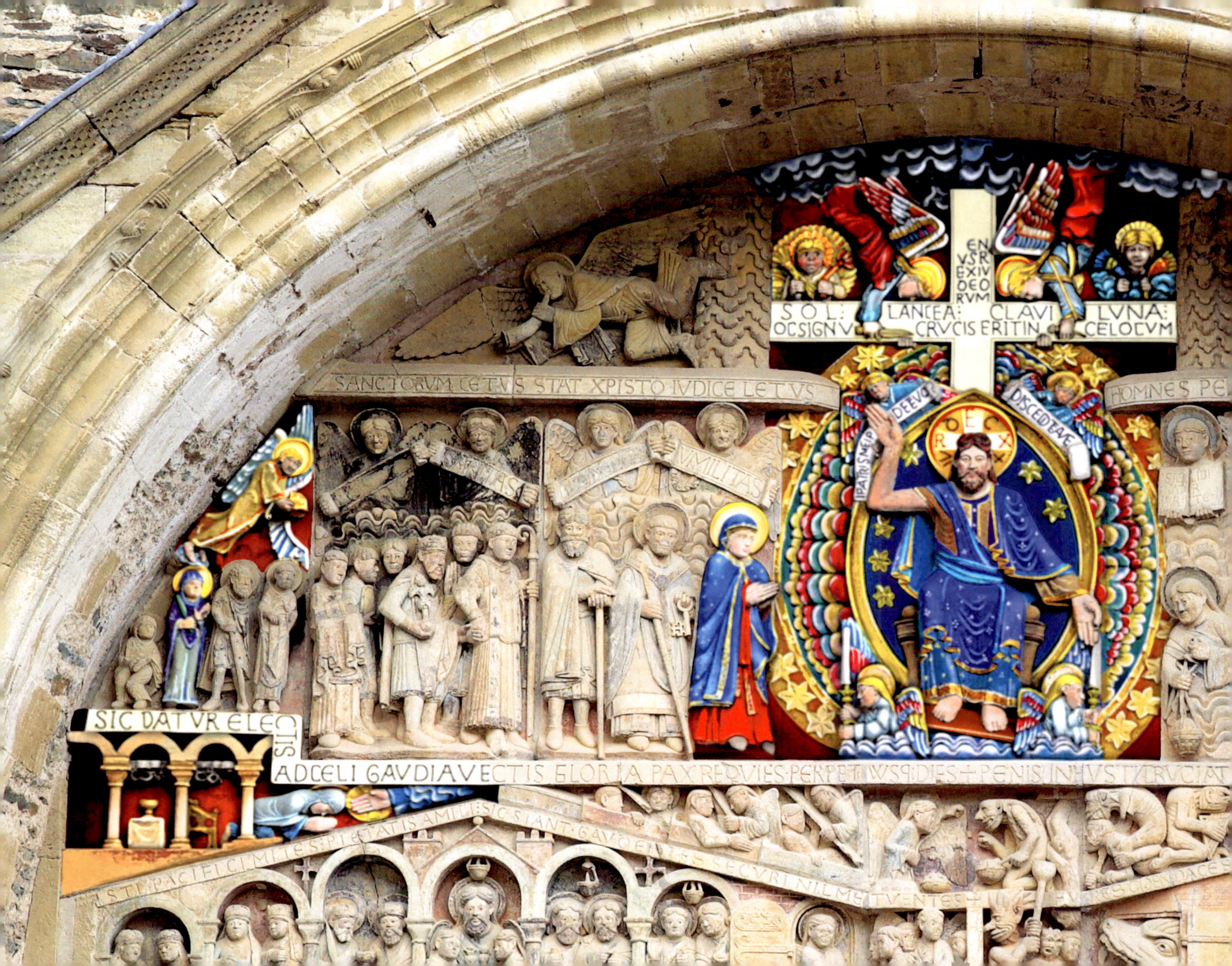

EN R VSR EXIV OEO RVM
SOL: LANCEA: CLAVI LVNA:
OCSIGNV CRVCIS ERITIN CELOCVM
SANCTORVM CETVS STAT XPISTO IVDICE LETVS
HOMNES PE
UMILITAS
SIC DATVR ELECTIS
ADCELI GAVDIA VECTIS GLORIA PAX REQVIES PERPET VSQ DIES PENIS INIVST CRVCIAT

PART FOUR

LOCUS (SACRED SPACE), ARCHITECTURE, *and* ACOUSTICS

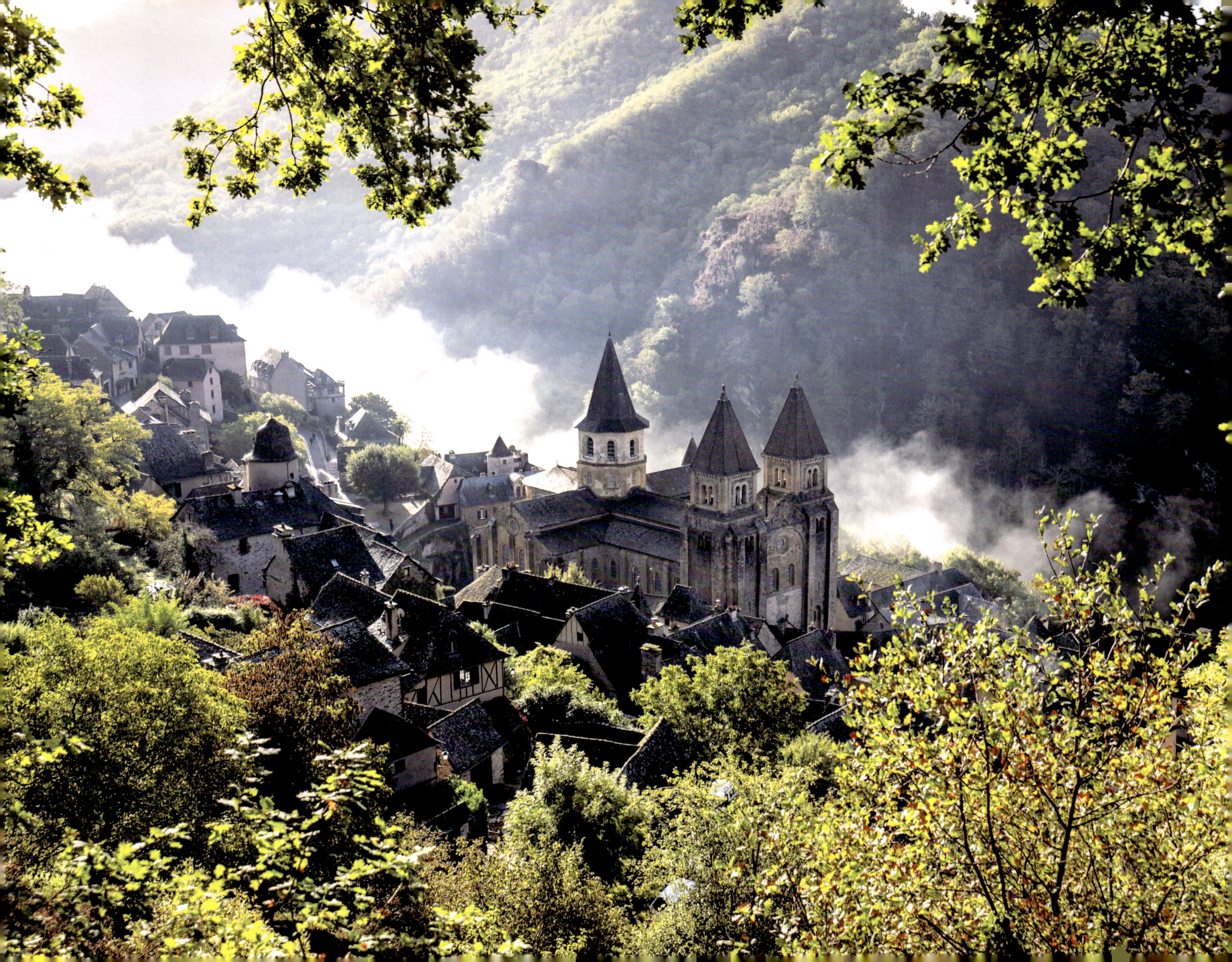

Nestling the Saint in the Landscape and the Church

Natural phenomena, fleeting and ephemeral, most eloquently convey the metaphysical presence at Conques, making the divine perceptible but resisting the tangible and anthropomorphic. The light fog, known as *brume* in French, appears frequently at the site in the early fall and coincides with the feast-day of Sainte-Foy, October 6. In the eleventh-century *Book of Miracles*, Sainte-Foy manifests herself in the clouds, moving through the upper air (*Liber Miraculorum*, bk. IV.1 and IV.8).

The Latin word *locus* designates a place and a vessel, where the divine can descend and pour out into the terrestrial. *Locus* thus marks the fleeting encounter of Spirit and matter. The landscape, the monastery, and the golden statue and its relics are all physical *loci*-vessels to which sacred energy adheres.

The modern name of the village "Conques" comes from the Latin *conca*, "shell." It is a toponymic originally identifying the area, and later on, the monastery. *Conca* captures the shape of the valley and the shell-like open space directly in front of the church. But there are other, less obvious shells. The monastery is a vessel/shell that holds Sainte-Foy. Fides, too, is a *conca-locus* for the encounter of the ultimate pearl: Christ.

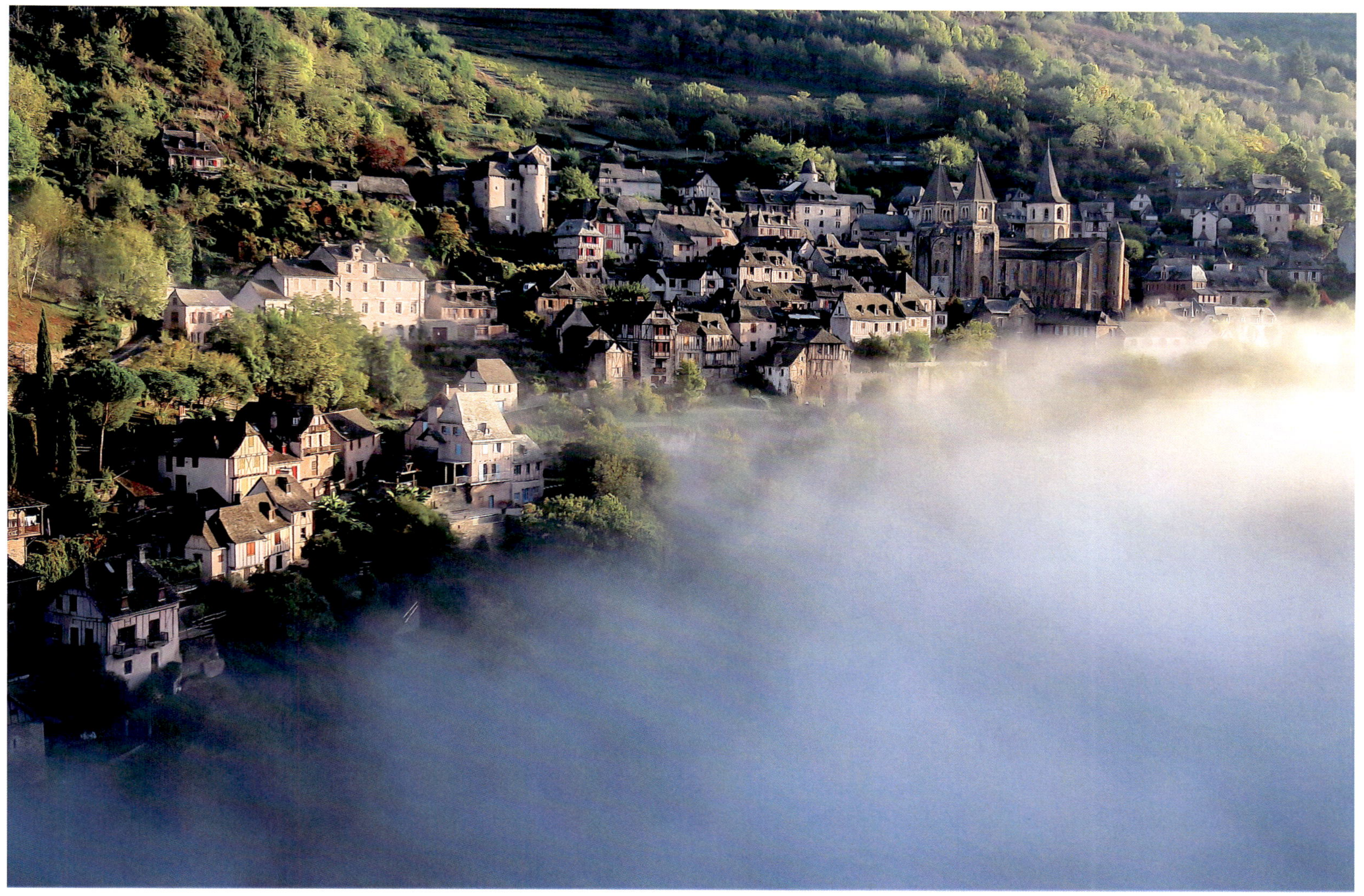

Photographs (above and page 127): Emeline and Nicolas Delsaut, Studio End, Naucelle, France, for Stanford's "Enchanted Images" Project

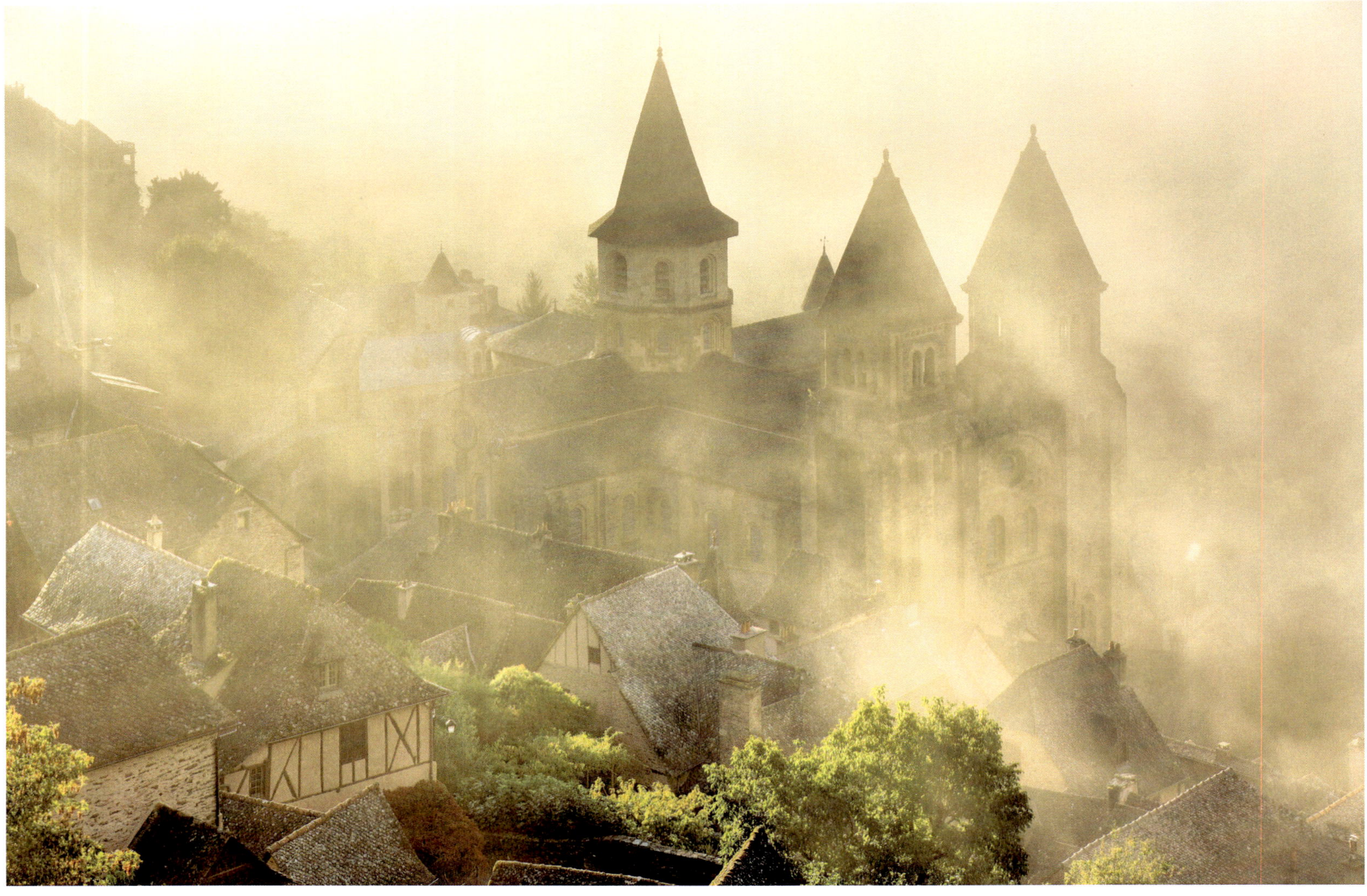

The Church of Sainte-Foy, Conques, in light fog (*brume*)

The Opalescence of Air and Pearl

The *brume* at Conques is another manifestation of the pearl: an opalescent vapor in the air produced by the conjoining of water (the river Ouche) and the sky. It creates a lustrous film veiling the church, the square, the village, and the valley. *Brume* as the atmospheric phenomenon of opalescent air transforms the appearance of Conques into a pearl.

The *margarita* is *candida* — shiny and radiant — as it channels *Pneuma* (Spirit) and as it brings together air and water. The shininess of the pearl makes it the perfect ornament for the crown, the very object of inspiriting that marks the transformation of the saint into Christ and the binding of earth with heaven. The chants for the Office of Sainte-Foy often describe the *chorona* as decorated with celestial pearls (*chorona celestibus margaritis ornata*). Similarly, the actual diadem of the golden statue of Sainte-Foy frames each element with pearls or with the gold filigree that imitates strings of pearls. The visual repetition amplifies the *margarita*-effect, saturating the crown with light (Pentcheva 2023b).

The Rise and Fall of Conques, 11th–12th Centuries

While in modern times Conques is linked to the pilgrimage to Santiago de Compostela in Spain, the monastery at Conques did not arise from international pilgrimage (Williams 2008). Pilgrimage to Santiago only became a prominent phenomenon after Conques lost its influence and wealth in the second half of the twelfth century (Desjardins 1879; Bousquet 1992). The monastery is a ninth-century Carolingian foundation that consolidated its land possessions in the late tenth and eleventh centuries. By investing further in its local artistic production — texts about the passion and miracles of Sainte-Foy, poetry and music for the liturgy, art, and architecture — Conques successfully magnified the aura of its patron saint (*Liber miraculorum*; Fau 1956; Bernoulli 1956; Bonne 1984; Bousquet 1997; Wirth 2004; Williams 2008; Vergnolle et al 2011; Huang 2014; de Mondredon 2015; Castiñeiras 2018; Fricke 2015). This artistic production catapulted Conques to the sphere of the *fideles* (the faithful/ loyal) — a network of powerful politicians including the pope, his legates, kings, bishops, and abbots who were active in the eleventh and twelfth centuries and who were of crucial importance for directing major international campaigns like the Reconquista, which identifies the gradual conquest of Islamic Spain starting in the 1060s (1063–1064 a brief capture of Barbastro) and reaching its climax in the middle of the thirteenth century (1248 conquest of Seville) (Rennie 2007; Rennie 2008; Giunta 2017). Conques profited from these military operations in Spain; it acquired lands in the area around Pamplona and the pass at Roncevaux. Monks from Conques were handpicked for important positions such as Pedro de Roda who became the bishop of Pamplona (1083–1115) and Pons, bishop of Roda and Barbastro (1097–1104) (Garland 2006; Giunta 2017; Pentcheva 2023c). But Conques lost its status and place among the *fideles* when it embezzled money in 1114 and was not able to regain its prominence. As a result, it never had the funds to update its art and architecture (Bousquet 1992). It thus preserved the form of its Carolingian statue and its Romanesque architecture and reliefs. Its financial and political failure paradoxically secured the legacy of its medieval art that remained unadulterated by subsequent styles.

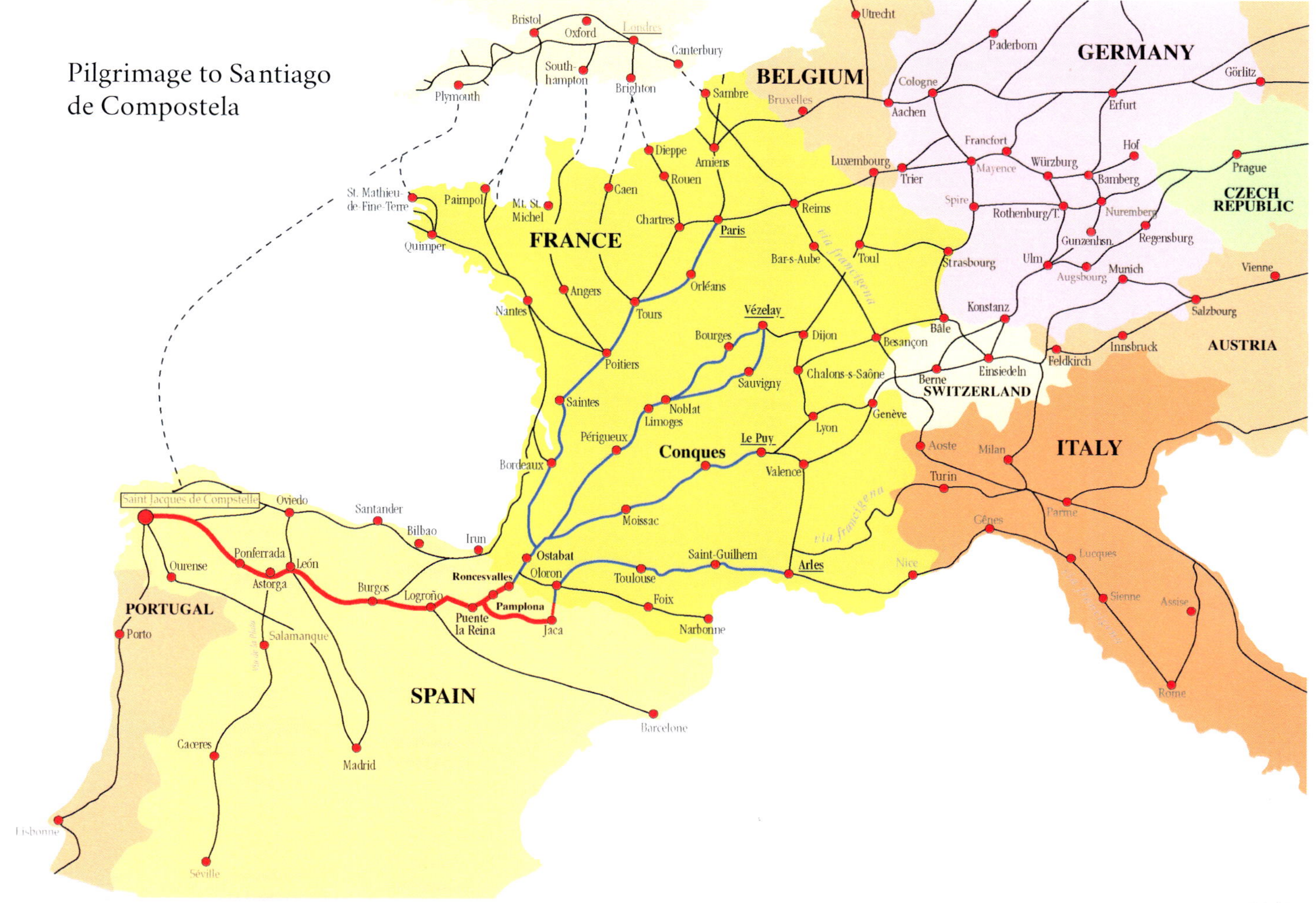

Map: Manfred Zentgraf, Volkach, Germany; image in the public domain

The lithographs in this volume illustrating scenes of Languedoc show the landscape and the exterior and the interior of the abbey church at Conques in the early nineteenth century. Because these images predate the visit of the writer, archaeologist, and preservationist Prosper Mérimée (1803–1870) in 1837, they offer unique insight into the state of preservation of this monument before the extensive restoration work that was carried out in the mid-nineteenth century (Merimée 1838; Vergnolle et al. 2011; Barral i Altet 2018). A dirt road leads to the church that towers over the valley. The ravages of time are more apparent on the east façade, where the building has sunken into the ground. Open sarcophagi of wealthy benefactors decorate the retaining wall. Thistles and bushes envelop the stones (on landscape at Conques, see Lešák 2022; Palladino 2022; Foletti 2022).

Pages 135–137

Lithographs of the Abbey Church of Sainte-Foy, Conques

Charles Nodier, Isidore-Justin-Séverin Taylor, and Alphonse de Cailleux, *Voyages pittoresques et romantiques dans l'ancienne France* (Scenic and Romantic Journeys in Ancient France) 18 vols. (Paris: P. Didot, 1833–1837); *Languedoc*, 2 vols. (Paris: P. Didot, 1835). Vol. 1, part 2, pp. 256–68.

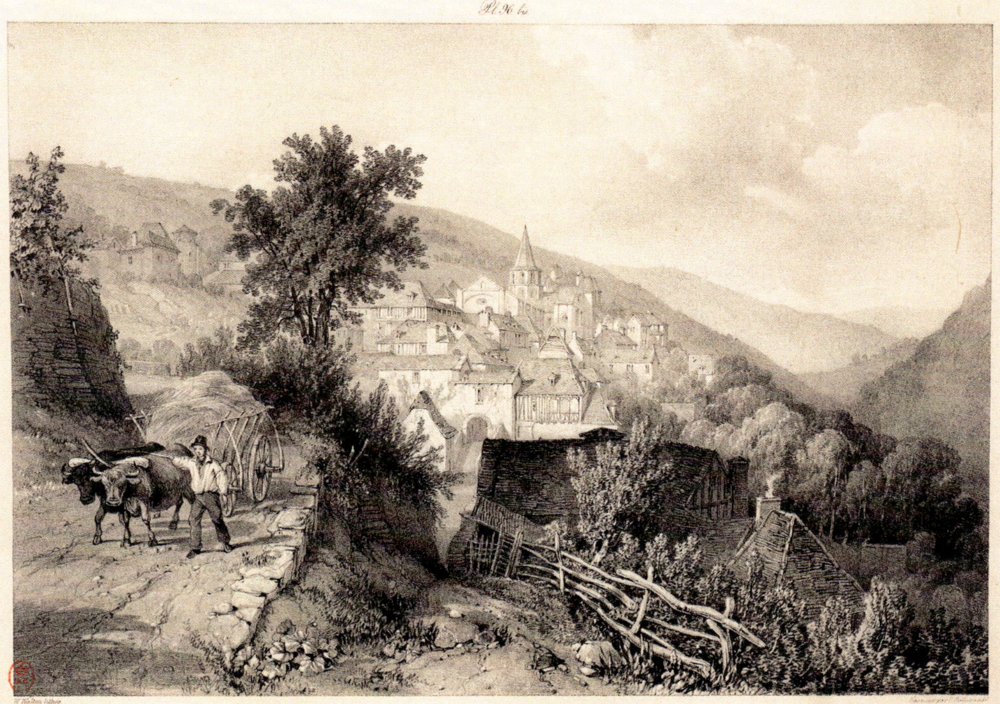

Vue générale du bourg de Conques.
(Aveyron.)

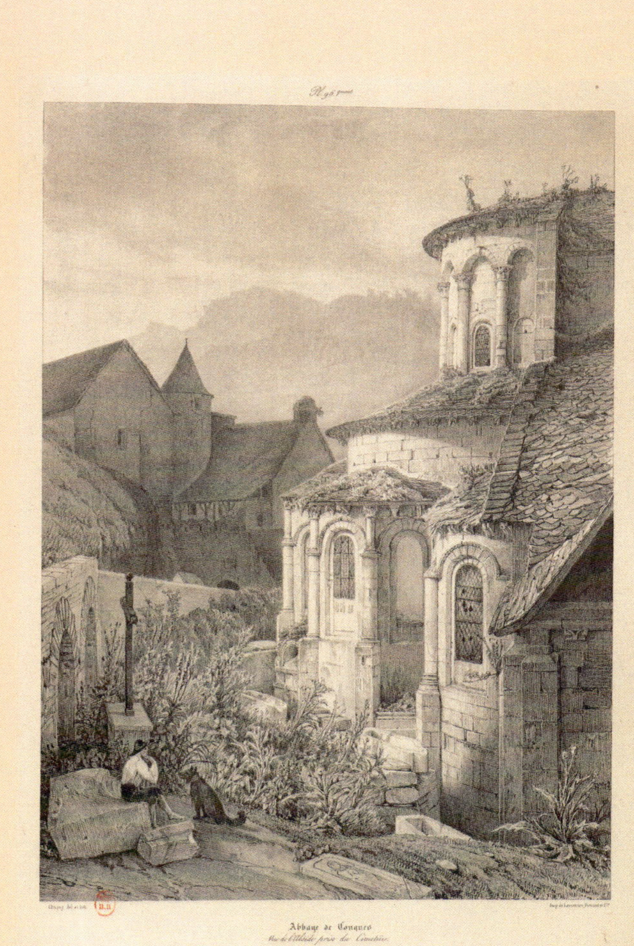

Imp. de Lemercier, Bernard et Cie

Abbaye de Conques
Vue de l'Abside prise du Cimetière.
(Rouergue)

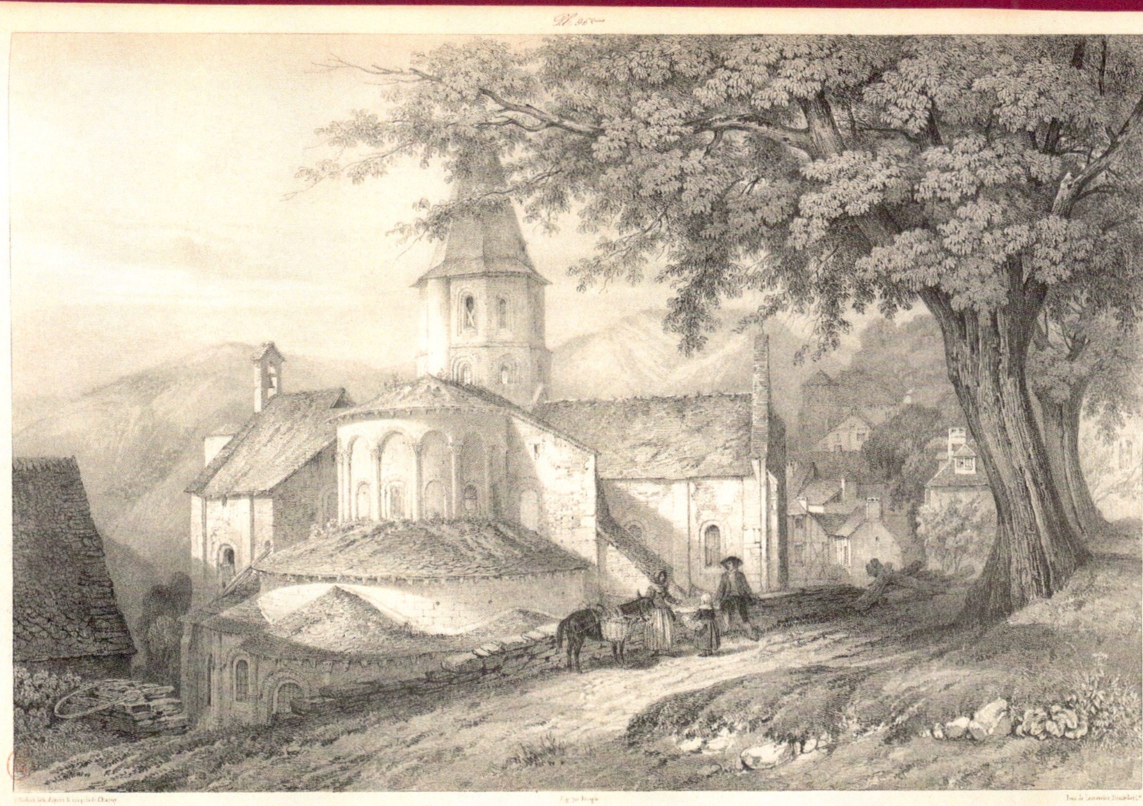

Ancienne Abbaye de Conques.
Rouergue.

Architecture, Acoustics, and Auralizations

The Romanesque church at Conques was planned and constructed during the eleventh century. The steep slope on which it was built ultimately created problems and destabilized the foundation, so it needed to be fundamentally rebuilt at the turn of the eleventh to the twelfth centuries. The resulting structure resembles other prominent Romanesque buildings, such as St. Sernin in Toulouse and Santiago de Compostela in Spain, especially in terms of its overall shape: a cross-shaped basilica with a prominent transept, a barrel-vaulted ceiling in the nave, groin vaults in the aisles, radiating chapels on axis with the sanctuary, and niches *en echelon* (arranged in a line) extending east of the transept (Vergnolle et al. 2011, Barral i Altet 2018).

In width and length (56 x 15 m; 183 ¾ x 49 ft.) Conques is much smaller compared to St. Sernin (115 x 64 m; 377 1/3 x 210 ft.) and Santiago (97 x 70 m; 318 ¼ x 229 ¾ ft.). Yet, in height (20.7m; 67.91 ft.) it is comparable to them (21 m; 68.89 ft. for St. Sernin and 22 m; 72.17 ft. for Santiago). It is the height of the church at Conques that impresses visitors today: the building is small but tall. The height also helps increase the overall volume of the interior, which is about 21,054 m³ (743,515 cu. ft.). A striking parallel also exists between the height of the church and the consistent tendency of the eleventh-century music composed for the feast of Sainte-Foy at Conques to push the chants into the higher register.

Plans of Saint-Sever, Toulouse, Santiago de Compostela, and Conques

From Georg Dehio and Gustav von Bezold, *Die kirchliche Baukunst des Abendlandes* (Church Architecture of the West), text, 2 vols.; atlas, 5 vols. (Stuttgart: J. G. Gotta, 1892–1901, atlas 1887–1901); Atlas vol. 2, plate 119.

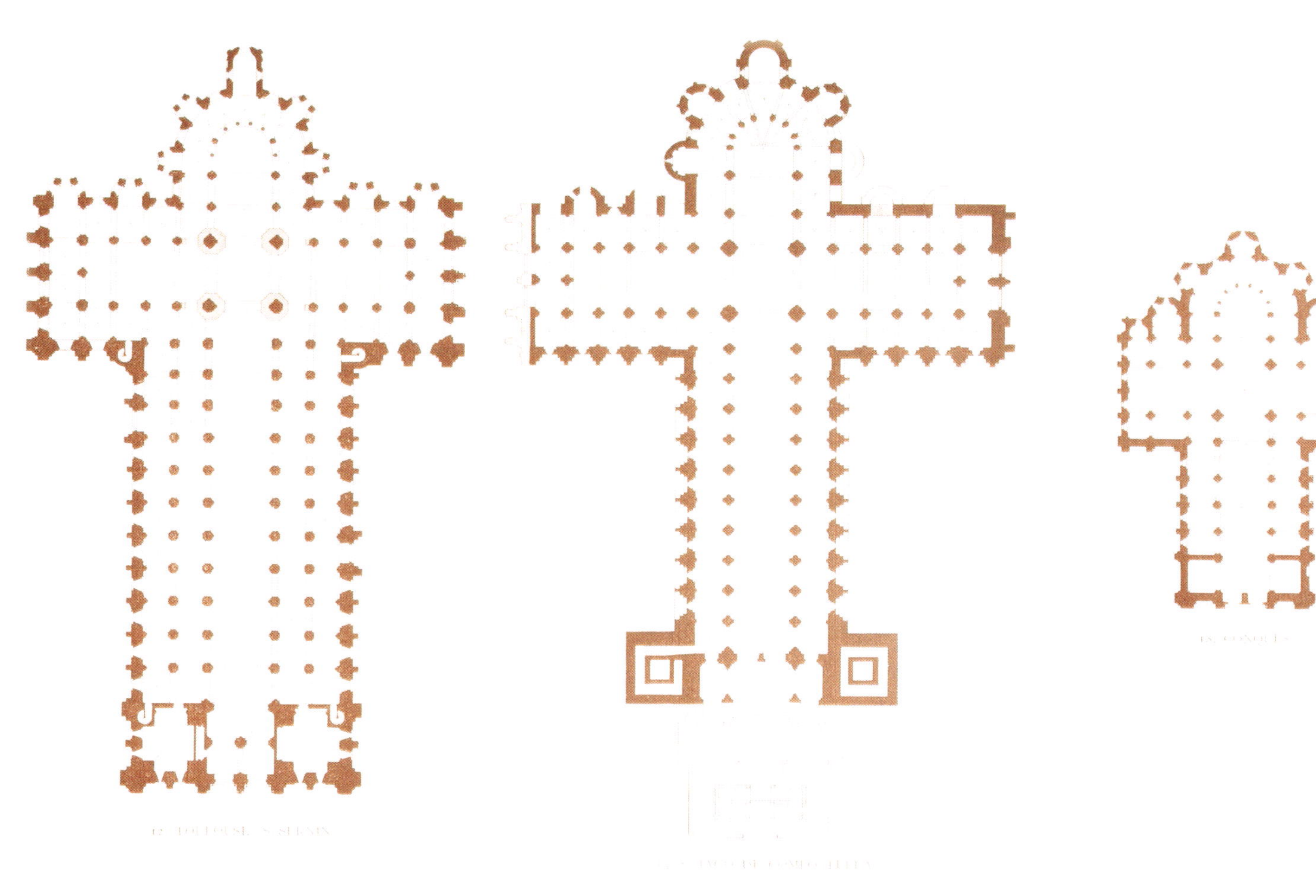

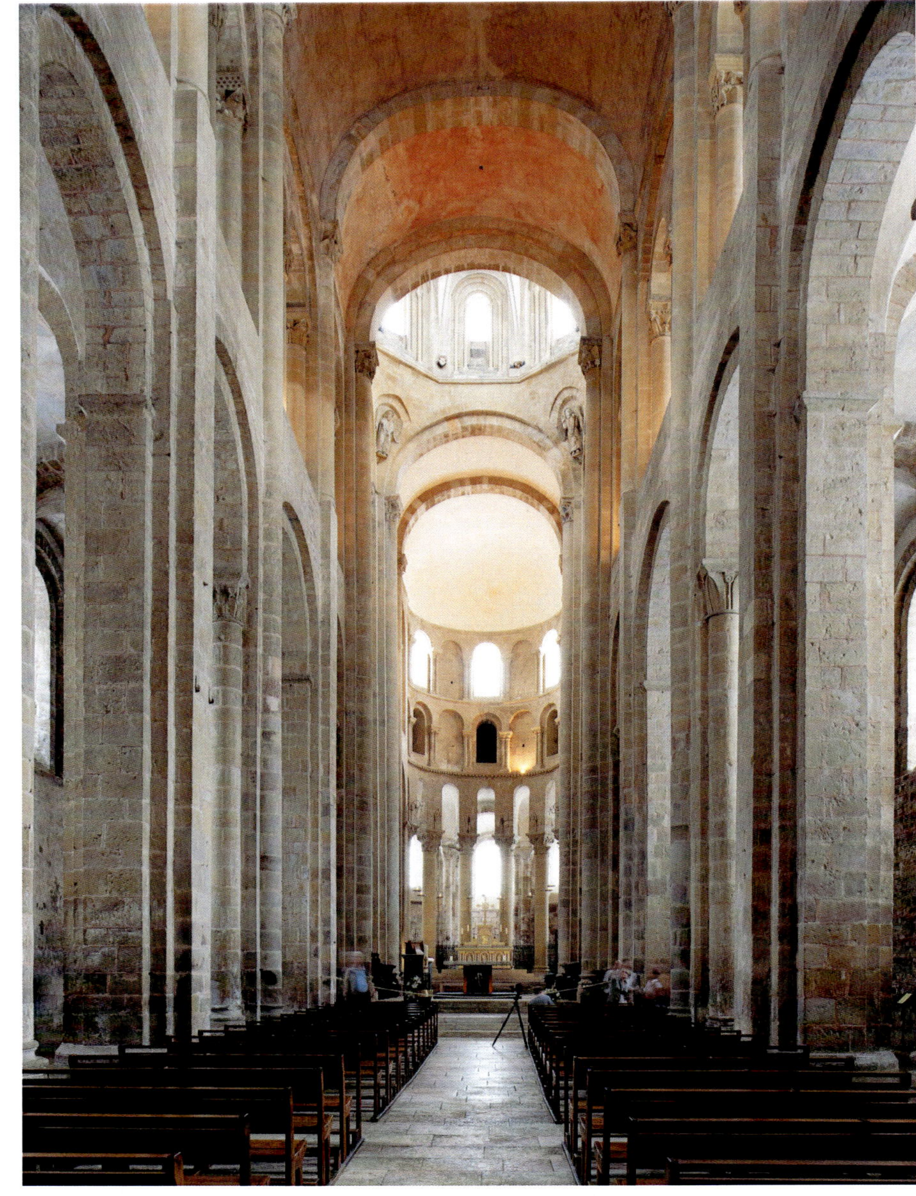

Abbey Church of Sainte-Foy,
Conques, view East towards
the apse

Photograph: Stephen Murray

Image Courtesy of the Mapping Gothic Project,
Media Center for Art History.
©The Trustees of Columbia University.

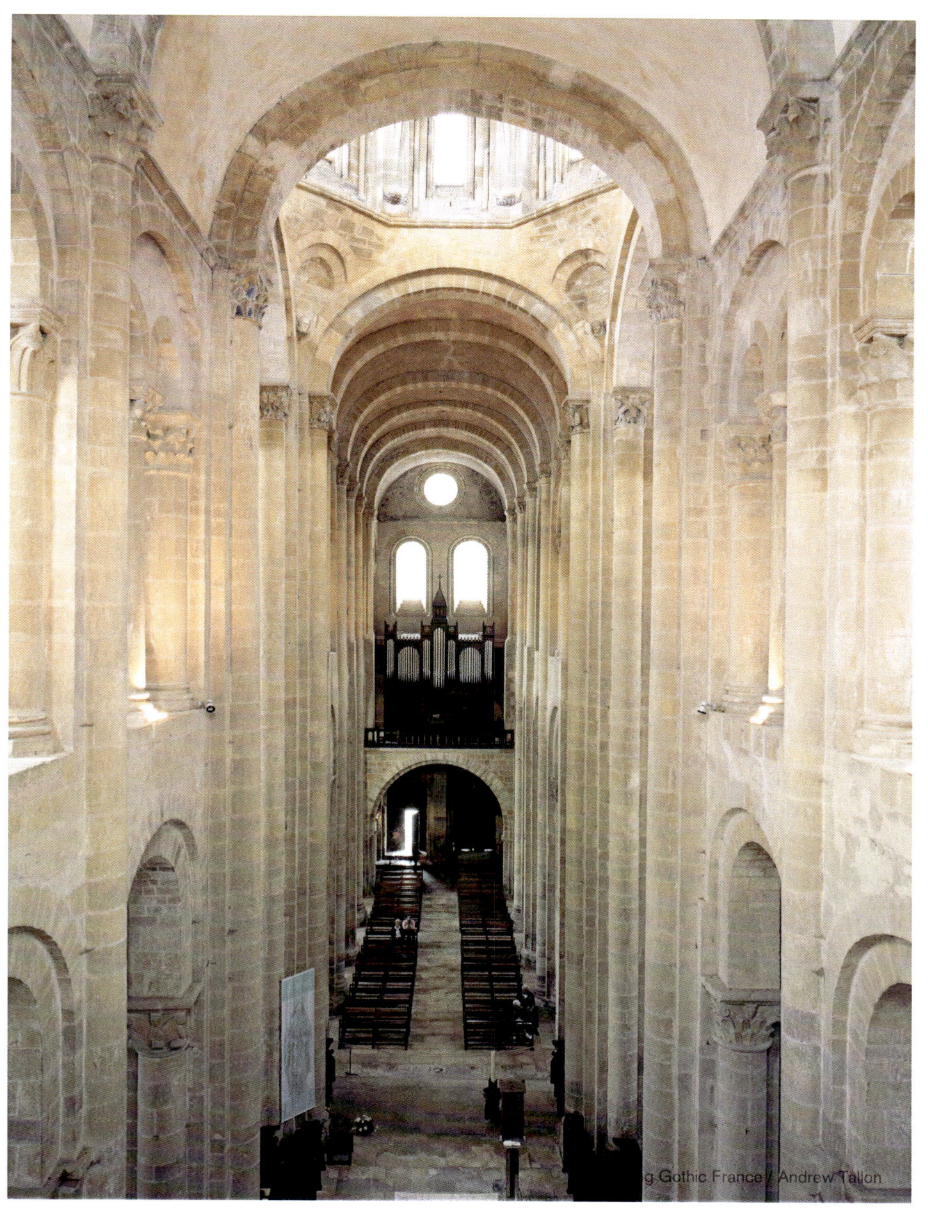

Abbey Church of Sainte-Foy, Conques, view West towards the entry

Photograph: Stephen Murray

Image Courtesy of the Mapping Gothic Project, Media Center for Art History.
©The Trustees of Columbia University.

Chart of the Reverberation
Time (RT$_{60}$) at Conques

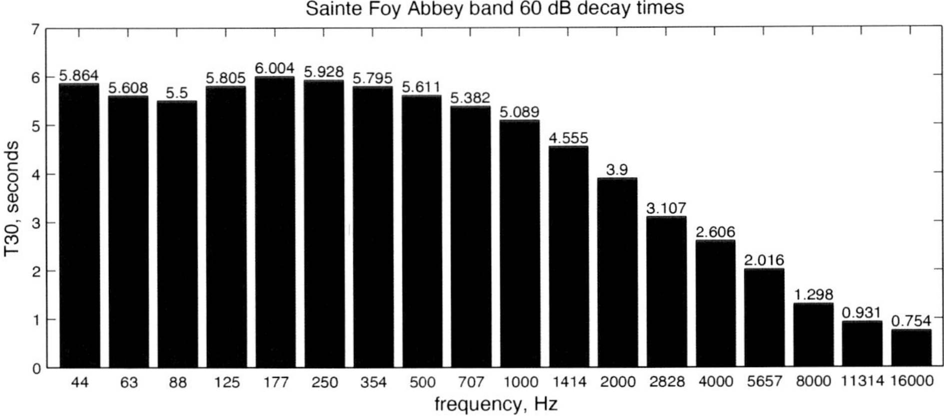

The reflective surfaces of the stone vaults and walls and the massive interior volume result in reverberant acoustics. For the frequencies in the range of the singing voice, the interior has around five seconds reverberation time (RT$_{60}$).

An earlier project, "Icons of Sound," focused on Hagia Sophia (Constantinople / Istanbul), co-directed by Bissera Pentcheva and Jonathan Abel, pioneered a new method of measuring acoustics by using balloon pops. They applied this method to Hagia Sophia to compensate for the governmental ban on singing in that building's interior. The only way to hear the sound of chant in the Great Church in Istanbul (Constantinople) was through auralizations (Pentcheva 2017).

Clearly, Conques is a different case. The church has a lively monastic community, the Premonstratensians, that sing in this church on a regular basis, although their singing does not follow the medieval repertoire. During the travel bans that were mandated during the

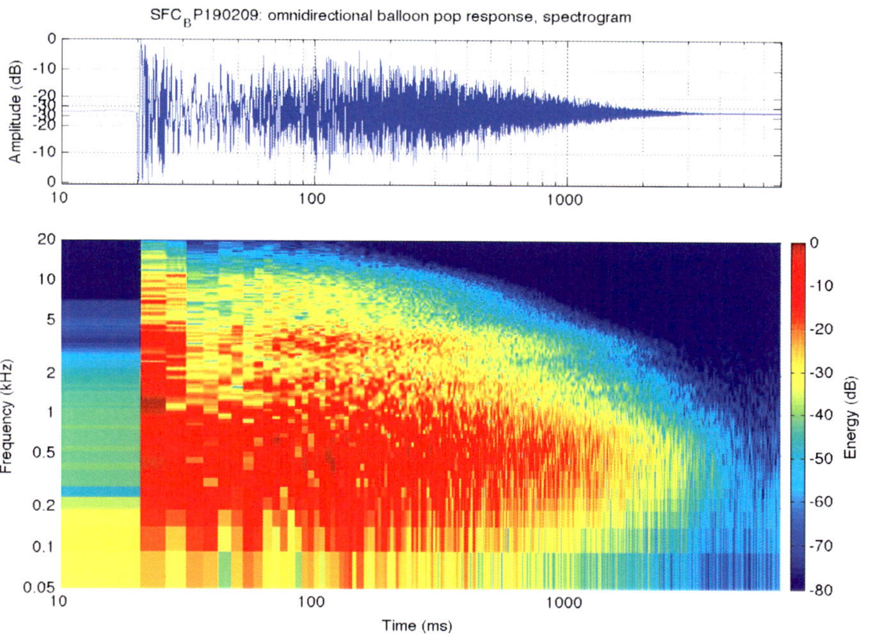

Spectrograms of the balloon pop done February 9, 2019

Graphs generated by Jonathan Abel, Center for Computer Research in Music and Acoustics (CCRMA), Stanford University

COVID-19 pandemic, however, auralizations became an important tool that helped the team of this project advance in its research. Because we were all stranded at home, interspersed in different corners of the United States, we could all work together virtually, despite the distance. Laura Steenberge transcribed the music from the medieval manuscripts and directed the recording and auralizations; Bissera Pentcheva translated the Latin poetry and recorded balloon pops at Conques in 2019 and 2022; the soprano Argenta Walther sang and recorded the repertoire, and Jonathan Abel prepared the impulse responses for the auralizations. Digital technology enabled us to hear and record the medieval chant in the very acoustics it was designed for: the Abbey Church of Sainte-Foy at Conques.

Auralizing the Medieval Image: Music from the Liturgy of Sainte-Foy at Conques

Bing Hall, Stanford Live, February 10, 2023

The concert at Bing Hall in 2023 brought to life the vespers of the eleventh-century Office of Sainte-Foy sung by Marcel Pérès and his *Ensemble Organum*. The stage was animated with the scrim projection of the statue of Sainte-Foy, floating over and behind the singers. She was the figure to whom the singers turned and sang. Gobo light projections on the sails of Bing Hall gave a glimpse into the Aquitanian music notation with its precisely heightened neumes sitting on invisible lines. The elaborate vegetal rinceaux of its initials drew the connections between music, fragrance, flowers, and the languorous wisps of smoke from burning incense, whose imagined slow rhythm fused with the tempo of the chants. Live auralizations immersed the voices of the singers in the resonant acoustics of Conques. The audience of Bing thus had the acoustic experience of hearing two places at once: the direct sound from the stage and the resonant late-field reverberation of the eleventh-century church. The team that produced this concert with its complex acoustics and visuals included:

Bissera V. Pentcheva, professor, Art History, Stanford University
Principal investigator

Laura Steenberge, DMA 2016, Stanford University
Transcription of the Liturgy of Sainte-Foy

Michael Ramsaur, emeritus professor, TAPS (Theatre and Performing Arts), Stanford University
Lighting design and scrim projection

Miguel Novelo, MFA 2022, Stanford University
Computer modeling and film sequencing of the gold statue of Sainte-Foy

Jonathan Abel, consulting professor, CCRMA (Center for Computer Research in Music and Acoustics), Stanford University
Virtual Acoustics Modeling of the Abbey of Sainte-Foy at Conques

CCRMA Team
Constantin Basica
Chris Chafe
Seán Ó Dálaigh
Hassan Estakhrian
Nette Worthey
Matt Wright

Ensemble Organum

Artistic Director: Marcel Pérès

Vocals
Jean-Christophe Candau
Jerome Pierre-Toussaint Casalonga
Jean Etienne Langianni
Marcel Jean-Marie Dominique Pérès,
Antoine Marie Gilles Jacques Sicot
Frederic Paul Tavernier

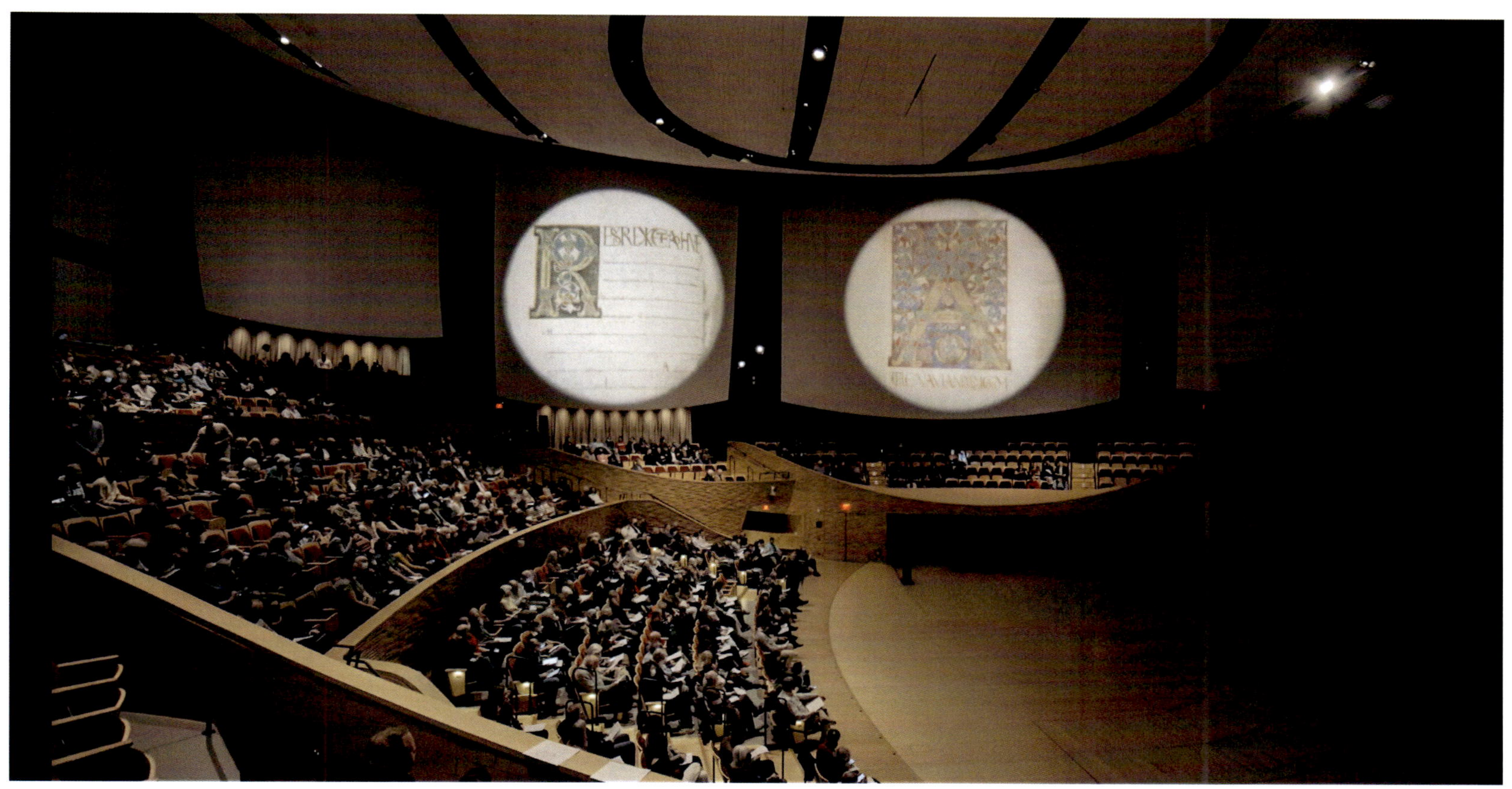

Photograph: Susana Barron

Bing Concert Hall, gobo lights with initials and vegetal ornament
coming from Aquitanian music manuscripts

Program

Music from the Liturgy for Sainte-Foy
Anonymous, mid-eleventh century
From Paris, BnF, MS Nouv. Acq. Lat.
443 and Paris, BnF, MS Lat. 1240
Transcription by Laura Steenberge

Vespers Antiphon
Haec est virgo prudens meritis

Vespers Responsory
Respond *Emissiones tue*,
"Your aromas"

Verse *Veni sponsa miscui*,
"Come my bride, mix"

Doxology *Gloria patri*,
"Glory to the Father"

Prosa *Candida tu quia*,
"You are brighter"

Vespers Magnificat Antiphon
Veneranda, "The Venerable Festivity"

Processional antiphon
O decus, "O Exceptional Glory"

———— INTERMISSION ————

*Seeing through Chant: Sainte-Foy
at Conques*
Documentary film, dir. Bissera V.
Pentcheva, 17:59 min, 2022

*Versus de Sancto Marcialis
Septuaginta Duo*
"72 Verses for St. Martial"
Adémar of Chabannes
(988/989–1034)
From Paris, BnF, MS Lat. 909
Polyphonic verses

Preconia Virginis Laudes
Anonymous (twelfth century)
From Paris, BnF, MS Lat. 3719
Transcription by Malcolm Bothwell
Polyphonic chant

Alleluia Justus germinabit
"The Just Will Sprout"
From Anonymous (twelfth century)
From Paris, BnF, MS Lat. 903
Alleluia and verse

Alma chorus
"Nourishing Choir"
Anonymous (twelfth century)
From Paris, BnF, MS. Lat. 3719
Transcription by Malcolm Bothwell
Polyphonic sequence

Stirps Jesse
"The Shoot of Jesse"
Anonymous (twelfth century)
From Paris, BnF, MS Lat. 3549
Transcription by Malcolm Bothwell
Polyphonic Benedicamus trope

Program notes:
https://live.stanford.edu/blog/february-2023/program-notes-auralizing-medieval-image

Concert Announcement:
https://live.stanford.edu/calendar/february-2023/auralizing-medieval-image

Featured story:
https://live.stanford.edu/blog/january-2023/bringing-spiritual-life-0

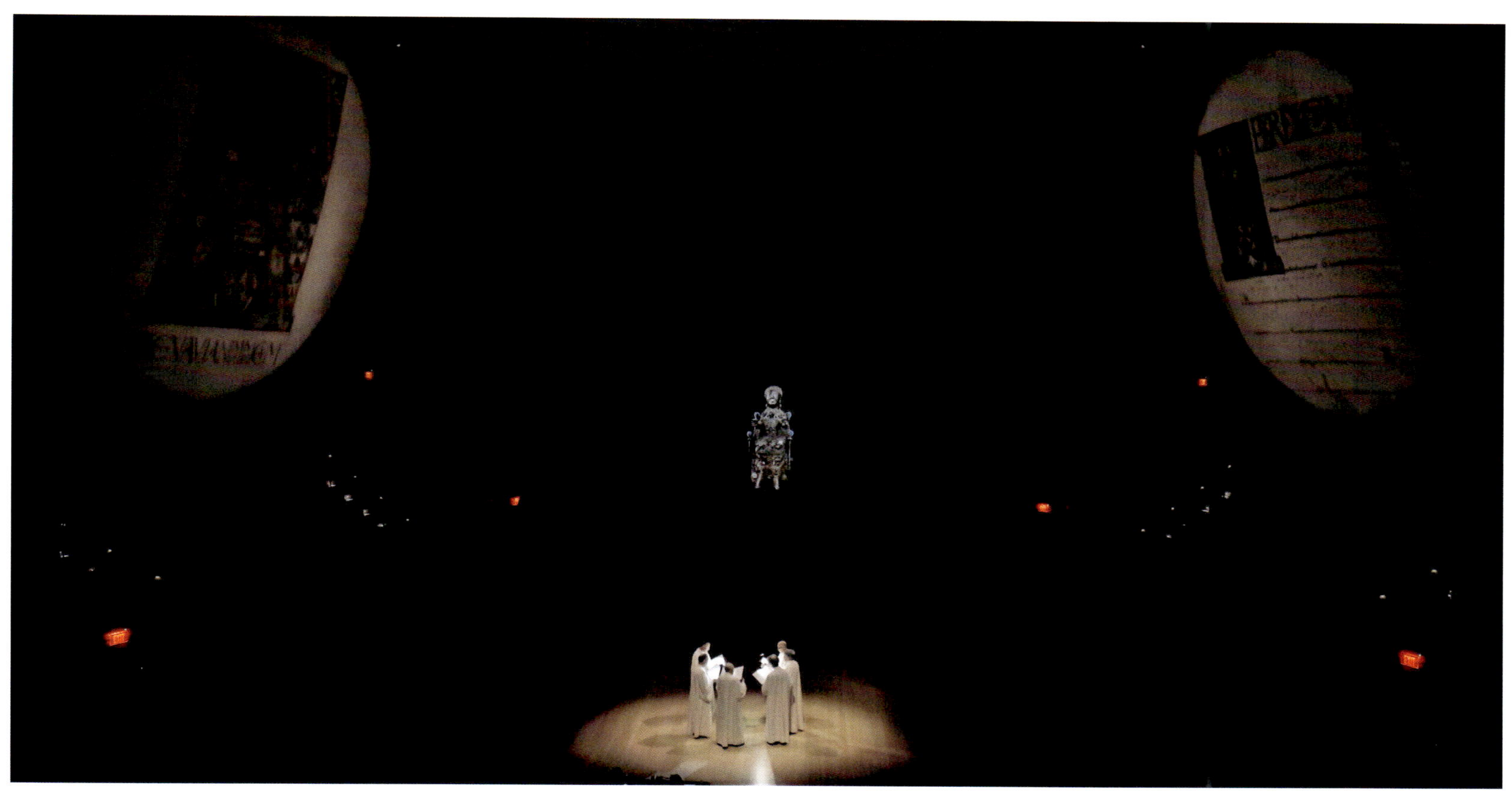

Photograph: Susana Barron

The singers of *Ensemble Organum* chanting towards the
rotating statue of Sainte-Foy projected on a scrim

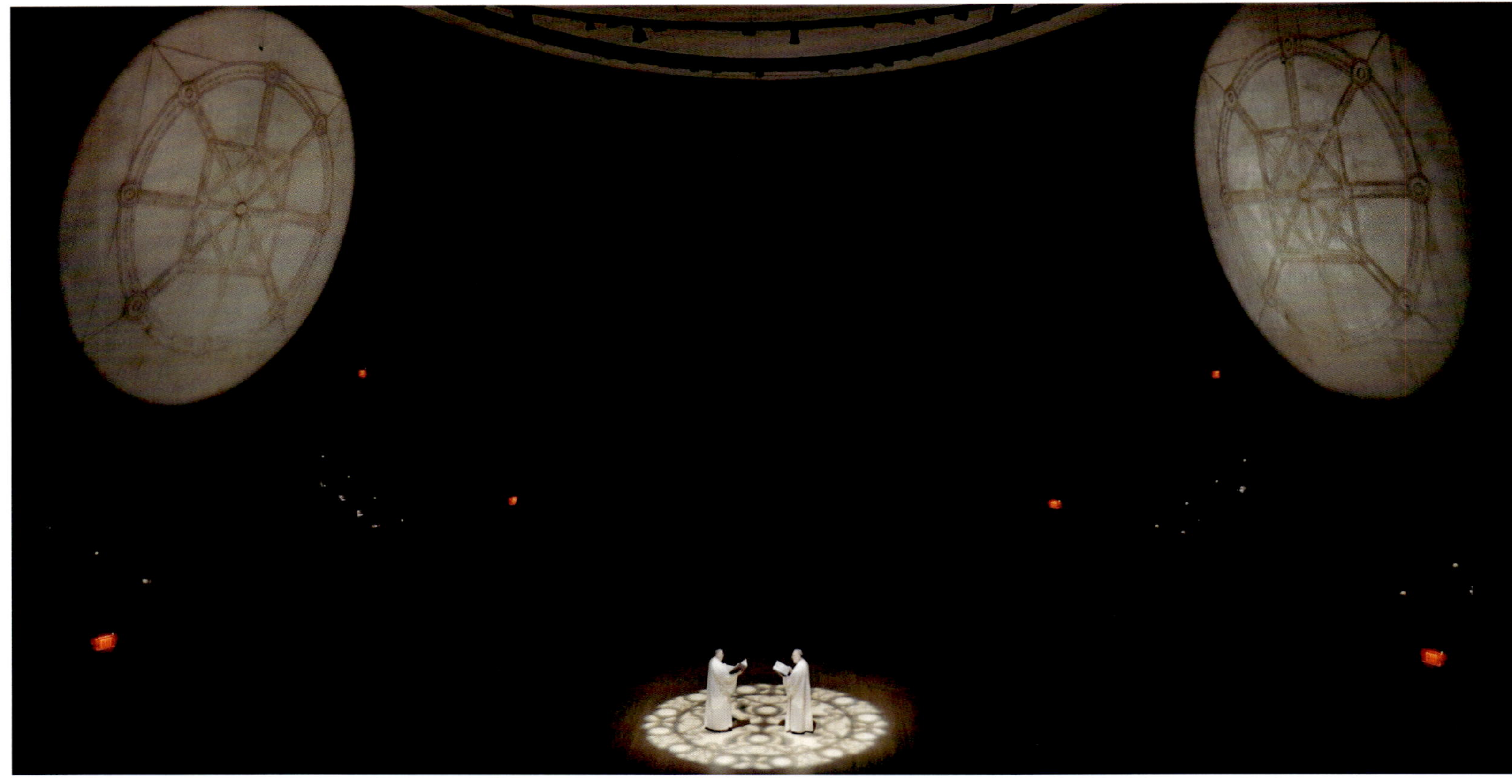

Gobo lights with the diagram of Paris, BnF, MS Lat. 776,
fol. 1v and a stencil of a Byzantine chandelier projected
at the feet of the singers

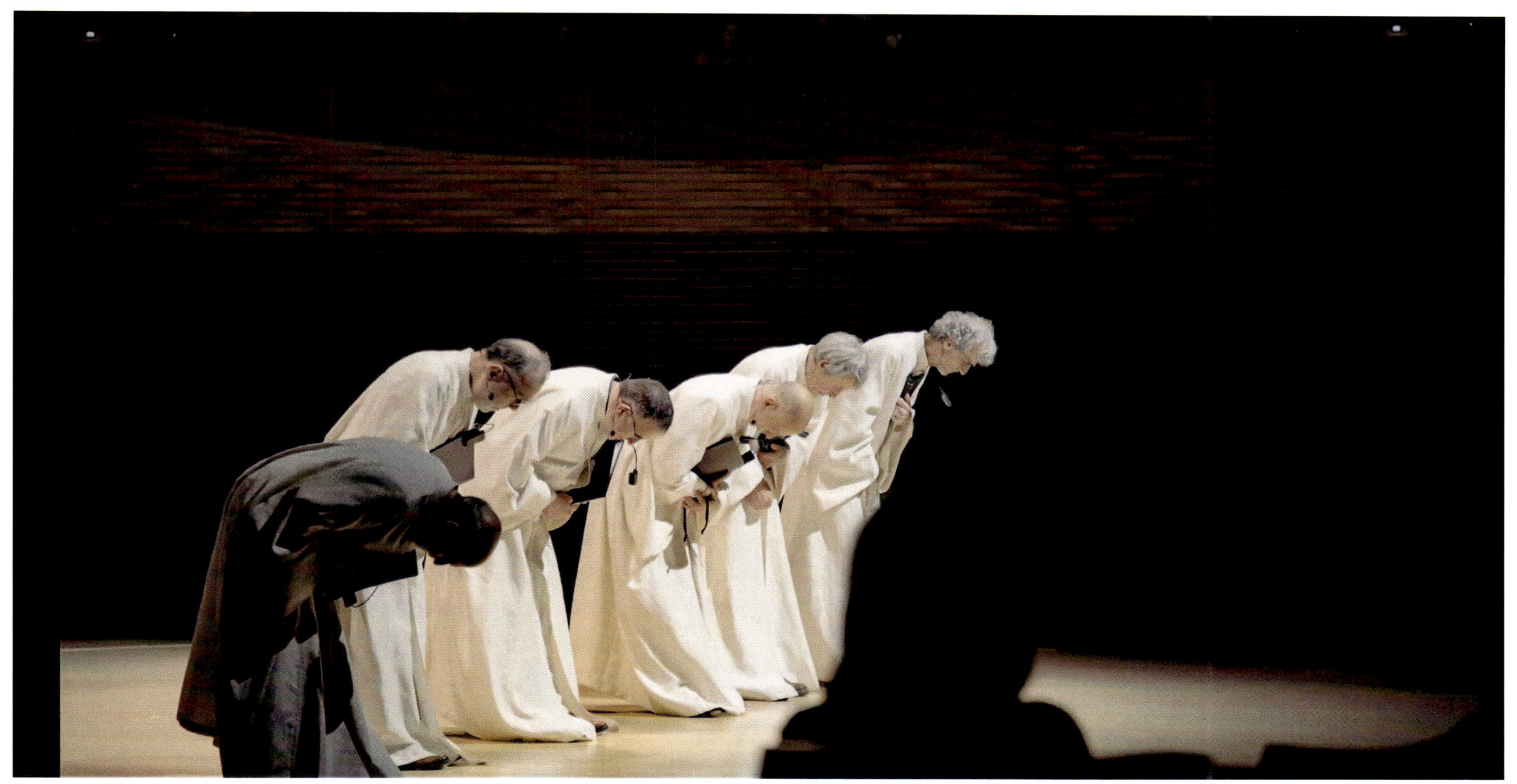

The singers of *Ensemble Organum* receiving applause

Seeing through Chant: Sainte-Foy at Conques

Documentary Film, directed by
Bissera V. Pentcheva, 17:59 min.

Just like film studies for decades did not include sound in its exploration of the moving image, so too art history for a century has only engaged with the visual without taking into consideration the sonic. The film — *Seeing Through Chant: Sainte Foy at Conques* — explores the story of a golden effigy, its monastery, its music, and its art, revealing the complex shared structures between chant and the visual. This film production offers a perfect blend between deep past and modern technology. It shows the relevance of premodern art in our times that are otherwise so focused on the present and the moment.

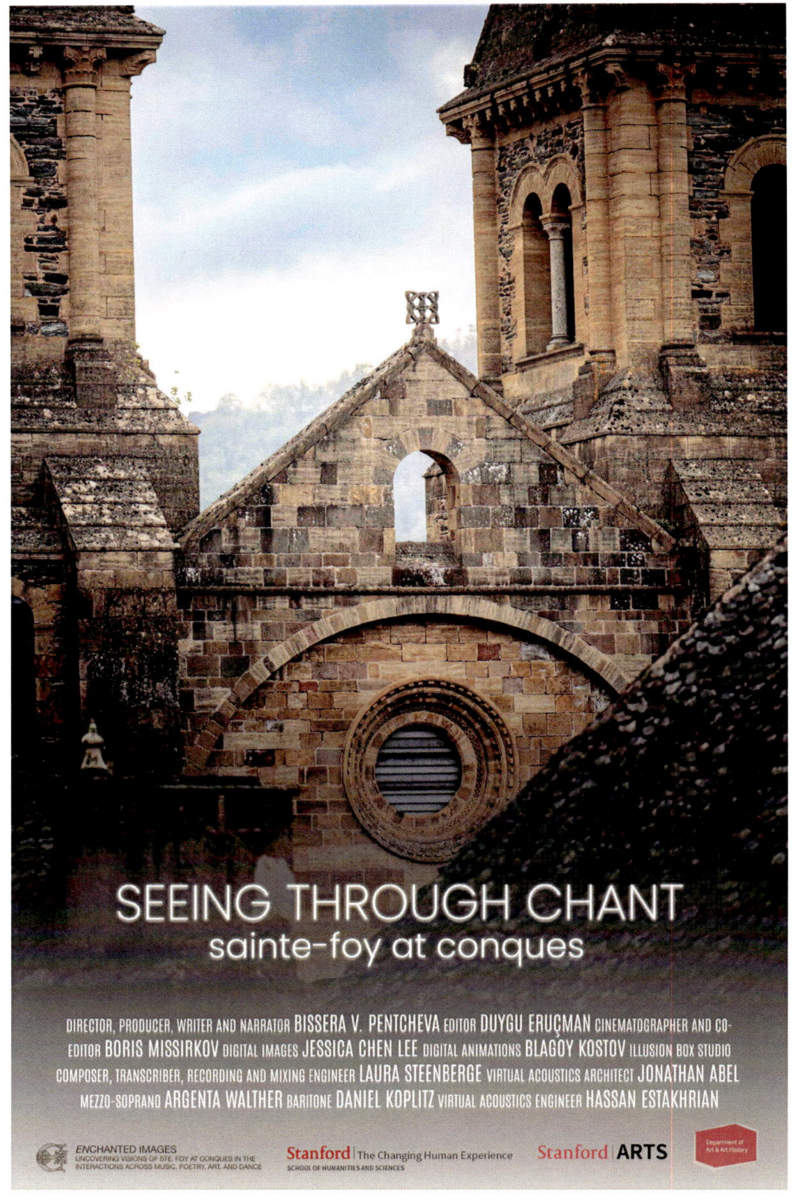

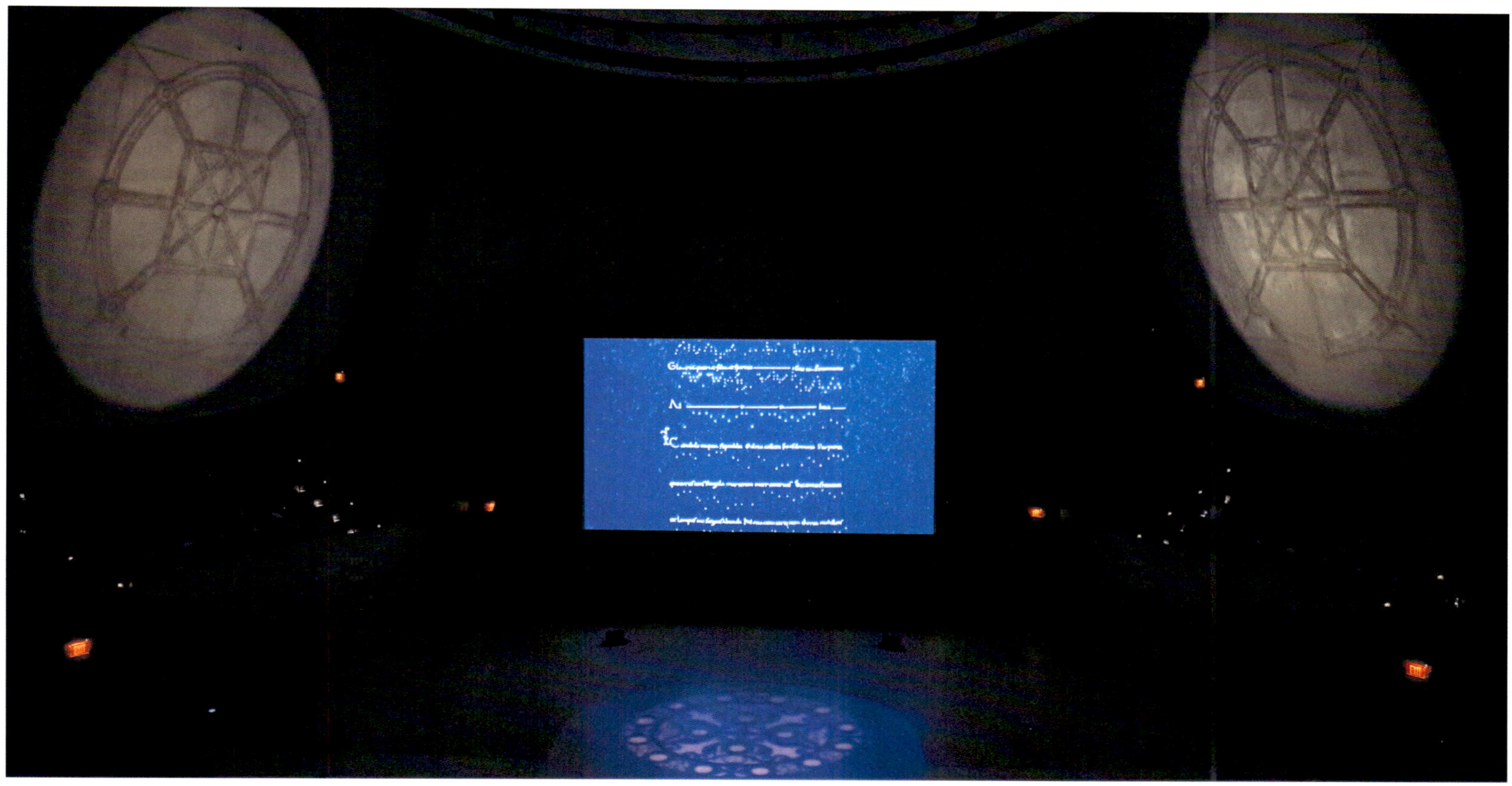

Photograph: Susana Barron

The film *Seeing Through Chant: Sainte-Foy at Conques*
projected in the second half of the concert

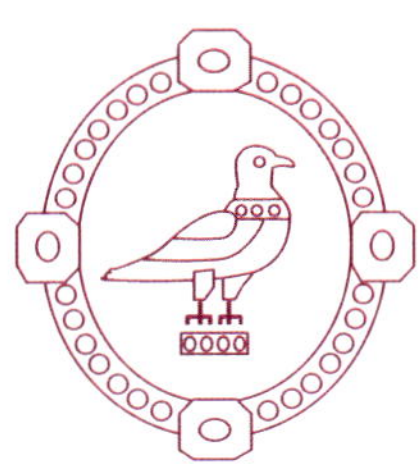

BIBLIOGRAPHY

Primary Sources

Liber miraculorum, 11th century
Robertini, Luca, editor, 1994. *Liber miraculorum Sancte Fidis, edizione critica e commento*. Spoleto: Centro italiano di studi sull'alto medioevo. English: Sheingorn, Pamela, translator, 1995. *The Book of Ste Foy*. Philadelphia: University of Pennsylvania Press.

Office of Sainte-Foy, 11th century
Bouillet, Auguste, and L. Servieres, editors. 1900. *Sainte Foy, Vierge et Martyre*. Rodez: E. Carrère, pp. 644–55.

Pseudo-Dionysius, 6th century
Luibhéid, Colm, translator. 1987. *Pseudo-Dionysius: The Complete Works*. London: SPCK.

Rule of Saint Benedict, 6th century
Venarde, Bruce, translator. 2011. *The Rule of Saint Benedict*. Cambridge. MA: Harvard University Press.

Thesauri hymnologici prosarium
Blume, Clemens, editor. 1911. *Thesauri hymnologici prosarium. Die Sequenzen des Thesaurus Hymnologicus H. A. Daniels und anderer Sequenzenausgaben. Part I.*

Liturgische Prosen erster Epoche aus den Sequenzenschulen des Abendlandes, insbesondere die dem Notkerus Balbulus zugeschriebenen nebst Skizze über den Ursprung der Sequenz. Series Analecta hymnica medii aevi. Edited by Clemens Blume and Henry Bannister. Leipzig: Reisland, vol. 53, no. 76, 132–34.

Secondary Sources

Barral i Altet 2018
Barral i Altet, Xavier, 2018. *Il cantiere romanico di Sainte-Foy de Conques. La ricchezza, i miracoli, e le contingenze materiali, dalle fonti testuali alla storia dell'arte*. Zagreb: University of Zagreb.

Bernoulli 1956
Bernoulli, Christoph. 1956. *Die Skulpturen der Abtei Conques-en-Rouergue*. Basel: Birkhäuser Verlag.

Berthod 2019
Berthod, Bernard and Gaël Favier. 2019. *Conques, un trésor millenaire*. Paris. Éditions CLD.

Bonne 1984
Bonne, Jean-Claude. 1984. *L'art roman, de face et de profil. Le tympan de Conques*. Paris: Le Sycamore.

Bonne 2012
Bonne, Jean-Claude. 2012. "Végétalité." In *Le monde roman: par-delà le bien et le mal. une iconographie du lieu sacré*. Edited by Jérôme Baschet, Jean-Claude Bonne; and Pierre-Olivier Dittmar. Paris: Arkhê, pp. 43–97.

Bouché 2006
Bouché, Anne-Marie. 2006. "Vox Imaginis: Anomaly and Enigma in Romanesque Art." In *The Mind's Eye. Art and Theological Argument in the Middle Ages*. Edited by Jeffrey Hamburger and Anne-Marie Bouché. Princeton: Princeton University Press, pp. 306–36.

Bousquet 1947
Bousquet, Abbé Louis. 1947. "L'enigme architectonique du portail de Conques." *Revue du Rouergue* 1: 491–502.

Bousquet 1992
Bousquet, Jacques. 1992. *Le Rouergue au Premier Moyen Âge (vers 800–vers 1250). Vol. 1. Les pouvoirs, leurs rapports et leurs domaines*. Rodez: Société des lettres, sciences et arts de l'Aveyron: pp. 273–345.

Bousquet 1997
Bousquet, Jacques. 1997. "Conques et l'art du premier Moyen Age: Trois mises au point." *Revue du Rouergue* 52: 561–80.

Busse-Berger 2005
Busse-Berger, Anna Maria. 2005. *Medieval Music and the Art of Memory*. Berkeley: University of California Press.

Bynum 2011
Bynum, Carolyn. 2011. *Christian Materiality: An Essay on Religion in Late Medieval Europe*. New York: Zone Books.

Cantus n.d.
Cantus: A Database for Latin Ecclesiastical Chant. n.d. Available online at the Cantus website: https://cantus.uwaterloo.ca (accessed December 14, 2022).

Carruthers 1990
Carruthers, Mary. 2008. *The Book of Memory: A Study of Memory in Medieval Culture*. Cambridge: Cambridge University Press.

Castiñeiras 2018
Castiñeiras, Manuel. 2018. "Ojo avizor: Porter, un Pantocrátor errático y la estela de Conques en Compostela." *Ad Lumina* 9: 247–68.

Chion 1994 and 2019
Chion, Michel. 1994 and 2019. *Audio-vision: Sound on Screen*. New York: Columbia University Press.

Collamore 2006
Collamore, Lila. 2006. "Reassessing the Manuscript Paris, BnF, MS Lat. 1118." *The 17th Congress of the International Musicological Society*. (Leuven, Belgium), August 6, 2002. Available on Academia.edu website at: https://www.academia.edu/33627289/Reassessing_the_Manuscript_Paris_Bibliothèque_Nationale_lat._1118

Constable 1995
Constable, John. 1995. "The Ideal of the Imitation of Christ." In *Three Studies in Medieval Religious and Social Thought*. Cambridge, UK: Cambridge University Press, pp. 143–248.

Constas 2014
Constas, Maximos. 2014. *The Art of Seeing: Paradox and Perception in Orthodox Iconography*. Alhambra, CA: Sebastian Press.

Crocker 1977
Crocker, Richard. 1977. *The Early Medieval Sequence*. Berkeley: University of California Press.

Cox-Miller 2009
Cox-Miller, Patricia. 2009. *The Corporeal Imagination: Signifying the Holy in Late Antique Christianity*. Philadelphia: University of Pennsylvania Press.

Dahl 1979
Dahl, Ellert. 1978. "Heavenly Images: The Statue of St. Foy of Conques and the Signification of the Medieval 'Cult-Image' in the West." *Acta ad Archaeologiam et Artium Historiam Pertinentia* 8: 175–92.

Dale 2019
Dale, Thomas. 2019. *Pygmalion's Power: Romanesque Sculpture, the Senses, and Religious Experience*. University Park, PA: Penn State University Press, pp. 95–103.

Danford 2014
Danford, Rachel. 2014. "'Cast Not to the Beasts the Souls That Confess You': Images of Mouths at the Cathedral of St. Lazare at Autun." *The Rutgers Art Review* 29: 4–21.

Deschamps 1941
Deschamps, Paul. 1941. "Étude sur sculptures de Sainte-Foy de Conques et de Saint-Sernin de Toulouse et leurs relations avec celles de Saint-Isidore de Léon et de Sainte-Jacques de Compostelle." *Bulletin monumental* 100 (3–4): 239–64.

Desjardins 1879
Desjardins, Gustave, editor. 1879. *Cartulaire de l'abbaye de Conques en Rouergue*. Paris: Picard.

Della Dora 2016
Della Dora, Veronica. 2016. *Landscape, Nature, and the Sacred in Byzantium*. Cambridge, UK: Cambridge University Press.

Dyer 1989
Dyer, Joseph. 1989. The Singing of Psalms in the Early Medieval Office. *Speculum* 64 (3): 535–78.

Fassler 1993
Fassler, Margot. 1993. *Gothic Song: Victorine Sequences and Augustinian Reform in Twelfth-Century Paris*. New York: Cambridge University Press.

Fassler 2000
Fassler, Margot. 2000. "Mary's Nativity, Fulbert's Chartres, and the Stirps of Jesse: Liturgical Innovation ca. 1000 and Its Afterlife." *Speculum* 75 (2): 389–434.

Fassler 2010
Fassler, Margot. 2010. *The Virgin of Chartres: Making History through Liturgy and the Arts.* New Haven and London: Yale University Press.

Fassler 2014
Fassler, Margot. 2014. *Music in the Medieval West.* New York and London: Norton and Company.

Fassler 2019
Fassler, Margot. 2019. "Women and Their Sequences: An Overview and a Case Study." *Speculum* 94 (3): 625–73.

Fau 1956
Fau, Jean-Claude. 1956. *Les chapiteaux de Conques.* Toulouse: É. Privat.

Favreau and Michaud 1984
Favreau, Robert, and Jean Michaud, editors. 1984. *Corpus des inscriptions de la France médiévale.* Paris: Éditions du Centre National de la Recherche Scientifique. Vol. 9, no. 12, pp. 17–55.

Foletti 2018
Foletti, Ivan. 2018. "Meeting Saint Faith." *In Migrating Art Historians on the Sacred Ways.* Edited by Ivan Foletti, Katarína Kravčíková, and Sabina Rosenbergová. Brno: Masaryk University, pp. 295–31.

Foletti 2019
Foletti, Ivan. 2019. "Dancing with Ste. Foy: Movement and the Iconic Presence." *Convivium* 6 (1): 70–87.

Foletti 2022
Foletti, Ivan. 2022. "Spaces for Miracles: Constructing Sacred Space through Body, from Conques to the Mediterranean and Beyond." *Convivium* 9 (1): 169–85.

Forsyth 1972
Forsyth, Ilene. 1972. *The Throne of Wisdom: Wood Sculptures of the Madonna in Romanesque France.* Princeton: Princeton University Press.

Franzé 2021
Franzé, Barbara. 2021. "Images et société à Reichenau vers l'an mil: les peintures d'Oberzell et les manuscrits apparentés." *Zeitschrift für Kunstgeschichte* 84 (2): 147–80.

Fricke 2015
Fricke, Beate. 2015. *Fallen Idols, Risen Saints: Sainte Foy of Conques and the Revival of Monumental Sculpture in Medieval Art.* Turnhout, BE: Brepols.

Gaborit-Chopin et al. 2001
Gaborit-Chopin, Danielle, Elisabeth Taburet, and Marie-Cécile Bardoz. 2001. *Le trésor de Conques: Exposition du 2 novembre au 11 mars 2002, Musée du Louvre.* Paris: Monum, Editions du patrimoine.

Garland 2006
Garland, Emmanuel. 2006. "L'autel portatif de l'Abbé Bégon à Conques et ses relations avec l'art somptuaire occidental." *Cahiers de Saint-Michel de Cuxa* 37: 221–37.

Giunta 2017
Giunta, Alexandre. 2017. *Les Francos dans la vallée de l'Èbre (XIᵉ–XIIᵉ siècles).* Toulouse: Presses universitaires du Midi Méridiennes.

Grémont 1969
Grémont, Denis. 1969. Le culte de Ste-Foi et Sainte-Marie Madeleine à Conques au IXᵉ siècle d'après le manuscrit de la Canson de Ste-Foi. *Revue du Rouergue* 23: 165–75.

Grier 2006
Grier, James. 2006. *The Musical World of a Medieval Monk: Adémar de Chabannes in Eleventh-Century Aquitaine.* New York: Cambridge University Press.

Hahn 2012
Hahn, Cynthia. 2012. *Strange Beauty: Issues in the Making and Meaning of Reliquaries, 400–circa 1204.* University Park, PA: Penn State University Press.

Harper 1991
Harper, John. 1991. *The Forms and Orders of Western Liturgy from the Tenth to the Eighteenth Century: A Historical Introduction and Guide for Students and Musicians.* Oxford, UK: Oxford University Press.

Harvey 2006
Harvey, Susan. 2006. *Scenting of Salvation: Ancient Christianity and the Olfactory Imagination.* Berkeley and Los Angeles: University of California Press.

Helsen 2008
Helsen, Kate. 2008. "The Great Responsories of the Divine Office: Aspects of Structure and Transmission." PhD diss., Regensburg, DE. Available online at University of Regensburg Publications website: https://epub.uni-regensburg. de/10769/1/PhDThesisKateHelsen.pdf (accessed December 19, 2022).

Hiley 1993
Hiley, David. 1993. *Western Plainchant: A Handbook.* Oxford, UK: Oxford University Press.

Huang 2014
Huang, Lei. 2014. "Le Maître du tympan de l'abbatiale Sainte-Foy de Conques: état de la question et perspectives." *Études Aveyronnaises.* Rodez: Société des lettres, sciences et arts de l'Aveyron, pp. 87–100.

Hughes 1983
Hughes, Andrew. 1983. "Modal Order and Disorder in the Rhymed Office." *Musica Disciplina* 37: 29–51.

Huglo 1971
Huglo, Michel. 1971. *Les Tonaires. Inventaire, Analyse, Comparaison.* Paris: Société française de musicologie, pp. 132–40.

Huglo 2009
Huglo, Michel. 2009. "Les 'libelli' de Tropes et les premiers Tropaires-Prosaires." In *Embellishing the Liturgy. Tropes and Polyphony.* Edited by Alejandro Enrique Planchart. Farnham, UK: Ashgate, pp. 85–94.

Isar 2006
Isar, Nicoletta. 2006. "Chorography (*Chôra, Chôros, Chorós*) — A performative paradigm of creation of sacred space in Byzantium." In *Hierotopy: The Creation of Sacred Spaces in Byzantium and Medieval Russia.* Edited by Alexei Lidov. Moscow: Indrik, pp. 59–90.

Isar 2011
Isar, Nicoletta. 2011. *Chorós: The Dance of Adam, the Making of Byzantine Chorography, the Anthropology of the Choir of Dance in Byzantium.* Leiden: Alexandros Press.

Iversen 2007
Iversen, Gunilla. 2007. "Biblical Interpretation in Tropes and Sequences." *Journal of Medieval Latin* 17: 210–25.

Iversen 2010
Iversen, Gunilla. 2010. *Laus angelica: Poetry in the Medieval Mass.* Edited by Jane Flynn. Translated by William Flynn. Turnhout, BE: Brepols, pp. 127–59.

Kelly 1974
Kelly, Thomas Forrest. 1974. "Melodic Elaboration in Responsory Melismas." *Journal of the American Musicological Society* 27 (3): 461–74.

Kelly 1977
Kelly, Thomas Forrest. 1977. "New Music from Old: The Structuring of Responsory Prosas." *Journal of the American Musicological Society* 30 (3): 366–90.

Kelly 2011
Kelly, Thomas Forrest. 2011. "Poetry for Music: The Art of the Medieval Prosula." *Speculum* 86 (2): 361–86.

Kendall 1989
Kendall, Calvin B. 1989. "The Voice in the Stone: The Verse Inscriptions of Ste.-Foy of Conques and the Date of the Tympanum." In *Hermeneutics and Medieval Culture.* Edited by Patrick J. Gallacher and Helen Damico. Albany: State University of New York Press, pp. 163–82.

Kendall 1998
Kendall, Calvin B. 1998. *The Allegory of the Church: Romanesque Portals and Their Verse Inscriptions.* Toronto: University of Toronto Press.

Lešák 2022
Lešák, Martin. 2022. "Transforming a Desert, Claiming the Domain: The Early Medieval Landscape of Conques." *Convivium* 9 (1): 148–67.

Lonsdale 1994–95
Lonsdale, Steven H. 1994–95. "'Homeric Hymn to Apollo': Prototype and Paradigm of Choral Performance." *Arion. A Journal of Humanities and the Classics* 3 (1): 25–40.

Mahrt 1990
Mahrt, William Peter. 1990. "Word-Painting and Formulaic Chants." In *Cum Angelis Canere.* Edited by Robert Skeris. St. Paul, MN.: Catholic Church Music Associates, pp. 113–44.

Méhu 2007
Méhu, Didier. 2007. "Locus, transitus, peregrinatio: Remarques sur la spatialité des rapports sociaux dans l'Occident médiéval (XIᵉ–XIIIᵉ siècle)." In *Actes des congrès de la Société des historiens médiévistes de l'enseignement supérieur public, 37ᵉ Congrès Mulhouse, 2006. Construction de l'espace au Moyen Age: practiques et representations.* Edited by Thomas Lienhard. Paris: Publications de la Sorbonne, pp. 275–93.

Mérimée 1838
Mérimée, Prosper. 1838. "Extrait d'un rapport adressé au Ministre de l'Intérieur sur l'abbaye de Conques." *Bulletin monumental* 4: 225–42.

de Mondredon 2015
de Mondredon, Térence Le Deschault. 2015. "Les modéles transpyrénéens de la sculpture du premier chantier de Compostelle: imitation, présence réelle et usage de l'imaginaire." *Ad Limina* 6: 33–65.

Nees 2016
Nees, Lawrence. 2016. "L'odorat fait-il sens?" In *Les cinq sens au Moyen Âge.* Edited by Éric Palazzo. Paris: Éditions du Cerf, pp. 333–65.

Nodier, et al. 1835
Nodier, Charles, Isidore-Justin-Séverin Taylor, and Alphonse de Cailleux. 1835. *Voyages pittoresques et romantiques dans l'ancienne France. Languedoc.* Vol. 1, part 2. Paris: P. Didot, pp. 256–68.

Palladino 2022
Palladino, Adrian. 2022. "Dynamics of Medieval Landscape: Measure, Environment, Conversion." *Convivium* 9 (1): 13–26.

Parkes 2020
Parkes, Henry. 2021. "Theology and Teleology in the Festal Night Office: What Performance Directions Reveal About the Design and Experience of Historiae." In *Historiae: Liturgical Chant for Offices of the Saints in the Middle Ages.* Edited by David Hiley. Venice: Edizioni Fondazione Levi, pp. 33–57. Available online at publisher's website: https://archivio.fondazionelevi.it/record/59248/files/HISTORIAE_4_2021.pdf (accessed January 3, 2023)

Pentcheva 2010
Pentcheva, Bissera. 2010. *The Sensual Icon: Space, Ritual and the Senses in Byzantium.* University Park, PA: Penn State University Press.

Pentcheva 2016
Pentcheva, Bissera. 2016. "Glittering Eyes: Animation in the Byzantine *Eikōn* and the Western *Imago*." *Codex Aquilarensis* 32: 209–36. Available online at the Santa Maria la Real Foundation website: https://www.romanicodigital.com/sites/default/files/2019-09/C32-9_Bissera%20Pentcheva.pdf (accessed January 3, 2023)

Pentcheva 2017
Pentcheva, Bissera. 2017. *Hagia Sophia: Sound, Space, and Spirit in Byzantium.* University Park, PA: Penn State University Press.

Pentcheva 2020a
Pentcheva, Bissera. 2020. "Performative Images and Cosmic Sound in the Exultet Liturgy of Southern Italy." *Speculum* 95 (2):

396–466. Available online at the University of Chicago Press Journals website: https://www.journals.uchicago.edu/doi abs/10.1086/708002 (accessed January 3, 2023)

Pentcheva 2020b
Pentcheva. Bissera. 2020b. "Optical and Acoustic Aura in Medieval Art: The Golden Retable of the Pentecost at Stavelot." *Material Religion* 16 (1): 9–40. Available online at University of Chicago Press Journals website: https://doi.org/10.1080/17432200.2019.1696558 (accessed January 3, 2023)

Pentcheva 2021a
Pentcheva, Bissera. 2021a. "The Liveliness of the Methexic Image." In *Medieval Art at the Intersection of Visuality and Material Culture: Studies in the "Semantics of Vision."* Edited by Raphaèle Preisinger. Turnhout, BE: Brepols, pp. 137–58.

Pentcheva 2021b
Pentcheva, Bissera. 2021b. "Imaging the Sacred in Virtuoso Chant and Dance: The Music of Ste. Foy and the Dancer/Singer of Almiphona (Paris, BnF, MS Lat. 1118)." *Codex Aquilarensis* 37: 335–56. Available online at the Santa Maria la Real website: https://www.romanicodigital.com/sites/default/files/2022-10/C37-16_Bissera.pdf (accessed January 3, 2023)

Pentcheva 2022a
Pentcheva, Bissera. 2022a. "Audiovision: Image and Chant at Ste. Foy in Conques." *Musiktheorie* 37 (1): 41–54.

Pentcheva 2022b
Pentcheva, Bissera. 2022b. "The Virgin and Sainte-Foy: Chant and the Original Design of the West Façade at Conques." *Religions* 13 (12): 1299. Available online at the MDPI website: https://mdpi.com/2077-1444/13/12/1299 (accessed January 3, 2023)

Pentcheva 2023a
Pentcheva, Bissera. 2023a. "The *Choros* of the Stars: Image, Chant, and Imagination at Ste. Foy at Conques." In *From Words to Space: Textual Sources for Reconstructing and Understanding Medieval Sacred Spaces.*

Edited by Elisabetta Scirocco and Sible de Blauuw. Rome: Bibliotheca Hertziana, pp. 125–58.

Pentcheva 2023b
Pentcheva, Bissera. 2023b. "Entwining Ephemeral with the Eternal: *Locus, Conca,* and *Margarita* at Conques." In *Routledge Companion to Literature and Art.* Edited by Neil Murphy, W. Michelle Wang, and Cheryl Julia Lee. New York: Routledge, forthcoming.

Pentcheva 2023c
Pentcheva, Bissera. 2023c. "Pedro de Roda and the Impulsive Success of Conques." *Convivium,* forthcoming.

Pentcheva 2023d
Pentcheva, Bissera. 2023d. "Vesseling the Metaphysical at Sainte Foy in Conques: *Locus, Choros, Corona, Conca, Margarita.*" In *Festschrift for Xavier Barral i Altet.* Edited by Milenko Jurkovic. Zagreb: IRCLAMA, pp. 47–68.

Prado-Vilar 2021
Prado-Vilar, Francisco. 2021. "The Marble Tempest: Material Imagination, the Echoes of Nostos, and the Transfiguration of Myth in Romanesque Sculpture." In *Icons of Sound: Voice, Architecture and Imagination in Medieval Art.* Edited by Bissera V. Pentcheva. New York: Routledge, pp. 152–205.

Rascol 1942–1945
Rascol, Abbé. 1942–1945. "Le problème du Portail de Conques." *Bulletin de la société archéologue de Midi de la France* 5: 451–65.

Remensnyder 1995
Remensnyder, Amy Goodrich. 1995. *Remembering Kings Past: Monastic Foundation Legends in Medieval Southern France.* Ithaca, NY: Cornell University Press, 1995.

Renner 1997
Renner, Hans-Georg. 1997. "Les chants pour les 1ères Vêpres: Anonymes du XIIIe siècle." *Annuaire. Les Amis de la Bibliothèque Humaniste de Sélestat* 47: 72–78.

Rennie 2007
Rennie, Kriston. 2007. "'Uproot and Destroy, Build and Plant': Legatine Authority under Pope Gregory VII." *Journal of Medieval History* 33 (2): 166–80.

Rennie 2008
Rennie, Kriston. 2008. "Extending Gregory VII's 'Friendship Network': Social Contacts in Late-Eleventh-Century France." *History* 93 (4): 475–96.

Roederer 1974
Roederer, Charlotte. 1974. "Can We Identify an Aquitanian Chant Style?" *Journal of the American Musicological Society* 27: 75–99.

Sauerländer 2004
Sauerländer, Willibald. 2004. "Sainte Foy in Conques." *Romanesque Art: Problems and Monuments.* London: Pindar Press, vol. 2, pp. 399–410.

Scarry 1990
Scarry, Elaine.1990. *Dreaming by the Book.* Princeton: Princeton University Press.

Sumi 2004
Sumi, Akiko. 2004. *Description in Classical Arabic Poetry: Wasf, Ekphrasis and Interarts Theory.* Boston and Leiden: Brill.

Steenberge 2020–present
Steenberge, Laura. 2020–present. Transcription of the Office of Sainte-Foy at Conques and Recording with Auralization in the Acoustics of Conques. Will be available on the project website: https://enchantedimages.stanford.edu/ (accessed December 20, 2022).

Taralone 1978
Taralone, Jean. 1978. "La Majesté d'or de Sainte-Foy du trésor de Conques." *Revue de l'art* 40–41: 9–22.

Taralone 1997
Taralone, Jean, with Dominique Taralon-Carlini. 1997. "La Majesté d'or de Sainte-Foy de Conques." *Bulletin monumental* 155: 11–73.

Treitler 2003
Treitler, Leo. 2003. "The Marriage of Poetry

and Music in Medieval Song." In *With Voice and Pen: Coming to Know Medieval Song and How It Was Made.* Oxford, UK: Oxford University Press, ch. 17, pp. 457–82.

Vergnolle et al. 2011
Vergnolle, Elaine, Henri Pradaier, and Nelly Pousthomis-Dalle. 2011. "L'abbatiale Romane de Conques." In *137e Congrès Archéologique de France, Aveyron.* Paris: Société Française d'Archéologie, pp. 71–160.

Williams 2008
Williams, John. 2008. "Framing Santiago." In *Romanesque Art and Thought in the Twelfth Century. Essays in Honor of Walter Cahn.* Edited by Colum Hourihane. University Park, PA: Penn State University Press, pp. 219–38.

Wirth 2004
Wirth, Jean. 2004. *La datation de la sculpture médiévale.* Geneve: Droz.

Exhibition, Concert, Film, and Project Website

https://enchantedimages.stanford.edu/

***

All the photographs of manuscripts kept in Paris at the Bibliothèque nationale de France (BnF) and the lithographs from the book of Charles Nodier, Isidore-Justin-Séverin Taylor, and Alphonse de Cailleux, *Voyages pittoresques et romantiques dans l'ancienne France,* 18 vols. (Paris: P. Didot, 1833–1837) were supplied by the Bibliothèque nationale de France.

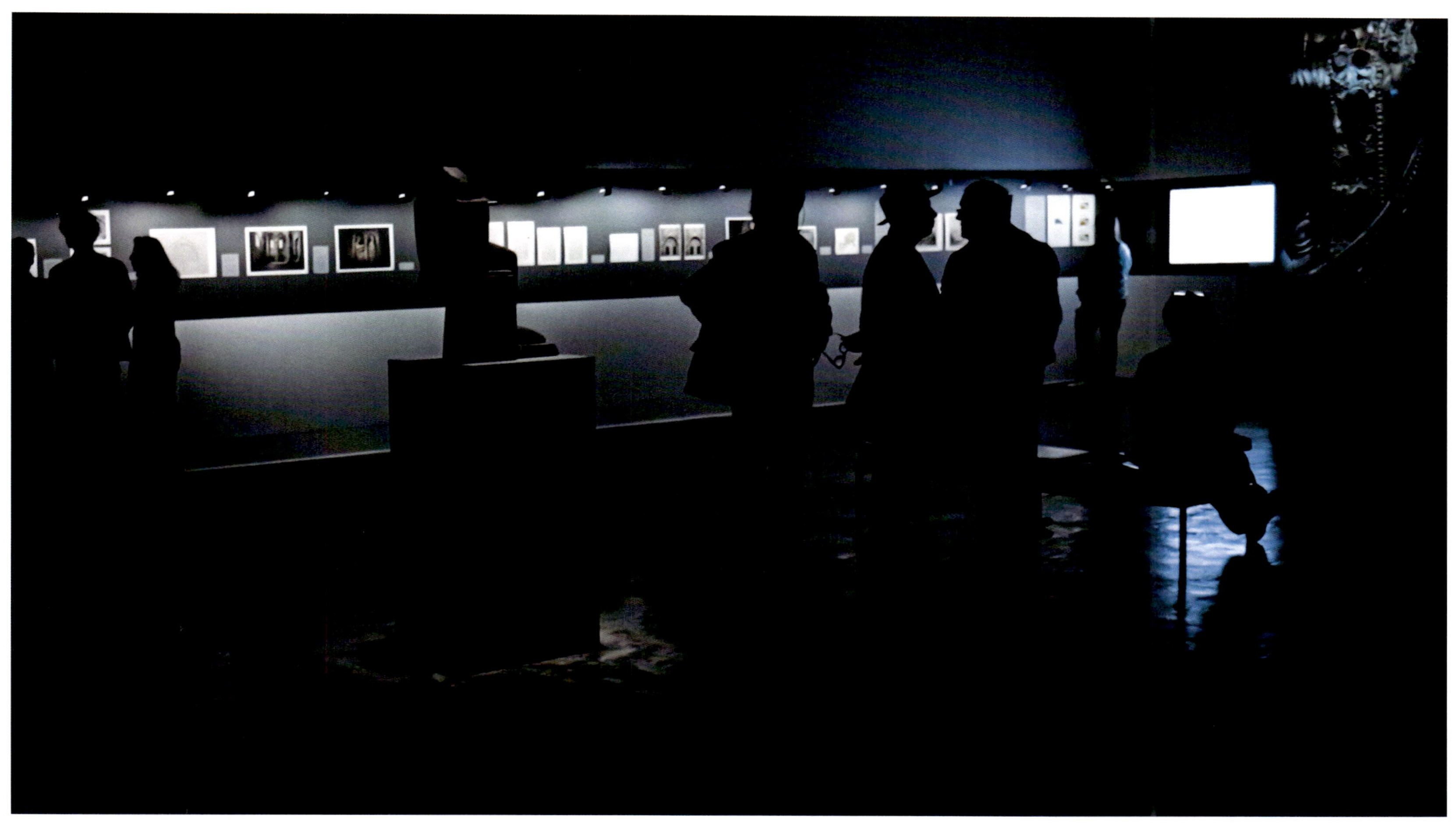

The singers of *Ensemble Organum* visiting the *AudioVision*
exhibition at Stanford